The Whole Duty of a Woman

BOOKS BY ANGELINE GOREAU

Reconstructing Aphra: A Social Biography of Aphra Behn

The Whole Duty of a Woman: Female Writers in Seventeenth-Century England

The Whole Duty of a Woman

FEMALE WRITERS IN
SEVENTEENTH CENTURY ENGLAND

Angeline Goreau

THE DIAL PRESS
Doubleday & Company, Inc., Garden City, New York
1985

Published by The Dial Press

Copyright © 1984 by Angeline Goreau

Manufactured in the United States of America
First printing

Library of Congress Cataloging in Publication Data
Main entry under title:

The Whole duty of a woman.

Bibliography: p. 333
1. English literature—Women authors. 2. Women—
Great Britain—History—17th century—Sources.
3. Feminism—Great Britain—History—17th
century—Sources. 4. English literature—17th
century. 5. Women—Literary collections. 6. Feminism
and literature. I. Goreau, Angeline.
PR1111.W6W53 1984 820'.9'099287 84-12042
ISBN 0-385-27878-0

For Bertha, Frances-Angeline, and Miss Eloise,
all well instructed in the whole duty.

Preface

A great deal has been written about women authors of the eighteenth and nineteenth centuries, but the substantial body of work produced by their seventeenth-century predecessors remains for the most part unfamiliar territory. The importance of these early figures to the evolution of the "female pen" ought not to be underestimated, however, for they preside over the crucial period of transition from the time when the woman writer was a bold exception to the time when she became an acknowledged "fact" of the literary world. Taken as a whole, seventeenth-century texts provide us with a startlingly articulate account of the intricate web of impediments, both external and self-imposed, that so often entangled a woman who aspired to write. The texts also reveal a surprising degree of feminist feeling, both the prefaces "To the Reader," in which literary women argue for their right to publish, and the polemical texts written by women in response to antifeminist attacks from the pens of male authors. Misogynist diatribes of the early seventeenth century seem, in fact, to have provided an important stimulus to the "female pen." When in 1615 Joseph Swetnam published *The Arraignment of Lewd, Idle, Froward, and Unconstant Women; or the Vanity of Them, Choose You Whether*, four women answered him in print within two years. These defenses of the female sex mark a significant turning point in the debate over women: there was a long tradition of works pointing out the defects of "Eve's daughters," but this was the first time that women had begun to reply in number—175 years before Mary Wollstonecraft published her *Vindication of the Rights of Women*. The feminist debate that continued to flare up in cycles throughout the seventeenth century adds an interesting perspective—one that is often missing—to the way we view the progress of feminism in history.

I have attempted in this collection of writings to document the education, social background, and circumstances under which seventeenth-century women wrote and in so doing to give some account of the extraordi-

narily complex, often contradictory set of attitudes toward publication
that these transitional figures expressed.

In order to make the texts more accessible to contemporary readers, I
have, with the exception of titles, modernized the spelling, punctuation
and capitalization where necessary, and cut out excessively repetitive
passages.

Acknowledgments

I wish first of all to acknowledge my large debt to the Humanities Council of Princeton University, which gave me time, freedom, and unstinting support while I was Hodder Fellow there. I owe a debt of gratitude also to the National Endowment of the Humanities, which unwittingly sowed the seeds of this book in funding my earlier study of Aphra Behn. Philippe Ariès and his seminar on the history of sexuality at the École Pratique des Hautes Études offered useful advice and criticism of some of the material here. Lawrence Stone, Natalie Davis, Keith Thomas, Ivon Asquith, and others kindly pointed out references I might not otherwise have come upon.

I could not have completed this book without the splendid assistance of the librarians and staff of the Bodleian Library, Oxford University. Walter Zervas and the New York Public Library helped immeasurably by granting me work space in the Frederick Lewis Allen Room. Other libraries who opened their collections and helped me in various ways were the British Library, the University Library, Cambridge, the University of London Library, the Institute of Historical Research, the London Library, the Friends Library, the Princeton University Library, the Yale University Library, the Barnard College Library, the Huntington Library, the Columbia University Library, the Houghton Library, Harvard University, the Folger Library and the Library of Congress. I also wish to thank the National Portrait Gallery, the Houghton Library, Harvard University, the Trustees of the British Museum, the Printed Books Division of the British Library, the Bodleian Library, Oxford University, for permission to reproduce photographs, and the Department of Manuscripts of the British Library for permission to quote from material in their collection.

Joyce Johnson and Berenice Hoffman have given me criticism, friendship, and support. Denise Barricklow helped with typing at a critical pass. Finally, there is my debt to my mother, whose aid was invaluable, and to my husband, Stephen McGruder, who nobly sustained and endured.

"Some crazy philosophers . . . have endeavoured to devance [women] from the same species with men."

J. Hall, *Paradoxes*, 1653.

Contents

Introduction

I

For women writers of the seventeenth century, one of the most prominent impediments to a literary career was the widely held view that knowledge (and therefore literature) belonged to the masculine province: "Books are a part of a man's prerogative," as Sir Thomas Overbury expressed it in 1614.[1] As a consequence of this prejudice, few parents felt it necessary to devote much effort to their daughters' formal education. In fact, Daniel Tuvil refers in 1616 to parents who "will by no means endure that their daughters should be acquainted with any kind of literature at all. The pen must be forbidden them as the tree of good and evil. . . ."[2]

Women writers of the period generally deplored their lack of training in arts and sciences and looked back with envy to the "golden age" of Tudor England, when a woman's learning was seen as one of her attractions. In the early part of the sixteenth century, the ideals of Renaissance humanism had extended to the female sex. The scholar Juan Luis Vives, who came to England as tutor to Princess Mary, wrote in 1523, at Queen Catherine's urging, a treatise entitled *De Institutione Feminae Christianae*, which argued in favor of classical training for women. In the next fifteen years, seven more tracts advocating women's education appeared, representing a significant departure from earlier indifference to the subject.[3] The effects of this shift in attitude became apparent in the generation of Tudor "paragons" famous for their learning: Lady Jane Grey, the Countess of Arundel, the daughters of Sir Thomas More, the daughters of the Duke of Somerset, the daughters of Sir Anthony Coke, Queen Mary, and Queen Elizabeth.

Unfortunately, however, the influence of this passion for educating women was much less extensive than legend might suggest. As Lawrence Stone has recently pointed out in *The Family, Sex and Marriage in England 1500–1800*, the number of women who actually benefited from this golden age of feminine instruction was limited to royalty and a handful of daughters of very eminent and privileged noblemen—the same few paragons always cited as representative of the whole. For the most part, Stone observes, the flowering of learning encouraged by the increasing availability of printed books significantly widened the breach between the literate (particularly those who could read Latin) and those who could not read or write at all. Despite the existence of a few exceptional learned women, the majority of women were still illiterate. In general, Stone concludes, "access both to sacred truth and to new learning was monopolized by men, thus increasing their prestige and influence and reducing that of women. In Elizabethan England this discrepancy between the sexes in terms of education was true at all levels of society, from the male artisans who could sign their names to the male elite who could write letters and read the Bible, and often also Cicero. Most of their wives were unable to emulate their husbands in these respects, which significantly reinforced their sense of inferiority."[4]

Furthermore, even those women who acquired learning in the golden age encountered limitations of the uses to which they might apply their education, as well as restrictions in the scope of the instruction itself. Noting the wide differences between the kinds of learning necessary to men and to women, Juan Vives remarked that "though the precepts for men be innumerable: women may yet be informed with few words. For men must be occupied both at home and abroad, both in their own matters and for the common weal. Therefore it cannot be declared in a few books, but in many and long, how they [men] shall handle themselves, in so many and diverse things. As for a woman, she hath no charge to see to, but her honesty and chastity. Wherefore when she is informed of that, she is sufficiently appointed."[5] Vives was, of course, only reflecting the conventional wisdom that a man's sphere of activity encompassed the business of the world, while a woman's was limited to the private circle of the home.

Vives, whose defense of education for women was the most widely read and influential of all the tracts on that subject, was careful to emphasize that under no circumstances should the classical training he advocated cause the subordinate role of the weaker sex to come into question. He cautioned that while women were well equipped to learn, they ought not to teach: "For it neither becometh a woman to rule a school, nor to live amongst men or speak abroad, and shake off her demureness and honesty [i.e., chastity], either all together, or else a great part; which if she be good, it were better to be at home within and unknown to other folks, and in company to hold her tongue demurely, and let few see her, and none at all hear her. The Apostle Paul . . . saith: Let your women hold their tongues in congregations. For they be not allowed to speak but to be subject as the law bideth. If they would learn any thing, let them ask their husbands at home. And unto his disciple, Timothy, he writeth on this wise: 'Let a woman learn in silence with all subjection.' But I give no license for a woman to be a teacher, nor to have authority of the man, but to be in silence."[6]

In the end Vives devoted only a small part of his *De Institutione Feminae Christianae* to academic study; the bulk of the "instruction" recommended has to do with proper deportment and moral education. Chapter titles like "Of Virginity," "Of the Keeping of Virginity and Chastity," "Of the Ordering of the Body in a Virgin," "Of the Raiments," "Of the Virtue of a Woman and Examples of Her Life," "How the Maid Shall Behave Herself Being Abroad," "Of Dancing," "Of Loving," "How the Maid Shall Seek a Husband," etc., give an idea of the sort of "education" Vives—one of the most progressive men of his age in his attitudes toward women—had in mind for young ladies. The reading of imaginative literature was firmly excluded: "When she shall be taught to read, let those books be taken in hand, that may teach her good manners. And when she shall learn to write, let not her example be void verses, nor wanton and trifling songs, but some sad sentences prudent and chaste, taken out of Holy Scripture, or the sayings of philosophers, which by often writing she may fasten better in her memory."[7] Vives warned particularly of the dangers of the imagination, telling his readers that women are by nature given to fantasy, their "swift" thought "walking and wandering out from home." Study of classical and sacred texts might serve as an antidote to this poetic leaning, but the young woman in question should never be left alone, lest "she should suffer her mind to muse."

Whatever the limitations of the Renaissance humanists' advocacy of learning for women, the prejudice against intellectual women was at least mitigated for a time. The period when scholarship was deemed an attractive addition to the education of a "happy few" young women lasted only about forty years, however, from about 1520 to 1560. After this time, there are fewer and fewer examples of learned ladies, and noticeably less enthusiasm for such accomplishment. Though Queen Elizabeth had been educated according to the ideals of an earlier age, and was fluent in both classical and modern languages, she did little to encourage similar training for women during her reign.

By the time Queen Elizabeth died, the vogue of feminine erudition had come to an end. The "learned lady" became a social misfit—a figure of ridicule whom parents were careful to prevent their daughters from imitating. Bathsua Makin, looking back nostalgically to the era of the Tudor "paragons of learning," deplored the sad neglect of women's education in her century (she was writing in 1673). In the "Dedication to the Ladies" that prefaced her *An Essay to Revive the Antient Education of Gentlewomen in Religion, Manners, Arts and Tongues*, she fulminated against the force of social custom: "Custom, when it is inveterate, has a mighty influence: it has the force of nature itself. The barbarous custom to breed women low, is grown general amongst us, and has prevailed so far, that it is verily believed (especially amongst a sort of debauched sots) that women are not endued with such reason as men, nor capable of improvement by education, as they are. It is looked upon as a monstrous thing to pretend the contrary. A learned woman is thought to be a comet, that bodes mischief whenever it appears."[8]

Accounts of individual women that can be culled from letters, diaries, and memoirs of the period generally support Mrs. Makin's contentions. Even in exceptional cases when particularly enlightened parents sought to "improve" their daughters by education, they often manifested extreme anxiety as to the effects this learning might have on the attractiveness of their offspring. Elizabeth Tanfield (later Lady Carew), who came of age at the end of the sixteenth century, was allowed a classical education by her parents, but when she showed too much enthusiasm for her studies, was forbidden light to read by, and had to buy candles secretly from her servants—she accumulated a debt of a hundred pounds by the time she married at fifteen. Lady Anne Clifford was fortunate enough to have the poet Samuel Daniel for her tutor, but her father, the Earl of Cumberland, was careful to specify that she should not be taught Latin. Sir Ralph Verney took the same line with regard to the education of his goddaughter, twelve-year-old Nancy Denton, advising her father: "Let not your girl learn Latin nor short hand: The difficulty of the first may keep her from that vice, for so I must esteem it in a woman; but the easiness of the other may be a prejudice to her; for the pride of taking sermon notes hath made multitudes of women unfortunate." The young woman herself objected, informing Sir Ralph that "i am a going whaar i hop i shal out rech [outreach] you in ebri grek and laten [Hebrew, Greek, and Latin]." Her godfather replied: "I did not think you had been guilty of soe much learning as I see you are; and yet it seems you rest unsatisfied or else you would not threaten Lattin, Greeke, and Hebrew too. Good sweet harte bee not soe covitous; beleeve me a Bible (with ye Common prayer) and a good plaine cattichisme in your mother tongue being well read and practised, is well worth all the rest and much more sutable to your sex; I know your Father thinks thise false doctrine, but be confident your husband will bee of my oppinion."9 Lucy Hutchinson's parents were more enlightened than Sir Ralph Verney, and gave her studies unusual encouragement, yet were horrified when she began to conceive intellectual ambitions: "My genius was quite averse too all but my book," she recounted in an autobiographical aside in her memoir of her husband, "so that my mother, thinking it prejudiced my health, would moderate me in it; yet this rather animated me than kept me back, and every moment I could steal from my play I would employ in any book I could find, when my own were locked up from me."10

During the time when standards for the education of young women were sinking, more and more of their male contemporaries were enjoying the advantage of grammar school (where Latin was taught) and university education. The number of grammar schools had been rapidly expanding (between 1480 and 1660 no less than eight hundred new ones were founded), and in consequence, the number of students who qualified for admission to university increased in measure. The hundred years between 1520 and 1620 saw the most rapid expansion in the history of Oxford University—the final degrees awarded every year increased by a multiple of six. There is evidence that in rare instances girls may have been permitted to attend grammar school, but only for a few early years. The statutes of Banbury Grammar School (1594) provided for the admission of a restricted number of girls, but none were permitted to attend "above the age of nine or longer than they may learn to read English." Richard Mulcaster, one of the sixteenth-century defenders of women's education, thought that girls ought to be admitted to grammar schools, but noted that since it was "a thing not used" in England at the time, there was no "president" [precedent] for doing so. A decade or so later, when John Lyon set out the charter of Harrow, he specifically stated that "no girls shall be received to be taught in the school."11 Clearly, no daughters ever made their way into the traditionally masculine domain of the university —there could be no question of admittance to Oxford or Cambridge. When the poet Abraham Cowley proposed the creation of a new college for the study of philosophy, the only females mentioned in his prospectus were "four old women to tend the chambers and such like services." These poor souls were to be paid the least of any of the servants: "To the four necessary women," Cowley allowed in the projected budget, "ten pounds."[12] The ten pounds were to be divided *among* them.

Women had traditionally been educated at home by tutors, but as the seventeenth century progressed, it became more and more the practice to send daughters to the increasing number of boarding schools that were being established. The curriculum of these "academies" for young ladies laid emphasis on practical rather than intellectual achievement, as marriage was to be the future occupation of the great majority of their scholars. At the end of the seventeenth century, the author of *An Essay in Defence of the Female Sex* described the standard "feminine education" that had been by then long established: ". . . after children can talk, they are promiscuously taught to read and write by the same persons, and at the same time. . . . When these are acquitted, which is generally about the age of six or seven years, they begin to be separated, and the boys sent to Grammar School, and the girls to boarding schools, or other places, to learn needlework, dancing, singing, music, drawing, painting, and other accomplishments. . . ."[13]

One of the earliest such schools was the Ladies' Hall at Deptford, where the principal educational concern seems to have been dancing. In May of 1617, the pupils' accomplishments were shown off to the court at Greenwich in a masque called *Cupid's Banishment,* where twelve "nymphs of Diana" (decked out in white "tinsie," artificial floral decorations, white pumps, and gloves) performed complicated "figures" designed by their dancing master. Two of the students presented the results of their instruction in needlework to the Queen. A similar school in the Kentish countryside was accepting students in 1620, and offered to teach the daughters of local gentry and nobility "to work [i.e., do needlework], write and dance and play upon some sorts of musick." Mrs. Perwich's school in Hackney, founded in 1643, was held in high esteem and attracted students from all over England. Much attention was given to music: there was instruction in singing, violin, lute, harpsichord, and organ, as well as country dancing. The "other parts of excellent well-breeding" that were taught at the school included housewifery, cookery, fine embroidery, black work, white work, work in colors, and various sorts of other "work" in silver, straw, glass, wax, and gum. Mrs. Hannah Woolley went even further in this last category, offering to teach "curious work" such as shellwork, mosswork, "transparent works," all manner of pretty toys, rocks made with shells, frames for mirrors, and other "household arts."[14]

Of all the "female academies," only Mrs. Bathsua Makin's school seems to have attempted a more serious academic program. Mrs. Makin expressed disdain for the standard schools of the day: they existed, she said, "merely to teach gentlewomen to frisk and dance, to paint their faces, to curl their hair, to put on a whisk, to wear gay clothes."[15] The young ladies who attended her school on Tottenham High Road in London studied grammar and rhetoric, logic, languages—especially Greek and Hebrew, "as these will enable the better understanding of the Scriptures"—as well as mathematics, geography, music, painting and poetry, among other subjects.

Most—in fact, nearly all—of the women who published either literary or other sorts of texts (philosophical, polemical, etc.) during this period lodged some kind of complaint about the inadequate instruction usually afforded their sex. The anonymous author of a feminist tract written about 1640 resentfully described the double educational standard that prevailed in her day: "When a father has a numerous issue of sons and daughters, the sons . . . must be first put to the Grammar School, and after perchance sent to the University and trained up in the liberal arts and sciences, and there (if they prove not blockheads), they may in time be booklearned. . . . When we, who may style by a name of weaker vessels, though of a more delicate, fine, soft and more pliant flesh, and therefore of a temper most capable of the best impression, have not that generous and liberal education, lest we should be made able to vindicate our own injuries. We are set only to the needle, to prick our fingers, or else to the wheel to spin a fair thread for our own undoings, or perchance to some dirty and debased drudgery. If we be taught to read, they then confine us within the compass of our mother tongue, and that limit we are not suffered to pass . . . thus, if we are weak by nature, they strive to make us more weak by our nurture. And if in degree of place low, they strive by their policy to keep us more under."[16] Writing in 1664, Margaret Cavendish, Duchess of Newcastle, protested that "for the most part women are not educated as they should be, I mean those of quality, for their education is only to dance, sing, and fiddle, to write complimental letters, to read romances, to speak some language that is not their native, which education, is an education of the body, and not of the mind, and shows that their parents take more care of their feet than their head, more of their words than their reason, more of their music than their virtue, more of their beauty than their honesty, which methinks is strange, as that their friends and parents would take more care, and be at greater charge to adorn their bodies, than to indue their minds. . . ."[17]

In 1675, Hannah Woolley, the author of *The Gentlewoman's Companion; or A Guide to the Female Sex* complained that "the right education of the female sex, as it is in a manner everywhere neglected, so it ought to be generally lamented. Most in this depraved later age think a woman learned and wise enough if she can distinguish her husband's bed from another's."[18] Her complaint was echoed more fiercely a year later by the author of "The Emulation," published in a collection entitled *Triumphs of Female Wit* (1683):

> They let us learn to work, to dance, or sing,
> Or any such trivial thing,
> Which to their profit may increase or pleasure bring.
> But they refuse to let us know
> What sacred sciences doth impart
> Or the mysteriousness of art.
> In learning's pleasing paths denied to go,
> From knowledge banished, and their schools,
> We seem designed alone for useful fools. . . .[19]

By the beginning of the eighteenth century, when Lady Damaris Masham was composing her *Occasional Thoughts in Reference to a Vertuous or Christian Life* (1705), the circumstances of women's education were still more or less the same. "The information and improvement of the understanding is commonly very little thought of in reference to [our] whole sex," she observed. Among her friends, she recounted, there was much dissatisfaction over this state of affairs: "As those persons who afforded that conversation I have mentioned, were the greatest part of them ladies, it was not strange if they expressed much displeasure at the too general neglect of the instruction of their sex—a reflection not easily to be avoided by them. . . ." Masham goes on to explain the reasons for this neglect by pointing out that parents deliberately kept their daughters from anything approaching "learning" out of apprehension that, should they manifest any fluency in a learned language, or be "conversant" in books, they might well fail to find husbands. Few men, Masham declared, "relish" these accomplishments in a lady: "For if it be considered that she who did seriously desire to make the least use of what she knew, would necessarily be obliged (for the gaining of time wherein she might do so) to order the course and manner of her life something different from others of her sex."[20]

The state of affairs which Damaris Masham described as the "norm" seemed hardly likely to create a favorable circumstance for the establishment of a room of one's own.

II

The sense of intellectual inferiority or illegitimacy that a superficial education could create constituted the most obvious impediment to literary ambition for a woman of the seventeenth century. There was, however, a much more subtle and complex inhibition that women repeatedly mentioned as a reason they hesitated to publish their work: feminine modesty.

In order to understand what sort of censorship "modesty" might impose in literary matters, it is important first to recognize the very specific meaning contemporaries assigned to it. A modest man was one who exhibited judicious self-restraint, but when "modesty" was used in connection with a woman, it referred specifically to chastity. In a similar fashion, the words "virtue," "honour," "honesty," "name," "fame," and "reputation" took on the same specifically sexual sense. Lady Damaris Masham speaks of virtue as "a term which, when applied to women, is rarely designed . . . to signify anything but the single virtue of chastity." As the writings of Juan Luis Vives illustrate, a good deal of the education of women in the sixteenth century was devoted to instructing them in the limits of their proper sphere (the "private circle" of the home) and impressing upon them the importance of a chaste posture. As Lady Damaris Masham put it, the principal object was "to persuade ladies that what they cannot want without being contemptible is the chief merit they are capable of having. . . ."[21]

The absolute insistence on chastity in women had its roots in concrete economic and social circumstance: under the patriarchal, primogenital inheritance system, the matter of paternity could most emphatically *not* be open to question, since, as the Duchess of Newcastle remarked, "women might bring forth branches from the wrong stock."[22] As the aristocracy's chief means of consolidating and perpetuating power and wealth was through arranged marriage, the undoubted chastity of daughters was a crucial concern. To be of value on the marriage market, girls had to deliver their maidenheads intact on the appointed day: a deflowered heiress could be disinherited, since her virginity was an indispensable part of her dowry; by its loss she would deprive her father of the possibility of selling her to a husband whose family line she would perpetuate. Legally, a woman's chastity was considered the property of either her father or her husband. A father could sue his daughter's seducer for damages; a husband could sue his wife's lover for trespassing on his property—and many did with success. In one case, a lover was ordered by the court to pay a husband ten thousand pounds for this indiscretion. As *The Whole Duty of Man* (1658) stated it: "The corrupting of a man's wife, enticing her to a strange bed, is by all acknowledged to be the worst sort of theft, infinitely beyond that of the goods."[23]

Though virginity could verifiably be preserved through the simple recourse of abstinence, the question of chastity was a far more complex matter in the sixteenth and seventeenth centuries. Though the necessity for "modesty" had its roots in concrete circumstance, it was interpreted by contemporaries in an abstract, or symbolic, fashion, and then reapplied to the circumstances of everyday life—thus enlarging its sphere of influence to cover the whole of experience. The anonymous female author of *The Whole Duty of a Woman* (1696) specified that "modesty . . . spreads itself in life, motions and words. . . . Your looks, your speech, and the course of your whole behaviour should own a humble distrust of yourselves; rather being willing to learn and observe, than to dictate and prescribe. . . . As you value your reputation, keep us to the strictures of this virtue . . . give no occasion for scandal or reproach; but let your conversation set an example to others. . . . Let neither your thoughts nor eyes wander."[24]

Through this figurative interpretation of "modesty," sexual significance could be assigned to every sphere of a woman's life, placing inhibitions on her way of speaking, looking, walking, imagining, thinking. The author of *The Ladies Calling* (1673) explains that "when we speak of modesty in our present notion of it, we are not to oppose it only to the grosser art of incontinency [i.e., "unchastity"], but to all those misbehaviours, which either discover or may create an inclination to it."[25] A popular reference book called *The Ladies Dictionary* (1694), which purported to include all knowledge requisite or pertinent to the female sex, supplied long descriptions of all the areas of restraint. Under "Gate or Gesture to be observed by Ladies," *The Ladies Dictionary* comments: "Great notice is taken of the gate and gesture of young ladies, and observations made thereon by the nice and censorious. They guess at the disposition of her heart by the dimension of her motion, concluding a light carriage most commonly discovers a loose inclination. . . . A swimming gate, or an affected pace, as if you were treading out . . . is to be avoided, lest it bee looked upon as a studied measure to be singular in your walking, and consequently draw more eyes upon you than others. A shuffling or rigling [wriggling] motion is likewise discommendable. . . . Beware of taking stradling steps, or running ahead, for those are indecent in a lady." Under the heading "Eye, how to govern it," readers of *The Ladies Dictionary* were counseled: "Eyes are the casements of the body, and many times by standing too much open, let in things hurtful to the mind. A wanton eye is the truest evidence of wandering and unsteadfast thoughts; we may see too much, if we be not careful in governing our eyes, and keeping them from going astray, and returning with vain objects to the fancy and imagination, which, making unhappy impressions, they cannot be easily obliterated. . . . Therefore, ladies, to prevent the malady, which like a spreading contagion disperses itself into most societies, you must keep your eyes within compass, from wandering as much as possible. . . . Consult chastity and modesty . . . give no occasion then, ladies, for any to tax your eyes with anything that is not modest, comely, and allowable. . . . The eyes are not the only dangerous things about you. The tongue many times for want of good government, betrays you into divers misfortunes."[26]

In the literature written for the "education" of women, much attention is also given to this danger of immodest tongues. Robert Codrington, in his very popular *The Second Part of Youth's Behaviour; or, Decency in Conversation Amongst Women* (1664), exhorts his readers to practice "Discretion, Silence, Modesty," and Richard Brathwaite's *The English Gentlewoman* (1631) reminds young women that "bashfull silence is an ornament to their sex. Volubility of tongue in these, argues either rudeness of breeding, or boldness of expression. The former may be reclaimed by a discreet tutor, but the latter, being grounded on arrogancy of conceit, seldom or never. . . . It suits not with her honour, for a young woman to be prolocutor." Modesty and honor, says Brathwaite, require that in public a woman "observe rather than discourse."[27] *The Ladies Calling* also opposes "this great indecency of loquacity in women . . . a symptom of a loose, impotent soul, a kind of incontinence of the mind," but goes on to emphasize that inward modesty is as important, if not more so, as its outward expression: "Every indecent curiosity, or impure fancy, is a deflowering of the mind, and every the least corruption of them gives some degree of defilement to the body too."[28]

Interestingly enough, though one finds the same sort of descriptions of and insistence upon "feminine modesty" over and over again in the guides, or advice books, addressed to women, the authors who put forth these opinions represent a wide range of moral, political, and social positions. The author of *The Ladies Calling* (who may have been Richard Allestree) was highly conservative as well as deeply religious. Robert Codrington, a popular writer who began his book by arguing that women's education was neglected, was far more liberal. The author of *The Ladies Dictionary* also argues for education, but goes still further in its defense of women's ability. Furthermore, despite its delivery of the conventional wisdom concerning the demands of modesty, *The Ladies Dictionary* contains an astonishingly frank discussion of certain aspects of female sexuality. Of the three authors, only Allestree can properly be called a moralist; yet, despite other differences in perspective, they all speak of modesty in more or less the same terms.

It is not necessarily true, of course, that these prescriptions for behavior represented actual practice, or even what was generally agreed upon as a model for it. There is evidence, however, that these books were widely read, some going into many editions. Hannah Woolley, a recognized authority on manners and household management whose practical manuals were much consulted, acknowledged in the preface of *The Gentlewoman's Companion* that she had found Codrington's *The Second Part of Youth's Behaviour; or, Decency in Conversation Amongst Women* very useful in the compilation of her own text—useful enough to borrow from liberally, apparently. The early feminist writer Mary Astell quotes admiringly from *The Ladies Calling* in *A Serious Proposal to the Ladies for the Advancement of Their True and Greatest Interest.* Furthermore, one finds the same interpretation of the demands of modesty either repeated or tacitly assumed in many private expressions of opinion—letters, diaries, family memoirs—as well as in texts written for publication. Lady Anne Twisden, who lived in Kent during the Civil War, was so careful of her reputation, even after all her children were grown and she was past the age of childbearing, that she never permitted herself any society that might cast doubt on her virtue. "Her maxim," wrote a friend after Lady Twisden's death, "was that the woman was to blame of whom there could be any suspicion, and therefore she was never with any man (except her husband) but she had some woman by in the room, or at least the doors open, and in sight of her."[29] Dorothy Denne, who lived a few miles away, testified to the necessity of such behavior. In a letter she reminded her lover that "a woman which has lost her good name is dead while she lives."[30] The Duchess of Newcastle recounts in the autobiographical fragment attached to her memoir of the Duke of Newcastle that when she went to court as a maid of honor during the Civil War she was so cowed by the danger of compromising her modesty that she hardly spoke or lifted her eyes: "I had heard that the world was apt to lay aspersions even on the innocent, for which I durst neither look up with my eyes, nor speak, nor be any way sociable, insomuch as I was thought a natural fool. . . . And, indeed, I was so afraid to dishonour my friends and family by my indiscreet actions, that I rather chose to be accounted a fool than to be thought rude or wanton."[31] Two generations later the author of a feminist tract referred ironically to the demands of modesty: ". . . as one great commendation of our sex is to know much and speak little, so an intelligent modesty informs my soul, I ought to put a period to the ensuing lines, lest censuring critics should measure my tongue by my pen, and condemn me for a talkative by the length of my poem."[32] Though the author was prepared to attack the inhibitions on a woman's tongue, however, she was not so immodest as to sign a name to her work.

The reinterpretation of "chastity" as a figurative rather than literal inhibition created an infinitely expanding architecture of self-restraint—often more far-reaching and effective than any form of external censorship might be. In this light, it is easier to see how the act of publishing one's work—"publishing one's private thoughts to the world"—would be seen as a violation of the requirements of modesty. Not only did such an act permit foreign eyes access to what ought to remain hidden and anonymous, but it also violated the requirement that women remain within the "private sphere," represented by "the home," while men occupied the public domain of "the world." Anna van Schurman, in her defense of learning for women, *The Learned Maid* (1659), brought up this point as though it were a "given" for women: "The study of letters is convenient for [women], for whom it is more decent to find themselves both business and recreation at home and in private, than abroad among others. . . . The Apostle requireth women to be 'keepers at home,' and moreover, experience testifies; whose ears, eyes often travail abroad, hunting after pleasures, their faith, diligence, and modesty too, is generally called into question."[33]

The irreconcilability of feminine modesty and making one's thoughts public is clearly described in a poem written by Lady Elizabeth Carey at the beginning of the seventeenth century. She begins by stating that duty requires "one that is a wife" not merely to "keep her [self] spotless from an act of ill," but also to avoid any appearance, or suspicion thereof, and "bare herself of power as well as will."[34] Rather than finding freedom "glorious," Lady Carey advises, a woman ought to seek "glory" through self-denial—"by her proper self restrained to be." The next two lines presumably refer to the desire for some sort of public recognition or fame, perhaps the "glory" of laurels: "When she hath spacious ground to walk upon,/Why on the ridge should she desire to go?" Once again, Carey repeats that a woman ought not to count herself truly virtuous merely because she avoids direct threats to her "honour" (read "chastity"). True "honour," for a woman, Carey says, requires that she forsake even "all lawful liberties."

Having established this standard for self-restraint, Elizabeth Carey proceeds in the next stanza to explain that "fame"—used here in its feminine sense, "chastity"—can be compromised merely by giving "more than to her lord alone . . . a private word to any second ear." Though in fact she might have been faithful to her husband, symbolically she "wounds her honour, though she kills it not." Chastity for women, Carey contends, includes chastity of the mind as well as body—and that precludes communication of thought:

> When to their husbands they themselves do bind,
> Do they not wholly give themselves away?
> Or give they but their body, not their mind,
> Reserving that, tho' best, for other's prey?
> No, sure, their thought no more can be their own,
> And therefore to none but one be known.

The last stanza of the poem reinforces Carey's point:

> Then she usurps upon another's right,
> That seeks to be by public language graced;
> And tho' her thoughts reflect with purest light
> Her mind, if not peculiar, is not chaste.
> For in a wife it is no worse to find
> A common body, than a common mind.

Paradoxically, the woman who wrote this condemnation of female "publication" may well have been (though the records are too incomplete to be considered definitive) the author of the first published play in the English language by a woman. Given the sentiments expressed in the poem, it is not surprising that the author chose not to sign her name to *The Tragedie of Mariam, the Faire Queen of Jewry* (1613).

The feeling that publication of one's work symbolically violated feminine modesty by exposing private thoughts to the world was implicit in the reaction expressed by Katherine Philips (later one of the most cited examples of female wit) when she claimed that an edition of her poems was published without her knowledge. Philips protested her innocence of this act in a letter written to her friend Sir Charles Cotterell: "The injury done me by that printer and publisher surpasses all the troubles that to my remembrance I ever had . . . who never writ a line in my life with the intention to have it printed . . . you know me, Sir, to have been all along sufficiently distrustful of whatever my own want of company and better employment, or the commands of others have seduced me to write, and that I have rather endeavoured never to have those trifles seen at all, than that they should be exposed to all the world . . . sometimes I think that to make verses is so much above my reach, and a diversion so unfit for the sex to which I belong, that I am about to resolve against it forever; and could I have recovered those fugitive papers that have escaped my hands, I had long since, I believe, made a sacrifice to them all to the flames. The truth is, I have always had an incorrigible vanity of rhyming, but intended the effects of that humour only for my own amusement in a retired life, and therefore did not so much resist it as a wise woman would have done."[35]

There was hardly anything shocking in Katherine Philips's published verses. The people that the poems were addressed to were disguised under names like "Lucasia" and "Silvander"; the subject matter was unimpeachable. The style was so literary that one wonders if the poems were in fact *not* written with publication in mind. Katherine Philips unquestionably cherished literary aspirations and found it perfectly natural that the male members of her literary "society of friends" should publish their work and receive recognition for it. Whether or not she really believed it was unthinkable for a woman to make herself "public" in this way, she nevertheless felt she had to write to all her friends to disclaim responsibility and to ask them to spread the word that she was not guilty of the immodest act of publication. To Dorothy Osborne she wrote: "I must never show any face among any reasonable people again, for some most dishonest person hath got some collection of my poems as I hear, and hath delivered them to a printer who I hear is just upon putting them out and this hath so extremely disturbed me, both to have my private folly so unhandsomely exposed and the belief that I believe the most part of the world are apt enough to believe that I connived at this ugly accident that I have been on the rack ever since I heard it, though I have written to Col. Jeffries who first sent me word of it to get the printer punished, the book called in, and me some way publicly vindicated; yet I shall need all my friends to be my champions to the critical and malicious that I am so innocent of the pitiful design of a knave to get a groat that I never was more vexed at anything and that I utterly disclaim whatever he hath so unhandsomely exposed."[36]

Mrs. Philips even went so far as to claim that this event had thrown her into a "fit of sickness." She finally succeeded in having the edition suppressed and forced the printer, Marriott, to apologize and publicly announce his intention to withdraw the book in an advertisement in the London *Intelligencer* of January 18, 1664. Six months later, she died of smallpox. Her poems were posthumously reedited, with her disclaimer of responsibility and her assertion that the activity of writing verses was "unfit for her sex" prefacing the new edition. She was thereafter held up as an example to her sex, having succeeded—despite the "accident" of publication—in preserving the description Sir Edward Dering had given of her: "No bolder thought can tax, those rhymes of blemish to the blushing sex; As chaste the lines, as harmless is the sense, as the first smiles of infant innocence."[37]

An example of a woman with a lively interest in literature and an evident gift and urge to write who shared Katherine Philips's feelings about the requirements of modesty was Dorothy Osborne. For seven whole years she kept up a steady stream of letters to her lover, articulate with descriptions of the countryside around her, of her reading, of whatever gossip she could garner in her isolated corner. Her "private correspondence" is, in fact, much more interesting than the highly artificial pastoral poetry Philips wrote. The idea of a woman's employing her pen for a public, however, seemed outrageous to her. When, in 1653, she heard that the Duchess of Newcastle had published a book of poetry, she considered that the duchess must have taken leave of her senses, since, as she wrote to her fiancé, "there are certain things that custom has made almost of absolute necessity, and reputation I take to be one of those; if one could be invisible I should choose that, but since all people are seen and known, and shall be talked of in spite of their teeth's, who is it that does not desire at least that nothing of ill may be said of them . . . no, not [even] my Lady Newcastle with all her philosophy."[38] Robert Codrington acknowledged the influence of this custom a few years later when in 1664 he wrote: "The tyranny of custom hath hindered many [women] from publishing their works. . . ."[39] The only exception to this rule that he could think of was the Duchess of Newcastle.

In 1617 the pseudonymous author of a feminist tract cited modesty as the principal obstacle to women's expressing themselves in print: "feminine modesty hath confined our rarest and ripest wits to silence," she wrote, but immediately added the qualification that even so "we acknowledge it our greatest ornament."[40] Much later in the century, when it was far more common for women to publish, many chose to omit their names from the title page for reasons of "modesty," "reputation," and other words that could be taken to stand for "chastity." The second edition of Elizabeth Singer Rowe's poetry was introduced by a long preface "To the Reader" (written by a woman friend), which ended by explaining why the author chose to remain anonymous: "Nothing more, I think, lies upon my hands, but to assure the reader, that they [the poems] were actually writ by a young lady . . . whose name had been prefixed, had not her own modesty absolutely forbidden it."[41] The anonymous author of *Triumphs of Female Wit* (1683) was well aware of the necessity of this expedient: "Gentlemen," she wrote in her preface, "your censures I know are ready . . . I expect to find my appearance in the behalf of injured females condemned not only as immodest and unfashionable, but as unnatural and unreasonable also. . . ."[42] The female author of the influential *An Essay in Defence of the Female Sex* (1696) wrote in the preface to that book: "I presume not upon the merits of what I have written, as to make my name public with it . . . [nothing could] induce me to bring my name upon the public stage of the world. . . . The tenderness of reputation in our sex . . . made me very cautious, how I exposed mine to such poisonous vapours. I was not ignorant, how liberal some men are of their scandal, whenever provoked, especially by a woman . . . and how ready the same men are to be so, tho upon never so mistaken grounds."[43]

III

If a woman managed to overcome obstacles of inadequate education or self-doubt and succeeded in publishing her writing, she could expect to be mocked, jeered, flouted, and attacked by critics. Prologues, epilogues, and prefaces to the reader are peppered with accounts of the hostile reception the "female pen" met with. Some women responded by apologizing, equivocating, or denying responsibility for the publication of their work.

Other women, however, were moved to take a feminist stance. Aphra Behn introduced her first play with a playful, nearly flirtatious prologue, but the violent detraction she was subjected to afterward prompted her to write a rousing defense of women's right to the pen, which she appended to the published text of her third play.

Despite all the formidable discouragements, the numbers of women who actually published work increased steadily in the seventeenth century, then exponentially in the eighteenth. It is interesting to speculate on the role which feminism may have played in this development, but the influence of feminist ideas is difficult to gauge. Many women were inspired to write by the desire to defend their sex from misogynist attacks; on the other hand, women who nursed literary ambitions were clearly moved to feminist feeling at least in part as a result of the difficulties they encountered. There is, however, a significant difference in the progress of feminism and feminine writing. The debate over women continued in more or less the same terms; interest in the question seems to have heated up and then cooled off in a cyclical pattern. There are shifts of style and language, but the content of the argument remains essentially the same. In some respects, the debate about women's writing follows the same pattern. Nearly every woman who takes up the pen feels that she must also take up the argument over women and wit. At the same time, it is clear that more and more women are settling into the profession of writing. The fact that "Orinda" and Aphra Behn published was obviously important to the next generation. By the middle of the eighteenth century, Eliza Haywood, though still concerned with the question of whether women and knowledge are inimical, nevertheless exhibits the relaxed attitude of a seasoned professional toward her own literary activity.

NOTES

1. Sir Thomas Overbury, "The Wife" (1614), reprinted in *The Overburian Characters*, ed. W. J. Paylor (Oxford, 1936), p. 105.
Not long after this was written, Sir Thomas Overbury was slowly poisoned to death by the agents of Frances Howard, Countess of Essex.
2. Daniel Tuvil, *Asylum Veneris, or A Sanctuary for Ladies* (London, 1616), p. 87.
3. Juan Vives's *De Institutione Feminae Christianae* was translated into English by Richard Hyrde and published under the title *The Instruction of a Christian*

Woman in 1540. There was another edition printed in 1541 and subsequent ones in 1557 and 1592. Passages of the six other treatises are reprinted in *Vives and the Renascence Education of Women*, ed. Foster Watson (London, 1912).

4. Lawrence Stone, *The Family, Sex and Marriage in England 1500–1800* (London, 1977), p. 158.

5. Foster Watson, ed., *Vives and the Renascence Education of Women* (London, 1912), p. 34.

6. Ibid., pp. 55, 56.

7. Ibid., p. 55.

8. Bathsua Makin, *An Essay to Revive the Antient Education of Gentlewomen*, see p. 25.

9. F. P. Verney and M. M. Verney, eds., *Memoirs of the Verney Family During the Seventeenth Century* (London, 1907) 1:501.

10. Lucy Hutchinson, *Memoirs of the Life of Col. Hutchinson*, ed. James Sutherland (Oxford, 1973), p. 288.

11. Roger Thompson, *Women in Stuart England and America* (London, 1974), p. 192.

12. Abraham Cowley, *Works* (London, 1693), p. 43.

13. *An Essay in Defence of the Female Sex* (London, 1696), pp. 32, 33.

14. Hannah Woolley, *The Gentlewoman's Companion* (London, 1675), pp. 10, 11.

15. Bathsua Makin, *An Essay to Revive the Antient Education of Gentlewomen* (London, 1673), p. 22.

16. *The Women's Sharpe Revenge* (London, 1640), pp. 40–42.

17. Margaret Cavendish, Duchess of Newcastle, *Sociable Letters*, see p. 23.

18. Hannah Woolley, *The Gentlewoman's Companion*, see p. 27.

19. *Triumphs of Female Wit*, see pp. 135–36.

20. Lady Damaris Masham, *Occasional Thoughts in Reference to a Vertuous Christian Life*, see pp. 29–30.

21. Ibid.

22. Margaret Cavendish, Duchess of Newcastle, *The World's Olio* (London, 1655), Preface, unpaginated.

23. [Richard Allestree,] *The Whole Duty of Man* (London, 1658, reprinted 1695), p. 87.

24. *The Whole Duty of a Woman*, see pp. 52–53.

25. [Richard Allestree,] *The Ladies Calling*, see p. 44.

26. *The Ladies Dictionary*, see pp. 57–58.

27. Richard Brathwaite, *The English Gentlewoman*, see pp. 38–39.

28. [Richard Allestree,] *The Ladies Calling*, see p. 55.

29. Henry F. Abell, *Kent and the Great Civil War* (Ashford, 1901), pp. 141, 142.

30. "Oxinden Correspondence," B.L., Additional Mss. 28, 003, fol. 173.

31. Margaret Cavendish, Duchess of Newcastle, "A True Relation of My Birth, Breeding and Life," appended to *The Life of William Cavendish, Duke of Newcastle*, ed. C. H. Firth (London, 1907), p. 161.

32. *The Female Advocate*, see p. 126.

33. Anna van Schurman, *The Learned Maid*, see p. 167.

34. Lady E[lizabeth]C[arey], *The Tragedie of Mariam, the Faire Queen of Jewry* (London, 1613), Act III, Chorus.

35. Katherine Philips, *Letters from Orinda to Poliarchus*, see pp. 196–99.

36. *Martha, Lady Giffard, Her Life and Correspondence* (1664–1722), ed. Julia G. Longe (London, 1911), pp. 38–42.

37. Katherine Philips, *Letters from Orinda to Poliarchus* (London, 1705), p. 232.

38. Dorothy Osborne, *Letters*, ed. E. A. Parry (London, 1914), p. 82.

39. Robert Codrington, *The Second Part of Youth's Behaviour; or, Decency in Conversation Amongst Women* (London, 1664), p. 62.

40. Constantia Munda, *The Worming of a Mad Dogge*, see p. 85.

41. [Elizabeth Singer Rowe,] *Poems on Several Occasions*, see p. 291.

42. *Triumphs of Female Wit*, see p. 133.

43. *An Essay in Defence of the Female Sex*, see pp. 142–43.

I
The Whole Duty of a Woman

EDUCATION: "LEARNING"

Margaret Cavendish, Duchess of Newcastle, here describes the usual sort of education given young women of her time. She was born in 1624, and came of age during the Civil War.

Sociable Letters. London, 1664.

For the most part women are not educated as they should be, I mean those of quality, for their education is only to dance, sing, and fiddle, to write complimental letters, to read romances, to speak some language that is not their native, which education, is an education of the body, and not of the mind, and shows that their parents take more care of their feet than their head, more of their words than their reason, more of their music than their virtue, more of their beauty than their honesty, which methinks is strange, as that their friends and parents should take more care, and be at greater charge to adorn their bodies, than to indue their minds, to teach their bodies arts, and not to instruct their minds with understanding; for this education is more for outward show, than inward worth, it makes the body a courtier, and the mind a clown, and oftentimes it makes their body a bawd, and their mind a courtesan, for though the body procures lovers, yet it is the mind that is the adulteress, for if the mind were honest and pure, they would never be guilty of that crime; wherefore those women are best bred, whose minds are civilest, as being well taught and governed, for the mind will be wild and barbarous, unless it be enclosed with study, instructed by learning, and governed by knowledge and understanding, for then the inhabitants of the mind will live peaceably, happily, honestly and honourably, by which they will rule and govern their associate appetites with ease and regularity, and their words, as their household servants, will be employed profitably.

The internalized sense of inferiority that this "education" could create in a woman who nursed literary ambitions is testified to by the duchess.

Sociable Letters. London, 1664.

Madam,

In your last letter you advised me to write a book of orations, but how should I write orations, who know no rules in rhetoric, nor never went to school, but only learned to read and write at home, taught by an ancient decayed gentlewoman whom my mother kept for that purpose—which my ill hand (as the phrase is) may sufficiently witness; yet howsoever, to follow your advice, I did try to write orations, but I find I want wit, eloquence, and learning for such a work, and though I had wit, eloquence, and learning, I should not find so many subjects, to write so many orations as will fill a book, for orations for the most part, are concerning war, peace, and matters of state, and business in the Commonwealth, all which I am not capable of, as being a woman, who hath neither knowledge, ability, nor capacity in state affairs, and to speak in writing of that I understand not, will not be acceptable to my reading auditors. . . .

Women's education in "learning" had not much improved by the second half of the seventeenth century, when Bathsua Makin wrote to protest its inadequacy and argue for its reform.

An Essay to Revive the Antient Education of Gentlewomen in Religion, Manners, Arts and Tongues. London, 1673.

Dedication to the Ladies. . . .
Custom, when it is inveterate, hath a mighty influence: it hath the force of Nature itself. The barbarous custom to breed women low, is grown general amongst us, and hath prevailed so far, that it is verily believed (especially amongst a sort of debauched sots) that women are not endued with such reason as men; nor capable of improvement by education, as they are. It is looked upon as a monstrous thing, to pretend the contrary. A learned woman is thought to be a comet, that bodes mischief whenever it appears. To offer to the world the liberal education of women is to deface the image of God in Man; it will make women so high, and men so low, like fire in the housetop, it will set the whole world in a flame.

These things and worse than these are commonly talked of, and verily believed by many, who think themselves wise men: to contradict these is a bold attempt; where the attempter must expect to meet with much opposition. . . . I verily think, women were formerly educated in the knowledge of arts and tongues, and by their education, many did rise to a great height in learning. Were women thus educated now, I am confident the advantage would be very great: the women would have honour and pleasure, their relations profit, and the whole nation advantage. I am very sensible it is an ill time to set foot on this design: [a time] wherein not only learning, but virtue itself is scorned and neglected, as pedantic things, fit only for the vulgar. I know no better way to reform these exorbitancies, than to persuade women to scorn these toys and trifles they now spend their time about, and to attempt higher things, here offered: this will either reclaim the men; or make them ashamed to claim the sovereignty over such as are more wise and virtuous than themselves.

Were a competent number of schools erected, to educate ladies ingeniously, methinks I see how ashamed men would be of their ignorance, and how industrious the next generation would be to wipe off their reproach.

I expect to meet with many scoffs and taunts from inconsiderate and illiterate men, that prize their own lusts and pleasure more than your profit and content. I shall be the less concerned at these, so long as I am in your favour, and this discourse may be a weapon in your hands to defend yourselves, whilst you endeavour to polish your souls, that you may glorify God, and answer to the end of your creation, to be meet helps [helpmeets] to your husbands. Let not your Ladyships be offended, I do not (as some have wittily done) plead for female pre-eminence. To ask too much is the way to be denied all. God hath made man the head, [and] if you be educated and instructed, as I propose, I am sure you will acknowledge it, and be satisfied that you are helps, that your husbands do consult you and advise with you (which if you be wise you will be glad of) and that your husbands have the casting-voice, in whose determinations you will acquiesce. That this may be the effect of this education in all ladies that shall attempt it, is the desire of [the author].

Hannah Woolley, a popular writer of cookery and advice books for women, also expressed disgust at the double standard in educational practice.

The Gentlewoman's Companion; or A Guide to the Female Sex. London, 1675.

The right education of the female sex, as it is in a manner everywhere neglected, so it ought to be generally lamented. Most in this depraved later age think a woman learned and wise enough if she can distinguish her husband's bed from another's. Certainly man's soul cannot boast of a more sublime original than ours; they had equally their efflux from the same eternal immensity, and therefore capable of the same improvement by good education. Vain man is apt to think we were merely intended for the world's propagation, and to keep its humane inhabitants sweet and clean; but, by their leaves, had we the same literature, he would find our brains as fruitful as our bodies. Hence I am induced to believe, we are debarred from the knowledge of humane learning, lest our pregnant wits should rival the towering conceits of our insulting Lords and Masters.

Pardon the severity of this expression, since I intend not thereby to infuse bitter rebellion into the sweet blood of females; for know, I would have all such as are entered into the honourable state of matrimony to be loyal and loving subjects to their lawful (though lording) husbands. I cannot but complain of, and must condemn the great negligence of parents, in letting the fertile ground of their daughters lie fallow, yet send the barren noddles of their sons to the university, where they stay for no other purpose than to fill their empty sconces with idle notions to make a noise in the country.

Pagans of old may teach our Christian parents a new lesson. Edesia, an infidel, taught her daughters learning and morality. Cornelia, hers (with the Greek tongue) piety. Portia, hers (with the learning of the Egyptians) the exemplary grounds of chastity. Sulpicia, hers (with the knowledge of several languages) the precepts of conjugal unity. These, though ethnics, were excellent informers of youth; so that their children were more bound to them for their breeding than bearing, nurturing than nursing. Emulation of goodness is most commendable; and though you cannot hang up the pictures of these worthy persons, so that their memories may live with you; however, imitate their virtues, that their memories may live fresher in you. All memorials, being materials, be they never so durable, are subject to frailty; only the precious monuments of virtue survive time, and breathe eternity.

Thus as ye take good example from others, be ye mother-patterns of virtue to your daughters: let your living actions be lines of their direction. While they are under your command, the error is yours not theirs, if they go astray. Their honour should be one of the chiefest things you are to tender, neither can it be blemished without some soil to your own credit.

Lady Damaris Masham echoed Bathsua Makin's objection to the frivolous education given women, and went on to further describe the ways in which prejudice against learned women perpetuated the old ills. Parents, she wrote, were reluctant to allow their daughters "booklearning" out of fear that they might then become less attractive to prospective husbands. Daughters, precisely because they were ill-equipped to reason, were therefore more likely to follow "custom" rather than think for themselves. It is this social circumstance that kept women from improving their minds, Masham argued, rather than the "fact" that they were naturally witless—as Jean de La Bruyère and others had endlessly pointed out.

Occasional Thoughts in Reference to a Vertuous or Christian Life. London, 1705.

The information and improvement of the understanding by useful knowledge (a thing highly necessary to the right regulation of the manners) is commonly very little thought of in reference to one whole sex. . . . [This omission is mistaken] since the actual assistance of mothers will (generally speaking) be found necessary to the right formation of the minds of their children of both sexes; and the impressions received in that tender age, which is unavoidably much of it passed among women, are of exceeding consequence to men throughout the whole remainder of their lives, as having a strong and oftentimes unalterable influence upon their future inclinations and passions.

As those persons who afforded that agreeable conversation I have mentioned, were the greatest part of them ladies, it was not strange if they expressed much displeasure at the too general neglect of the instruction of their sex: a reflection not easily to be avoided by them. . . .

How few parents are there of quality, even among such as are esteemed the most virtuous, who do not permit their daughters to pass the best part of their youth in that ridiculous circle of diversions, which is pretty generally thought the proper business of young ladies, and which so engrosses them that they can find no spare hours, wherein to make any such improvements of their understanding, as the leisure which they have for it exacts from them as rational creatures. . . .

The improvements of reason, however requisite to ladies for their accomplishment as rational creatures; and however needful to them for the well educating of their children, and to their being useful in their families, yet are rarely any recommendation of them to men, who foolishly thinking that money will answer to all things, do, for the most part, regard nothing else in the woman they would marry: and not often finding what they do not look for, it would be no wonder if their offspring should inherit no more sense than themselves. But be nature ever so kind to them in this respect, yet through want of cultivating the talents she bestows upon those of the female sex, her bounty is usually lost upon them; and girls, betwixt silly fathers and ignorant mothers, are generally so brought up, that traditionary opinions are to them, all their lives long, instead of reason. . . .

Ladies would do well, if, before they came to the care of families, they did employ some of their many idle hours in gaining a little knowledge in languages, and the useful sciences, would be, I know, to contradict the sense of most men; but yet, I think, that such an assertion admits of no other confutation than the usual one which opposite opinions to theirs are wont to receive from people who reason not, but live by fancy and custom; viz. being laughed at. For it cannot be denied that this knowledge would hereafter be more or less useful to ladies in enabling them either themselves to teach their children, or better, oversee and direct those who do so. . . .

Parents sometimes do purposely omit [learning] from an apprehension that should their daughters be perceived to understand any learned language, or be conversant in books, they might be in danger of not finding husbands; so few men, as do, relishing these accomplishments in a lady. . . . For if it be considered that she who did seriously desire to make the least use of what she knew, would necessarily be obliged (for the gaining of time wherein she might do so) to order the course and manner of her life something differently from others of her sex and condition, it cannot be doubted but that a conduct which carried with it so much reproach to woman's idleness, and disappointment to men's vanity, would quickly be judged fit to be ridiculed out of the world before others were infected by the example. So that the best fate which a lady thus knowing and singular could expect, would be that, hardly escaping calumny, she should be in town the jest of the would-be-wits, the wonder of fools, and a scarecrow to keep from her house many honest people who are to be pitied for having no more wit than they have, because it is not their own fault that they

have no more. But in the country she would, probably fare still worse.
. . . Her prudent conduct and management of her affairs would probably
secure her from being thought out of her wits by her near neighbours; but
the country gentleman that wished her well, could not yet choose but be
afraid for her, lest too much learning might in time make her mad.

Monsieur Bruyère says indeed, and likely it is, that men have made no
laws, or put out any edicts whereby women are prohibited to open their
eyes; to read; to remember what they read; and to make use thereof in
their conversation, or in composing of works. But surely he had little
reason to suppose, as he herein does, that women could not otherwise than
by laws and edicts be restrained from learning. It is sufficient for this that
nobody assists them in it; and that they are made to see betimes that it
would be disadvantageous to them to have it. For how many men are
there, that arrive to any eminence therein? Though learning is not only
not prohibited to them by laws and edicts; but that ordinarily much care,
and pains [are] taken to give it them; and that great profits, oftentimes,
and always honour attends their having it.

The law of fashion, established by repute and disrepute, is to most
people the powerfullest of all laws, as Monsieur Bruyère very well knew,
whose too satirical genius makes him assign as causes of women's not
having knowledge, the universally necessary consequences of being bred in
the want thereof. But what on different occasions he says of the sex, will
either on the one part vindicate them, or else serve for an instance that
this ingenious writer's reflections, however witty, are not always instructive
or just corrections. For either women have generally some other more
powerful principle of their actions than what terminates in rendering
themselves pleasing to men (as he insinuates they have not), or else they
neglect the improvement of their minds and understandings, as not finding them of any use to that purpose; whence it is not equal in him to
charge it peculiarly (as he does) upon that sex (if it be indeed so much
chargeable on them as on men). . . . Yet I think it is but natural, and
alike so in both sexes, to desire to please the other, I may, I suppose,
without any injurious reflection upon the ladies, presume that if men did
usually find women the more amiable for being knowing, they would
much more commonly than now, be so.

The anonymous author of *An Essay in Defence of the Female Sex*
pointed out that knowledge of classical languages afforded members
of the masculine sex "a vaster field for their imaginations to rove
in," but then argued that women's ignorance of these languages was
not as great a disadvantage as it was made out to be by men.

An Essay in Defence of the Female Sex. London, 1696.

Let us look into the manner of our education, and see wherein it falls
short of the men's, and how the defects of it may be, and are generally
supplied. In our tender years they are the same, for after children can talk,
they are promiscuously taught to read and write by the same persons, and
at the same time both boys and girls. When these are acquired, which is
generally about the age of six or seven years, they begin to be separated,
and the boys are sent to the grammar school, and the girls to boarding
schools, or other places, to learn needle work, dancing, singing, music,
drawing, painting, and other accomplishments, according to the humour
and ability of the parents, or inclination of the children. Of all these,
reading and writing are the main instruments of conversation; though
music and painting may be allowed to contribute something towards it, as
they give us an insight into two arts, that make up a great part of the
pleasures and diversions of mankind. Here then lies the main defect, that
we are taught only our mother tongue, or perhaps French, which is now
very fashionable, and almost as familiar amongst women of quality as men;
whereas the other sex by means of a more extensive education to the
knowledge of the Roman and Greek languages, have a vaster field for their
imaginations to rove in, and their capacities thereby enlarged. To see
whether this be strictly true or not, I mean in what relates to our debate, I
will for once suppose, that we are instructed only in our own tongue, and
then inquire whether the disadvantage be so great as is commonly imagined. You know very well, Madam, that for conversation, it is not requisite
we should be philologers, rhetoricians, philosophers, historians or poets;
but only that we should think pertinently and express our thoughts properly, on such matters as are the proper subjects for a mixed conversation.

Contemporary accounts of girls' boarding schools substantiate what women like Margaret Cavendish, Duchess of Newcastle, Bathsua Makin, and Lady Damaris Masham say about the lesser importance assigned to "learning" in the education of girls. This letter, written during the Civil War by a lady in Kent to a neighbor of hers, describes the curriculum of a local school for girls and brings up another important aspect of "feminine education": modesty.

Letter from Lady Dering to Henry Oxinden on the education of his daughters Margaret and Elizabeth, aged twelve and eleven, born in 1635 and 1636. Letter dated 1647, during the Civil War.*

Sir,
    According to your desire, I have spoken with Mr. Beven of Ashford concerning your daughters being with him; he is very willing to do you and them any service in his power, and I am confident you will receive very good satisfaction in your charge, for he is a conscienable [sic], discreet man, and one that stands upon this credit; and so industrious for the benefitting of his scholars as if they be willing to receive, he will spare no pains to bring them to perfection; as I can witness by experience, when he taught my daughter. And besides the qualities of music both for the virginals and singing (if they have voices) and writing (and to cast account, which will be useful to them hereafter) he will be careful also that their behaviour be modest and such as becomes their quality; and that they grow in knowledge and understanding of God and their duty to him, which is above all. . . . I presume you will think thirty pounds a year for both reasonable, when you consider the hardness of the times and that there is more trouble with girls than boys. . . .

* B.L., Additional Mss. 28,001, fol. 276.

EDUCATION: "MODESTY"

Training in "virtue," "modesty," and humility was viewed by most parents of the seventeenth century as the most important aspect of a young woman's education. Even advocates of learning for women like Juan Luis Vives held this view. Others, as Daniel Tuvil points out, saw learning as a potentially dangerous threat to feminine modesty.

Asylum Veneris, or A Sanctuary for Ladies. London, 1616.

Learning in the breast of a woman is likened by their stoical adversaries to a sword in the hand of a mad man, which he knoweth not how to rule as reason shall inform him, but as the motions and violent fits of his distemperature shall enforce him. It doth not ballast their judgements, but only addeth more sail to their ambition; and like the weapon of Goliah, serveth but as an instrument to give the fatal period to their honour's overthrow. And surely this fond imagination hath purchased a free inheritance to itself in the bosoms of some undiscreeter parents, who hereupon will by no means endure that their daughters should be acquainted with any kind of literature at all. The pen must be forbidden them as the tree of good and evil, and upon their blessing they must not handle it. It is a pander to a virgin chastity, and betrayeth it, by venting forth those amorous passions that are incidents to hotter bloods, which otherwise, like fire raked up in embers, would peradventure in a little space be utterly consumed.

Books written for the "education of young ladies" in the seventeenth century repeatedly emphasized the large requirements of "modesty" and its connection to obedience, submission, humility, etc.

Richard Brathwaite, *The English Gentlewoman.* London, 1631 (reprinted 1641).

As I formerly advertised your husbands, not to intermeddle in those feminine employments, which concern your charge: so be it your modesty to decline from those interests, which properly admit their care. It is a hateful thing, saith that devout Father, to see a man practise the spindle, and a woman to handle the spear. You have peculiar offices equally designed; let them not be improperly mixed. That Roman was much condemned for imparting secrets of state to his wife; but his wife was more publicly taxed for laying down grounds how to rectify the state to her husband. This is a presuming evil, and too largely spreading, said that cynic, to be cured, till self-conceit, by a timely reproof, be rebaited. Humility is the way to prevent it: for though pride be a dangerous mate to accompany man: yet it is never so domineering, as when it please for sovereignty in a woman's mind. Remember then that divine mandate; it will be a means to calm it: *Thy desire shall be subject to thine husband, and he shall rule over thee.* (Gen. 3.16.) Which subjection, as it implies a distinct condition, so it begets in every family a harmonious order, or disposition. If there be danger in civil wars, there can be no great security in domestic brawls: where both the conqueror and conquered become equally endamaged. Do not contest then for precedency, since the divine law hath given your consort the priority. And in one word, to the end you may appear more amiable in his sight who made you; and in his choice, for whom he made you; retain in memory that divine lesson, for it prescribes you a perfect rule of direction, how to behave yourselves in your whole course or conversation: "In your very motion, gesture, and gate, observe modesty; it will infinitely become you, and attract a kind of reverend esteem in those who eye you."

Decency

Decency takes discretion ever along with her to choose her fashion. She accommodates her self to the place wherein she lives, the persons with whom she consorts, the rank or quality she partakes. She is too discreet to affect aught that may not seem her: too constant to change her habit for the invention of any phantastic wearer. What propriety she expresseth in her whole posture or carriage, you shall easily perceive, if you will but with a piercing eye, a serious survey, reflect upon her demeanour in her gate, look, speech, habit. Of which, distinctly, we purpose to entreat, in our entry to this observation; that by these you may probably collect the excellency of her condition.

Gate

That wherein we should express ourselves the humblest, many times transports us most, and proclaims us proudest. It is no hard thing to gather the disposition of our heart, by the dimension of our gate. What a circular gesture we shall observe some use in their pace, as if they were troubled with the vertigo! Others make a tinkling with their feet, and make discovery of their light thoughts, by their wanton gate. Others with a jetting and strutting pace, publish their haughty and self-conceited mind. Thus do our wantons (as if they had transparent bodies) display their folly, and subject themselves to the censure of levity. This cannot decency endure. When she sees women, whose modesty should be the ornament of their beauty, demean themselves more like actors than civil professants, she compassionately suffers with them, and with choice precepts of moral instruction (wherein she hath ever shown herself a singular proficient) she labours to reclaim them: with amorous, but virtuous rhetoric, she woos them, hoping by that means to win them. She bids them look back to preceding times, yea those, on which that glorious light which shines in these Christian days, never reflected; and there they shall find women highly censured, for that their outward carriage only made them suspected. A veil covered their face, modesty measured out their pace; their spectators were as so many censors: circumspect therefore were they of their carriage, lest they should become a scandal or blemish to their sex. Their repair to their temples was decent, without any loose or light gesture entering their temples, constant and settled was their behaviour. Quick was their pace in dispatch of household affairs; but slow in their epicureal visits or sensual gossipings.

Look

It is most true, that a wanton eye is the truest evidence of a wandering and distracted mind. The Arabians' proverb is elegant; "Shut the windows, that the house may give light." It is death that enters in by the windows. The house may be secured, if these be closed. Whence it was, that princely prophet prayed so earnestly, *Lord turn away mine eyes from vanity.* And hence appears man's misery: that those eyes, which should be the cisterns of sorrow, limbecks of contrition, should become the lodges of lust, and portals of our perdition. That those which were given us for assistants and associates, should become our assassinants. Our eye is made the sense of sorrow, because the sense of sin; yet more apt is she to give way to sin, than to find one tear to rinse her sin. An unclean eye is the messenger of an unclean heart: confine the one, and it will be a means to rectify the other. Many dangerous objects will a wandering eye find, whereon to vent the disposition of her corrupt heart. No place is exempted, no subject freed.

Speech

Without speech can no society subsist. By it we express what we are, as vessels discover themselves best by their sound. Discretion makes opportunity her anvil, whereon is wrought a seasonable discourse. Otherwise, howsoever we speak much, we discourse little. That sage Stagirian debating of the convenience and propriety of discourse before Alexander, maintained, that none were to be admitted to speak (by way of positive direction) but either those that managed his wars, or his philosophers which governed his house. This opinion tasted of too much strictness, will our women say, who assume to themselves a priviledge in arguments of discourse, be the argument never so coarse wherein they treat. Truth is, their tongues are held their defensive armour; but in no particular detract they more from their honour, than by giving too free scope to that glibbery member. . . . The direction is general, but to none more consequently useful than to young women; whose bashful silence is an ornament to their sex. Volubility of tongue in these, argues either rudeness of breeding, or boldness of expression. The former may be reclaimed by a discreet tutor, but the latter, being grounded on arrogancy of conceit, seldom or never. It will beseem you, gentlewomen, whose generous education hath estranged you from the first, and whose modest disposition hath weaned you from the last, in public consorts, to observe rather than discourse. It suits not with her honour for a young woman to be prolocutor: but especially when either men are in presence, or ancient matrons, to whom she owes a civil reverence, it will become her to tip her tongue with silence. Touching the subject of your discourse, when opportunity shall exact it of you, and without touch of immodesty expect it from you; make choice of such arguments as may best improve your knowledge in household affairs, and other private employments. To discourse of State-matters, will not become your auditory: nor to dispute of high points of Divinity, will it sort well with women of your quality. These she-clarks many times broach strange opinions, which, as they understand them not themselves, so they labour to entangle others of equal understanding to themselves.

Habit

There is nothing which moves us more to pride it in sin, than that which was first given us to cover our shame. The fruit of a tree made man a sinner; and the leaves of a tree gave him a cover. In your habit [i.e., dress] is your modesty best expressed. . . .

Robert Codrington, *The Second Part of Youth's Behaviour; or, Decency in Conversation Amongst Women.* London 1664.

Of the Behaviour of Young Ladies and Gentlewomen:

Zeuxis being to paint a perfect beauty, proposed to himself five of the most accomplished ladies in all Greece, to take from every one of them those charms and representations which he conceived to be most powerful: but to frame the model of a woman, whose behaviour should be such as to please in all companies, he had need of greater assistance; all that nature affords, or morality teacheth is too little for this end. In this subject the fairest ornaments are most necessary, and an aggregation of all the best qualities that can be desired, since they do all terminate and end in conversation as in their center.

To say then what seemeth to me to be at the first most necessary, I could content my self to wish in young gentlewomen those three perfections which Socrates desired in his disciples, *discretion, silence,* and *modesty;* I would not have them think that I purpose to take away from them the use of speech in the stead of ruling it, I should not do well to go about to frame a conversation of dumb persons, but to make a powerful war against all noise and clamour, a most dangerous enemy in human society; silence gives I know not what grace to speech itself, and there is nothing truer, than as rests in music, so pauses in discourse being well used, do make that more plainly appear, which is the best of all and the sweetest in it.

Behaviour belongeth both to the body and the soul, and society is the comfort of the living; life without it is a kind of death; no hour can be so tedious which conversation and discourse cannot pass over with delight. What a desert is the world without society and behaviour? Gentlewomen who would be observed for their behaviour, ought to beware whom they elect into the number of their companions, for the world will be apt to judge of them according to the company they do keep. Augustus Caesar discerned the inclinations of his two daughters Livia and Julia, by the disposition of those who professed courtship to them, for ladies of honour and of eminence came to attend upon Livia, and those who were more licentious on his daughter Julia. "Young virgins (saith Plutarch) above all things are to consort with those whose lives were never tainted with any suspicion of incontinence, and whose tongues were never stained with any immodest language." Many questions are oftentimes asked them by those that profess love unto them, which are not to be answered but by silence.

Samuel Torshell, *The Woman's Glorie; A Treatise Asserting the Due Honour of That Sex, and Directing Wherein That Honour Consists.* London, 1645.

Modesty:

This is one of the most natural and most useful tables of the mind, wherein one may presently read what is printed in the whole volume. It is as proper, in the opinion of some, to the woman's sex as flying to a bird, swimming to a fish, beauty to a flower. Certainly a good heart looks out through modest eyes, and gives an answer to any that asks "who is within" with modest words, and dwells not at the sign of the bush or red lattice or painted post. A glorious soul is above dresses, and despiseth such as have no higher or other thoughts, than what concern[s] their gorget and their hair. The calm-constant-watchful-modest-composed-disposition is surely the most excellent temper, and the most useful, for this governs the heart, and makes one fit and able to entertain those pleasures by which others are lost and undone. Such a one may pledge even Circe in her cup and yet not be transformed: for such a one will only sip, but not drink deep of pleasures lawful. This preserves in tune and keeps the scale of affections even. This teaches a denying and preventing behaviour towards tentations *[sic]*. 'Tis much better than philosopher's wool to stop the ear with. It is the best guardian both of the eye and ear.

The dire tone and pious language of *The Ladies Calling* (1673) make it hard for the modern reader to believe that this book was probably, along with Lord Halifax's *The Lady's New-Year's-Gift: or, Advice to a Daughter*, the most influential "guide for the female sex" written in the seventeenth century. It is quoted as an authority on the subject by several women writers and was one of the two volumes written especially for women listed in the survey of a *Ladies' Library* published in the *Spectator* in 1711 (the other was Lord Halifax's *The Lady's New-Year's-Gift*).

The repeated emphasis here on the large requirements of "modesty" is to be found over and over again in most of the books on "feminine education" that precede *The Ladies Calling*.

[Richard Allestree,] *The Ladies Calling*. London, 1673 (reprinted 1675).

The two grand elements essential to the virgin state, are modesty and obedience, which though necessary to all, yet are in a more eminent degree required here . . . [it] should appear in its highest elevation, and should come up to shamefacedness. [A virgin's] look, her speech, her whole behaviour should own a humble distrust of herself; she is to look on herself but as a novice, a probationer in the world, and must take this time rather to learn and observe, than to dictate and prescribe. Indeed there is scarce anything looks more indecent, than to see a young maid too forward and confident in her talk. . . .

But modesty confines not itself to the face, she is there only in shadow and effigy: but is in life and motion in the words, whence she banishes all indecency and rudeness, all insolent vauntings, and supercilious disdains, and whatever else may render a person troublesome or ridiculous to the company. Nor does she only refine the language, but she tunes it too, modulates the tone and accent, admits no unhandsome earnestness, or loudness of discourse. . . . A woman's tongue should indeed be like the imaginary music of the spheres, sweet and charming, but not to be heard at a distance. And as modesty prescribes the manner, so it does also the measure of speaking, restrains all excessive talkativeness, a fault incident to none but the bold.

If we consider modesty in this sense, we shall find it the most indispensable requisite of a woman, a thing so essential and natural to the sex, that even the least declination from it, is a proportionable receding from womanhood, but the total abandoning it ranks them among brutes, nay sets them as far beneath those, as an acquired vileness is below a native. I need make no collection of the verdicts either of the philosophers or divines in the case, it being so much an instinct of nature, that though too many make a shift to suppress it in themselves, yet they cannot so darken the notion in others, but that an impudent woman is looked on as a kind of monster, a thing diverted and distorted from its proper form. That there is indeed a strange repugnancy to nature, needs no other evidence than the struggling, and difficulty in the first violations of modesty, which always begin with regrets and blushes, and require a great deal of self-denial, much of vicious fortitude, to encounter with the recoilings and upbraidings of their own minds. . . . When we speak of modesty in our present notion of it, we are not to oppose it only to the grosser act of incontinency, but to all those misbehaviours, which either discover or may create an inclination to it. . . .

But there is another breach of modesty, as it relates to chastity, in which [virgins] are yet more especially concerned. The very name of virgin imports a most critical niceness in that point. Every indecent curiosity, or impure fancy, is a deflowering of the mind, and every the least corruption of them gives some degrees of defilement to the body too. For between the state of pure immaculate virginity and arrant prostitution, there are many intermedial steps, and she that makes any of them is so far departed from her first integrity. She that listens to any wanton discourse has violated her ears, she that speaks any, her tongue, every immodest glance vitiates her eye, and every the lightest act of dalliance leaves something of stain and sulliage behind it. There is therefore a most rigorous caution requisite herein: for as nothing is more clean and white than a perfect virginity, so every the least spot or soil is the more discernable.

George Savile, Marquess of Halifax, *The Lady's New-Year's-Gift: or, Advice to a Daughter.* London, 1688 (reprinted 1700).

You must first lay it down for a foundation in general, that there is inequality in the sexes, and that for the better oeconomy of the world, the men, who were to be the law-givers, had the larger share of reason bestowed upon them; by which means your sex is the better prepared for the compliance that is necessary for the better performance of those duties which seem to be most properly assigned to it.

> Halifax goes on to acknowledge that there may be some injustice in the double standard of behavior and the subjection required by women, but nevertheless advises his daughter to "make your best of what is settled by law and custom, and not vainly imagine, that it will be changed for your sake." He then describes the most common form of dissatisfaction wives experience in marriage:

You are to consider, you live in a time which hath rendered some kind of frailties so habitual, that they lay claim to large grains of allowance. The world in this is somewhat unequal, and our sex seemeth to play the tyrant in distinguishing partially for ourselves, by making that in the utmost degree criminal in the woman, which in a man passeth under a much gentler censure. The root and the excuse of this injustice is the preservation of families from any mixture which may bring a blemish to them: and whilst the point of honour continues to be so placed, it seems unavoidable to give your sex, the greater share of the penalty. But if in this it lieth under any disadvantage, you are more than recompensed, by having the honour of families in your keeping. The consideration so great a trust must give you, maketh full amends; and this power the world hath lodged in you, can hardly fail to restrain the severity of an ill husband, and to improve the kindness and esteem of a good one. This being so, remember, that next to the danger of committing the fault yourself, the greatest is that of seeing it in your husband. Do not seem to look or hear that way: if he is a man of sense, he will reclaim himself; the folly of it, is of itself sufficient to cure him: if he is not so, he will be provoked, but not reformed. To expostulate in these cases, looketh like declaring war, and preparing reprisals; which to a thinking husband would be a dangerous reflexion. Besides, it is so coarse a reason which will be assigned for a lady's too great warmth upon such an occasion, that modesty no less than prudence ought to restrain her; since such an undecent complaint makes a wife much more ridiculous, than the injury that provoketh her to it. But it is yet worse, and more unskilful, to blaze it in the world, expecting it should rise up in arms to take her part: whereas she will find, it can have no other effect, than that she will be served up in all companies, as the reigning jest at that time; and will continue to be the common entertainment, till she is rescued by some newer folly that cometh upon the stage, and driveth her away from it. The impertinence of such methods is so plain, that it doth not deserve the pains of being laid open. Be assured, that in these cases your discretion and silence will be the most prevailing reproof.

Nahum Tate held a much more positive view of women than the author of *The Ladies Calling*, and in a book published in 1693 argued from historical example that women were indeed capable of learning. In the matter of "modesty," however, he fell back on the more conservative view.

A Present for the Ladies: Being an Historical Account of Several Illustrious Persons of the Female Sex. London, 1693.

To descend from these austere and philosophical heights, to the more cheerful walks of temperance, mildness, innocency, modesty, chastity, and the rest, which may as properly be called graces as virtues, we shall find them chiefly possessed by, as being the natural inheritance of the female sex. That no women have forfeited their birth-right in any of these, is no more to be affirmed than that none of the angels have fallen: every woman is born to, I may say, every woman is born with them. The sex is no more to be reproached for some delinquents, than the innocent among the forementioned angels. The legions that kept their station, shone the brighter for those that fell.

Intemperance is visible in but few of the very worst amongst them; meekness is seldom disordered in them without great provocation; and as their sex is generally more difficult to be exasperated, they are more easy to forgive than ours: 'tis for the most part our fault if they injure us; modesty is so inherent to their frame, that they cannot divest themselves of it without violence to their nature. We have heard of some ladies who have been modest almost to a crime.

Candaules had the vanity to expose his Queen naked to the view of his favorite Gyges, to show him what a treasure of beauty he was possessed of; the practice was not so dexterously managed, but the lady was sensible of the abuse, and requested her husband to kill the conscious spectator: which he refusing, she applied herself to the other, engaging him to kill the King. We hear of no former disgust that she had to her husband, but since he would not dispatch his friend, her modesty could not bear to have two witnesses of her undressing alive at the same time.

The Thyades or Bacchanal women, whose religion obliged them sometimes to drink to excess, as they wandered up and down in the fury of their wine, it happened once that they came unwittingly into the city of Amphissa, where being wearied with their ramblings, they cast themselves dispersedly in the marketplace, where they fell asleep. The matrons of the town fearing lest some injury might be offered them by the souldiers there in garrison, watched by them in person till morning, guarding and girting their clothes about their feet, that no indecency might happen, and with a reverent silence attended them till they awaked: then finding them returned to their senses, they ministered to them all such necessaries as the city afforded, and trusted them only to the charge and care of their husbands to conduct them safely home to their own cities. These Bacchanals were the wives of their enemies who were then actually in war with the Amphissans; but this was no consideration with these matrons to make them neglect their just care for the common modesty of their sex.

Some have been so tender in this point, that they have severely revenged the most harmless accidents upon themselves. In most uncultivated nations, the women are not without a sense of this virtue. An Indian girl in one of our plantations, while she was ministering at table, according to her custom, it happened that in taking off a dish, she slipped upon the handle of a knife that dropped out of her hand, and in her falling discovered part of her body, whereof being sensible by the company's laughing, she gave them as sudden occasion to be serious; for she was no sooner removed from their sight, but she drenched the same knife in her lifesblood.

Fame is grown hoarse with reciting the story of Lucretia; 'tis true, she acted the part of a Roman lady under her misfortune: but how many thousands of the sex have been beforehand with fate, who by a timely dispatch to the grave, did not suffer the threatened violence to approach them; by which means they left their bodies as unspotted as their souls. How many both of matrons and virgins have forever celebrated their names by running to the arms of death, to avoid the lawless embraces of tyrants? For the honour of our nation, give me leave to mention our own fair nuns of Winchester, in the time of the Danish invasion: they were disciplined in a severer religion than that of the Roman ladies; the faith and conscience they professed, not permitting to take the refuge of a voluntary fate. In this difficulty, their chastity taught them a way that was at once more daring and innocent than a voluntary destruction of their own lives. For before the approach of the ravishers, they so disfigured their beauties by cutting off their own noses and mangling their faces, that they rendered themselves spectacles of horrour, and converted the lust of the assassins into pity.

The Ladies Dictionary was another book which defended some very advanced views on women's education, but when it came to the "duties" of a woman, the author simply turned to *The Ladies Calling* and copied.

The Ladies Dictionary. London, 1694.

Virgins:

Virgins of tender years in the spring and bloom of their beauties and sprightly blood many will say, have various difficulties to struggle with; modesty and obedience is *[sic]* necessarily required to guard the forts of their chastity, and to give a power to their parents to hinder those assaults, which tender years may not be so capable of avoiding, without good counsel and wholesome advice. . . . Modesty [in virgins] should appear in its highest elevation, coming up even to shamefacedness: her looks, her speech, her whole behaviour should own an humble distrust of herself. She is to look on herself but as a novice or probationer in the world, and must take this time rather to observe and learn than to dictate: for we must aver, there is scarcely any thing looks more innocent,* than to see a young maid too confident, or forward in gestures and discourse. But there is another breach of modesty, as it relates to her chastity which more nearly concerns them; the very name of virgins, imports a critical niceness in that point, every impure fancy or indecent curiosity is a deflowering of the mind, and every the least corruption of them, gives some degree of defilement to the body likewise; for between the state of a pure, immaculate virgin, and a common prostitute, there are many intermedial steps, and she that takes any of them has so far departed from her first integrity, that if she listens to any wanton discourse, her ears are violated; and if she talks any, her tongue suffers no less a violation: her eyes placed on wanton objects run the same risk, and every the lightest daliance of action, leaves something of a sullying or stain behind it; there is therefore a most rigorous caution requisite herein. For as nothing is more clear and candid than perfect virginity, so the very least spot or soil is the most discernable. . . .

Pardon us, ladies, if you think we are now writing to nuns; no, we design

---

* This is probably a misprint of "indecent," or a similar word.

not to confine you to a cloister, but leave you all manner of civil freedom, yet would [not] have it turn to your injury or disadvantage; for those that are desirous of marriage, may by modest and reserved ways sooner procure it to their happiness, than by any other means whatsoever. . . .

Elaborate directions in all of these books are given on every aspect of life in which the question of "modesty" was concerned. A woman's entire relation to the world—walking, looking, talking—was properly subject to the restraints of a chaste posture, according to these texts.

The Whole Duty of a Woman. London, 1696.

Modesty is properly termed, the science of decent motion; as being a guider and regulator of all decent and comely carriage and behaviour, checking and controuling rudeness, and any thing tending to confidence and unmannerliness, and is held the great civilizer of conversation: balancing the mind with humble and sober thoughts of your selves, and ordering every part of the outward frame, in the most winning and obliging manner.

It appears in the face in calm and comely looks, where it makes due impressions; so that it seems from thence to have acquired the name of shamefacedness. And truly whatever the modern opinion of some may be, there is nothing adds a greater luster to feminine beauty.

Modesty confines itself not to the face only, for there it may in some sense, be said to be in shadow and effigy, but spreads it self in life, motion and words: banishing all indecency and rudeness, all insolent vauntings and superciliousness, or whatever else may render our sex troublesome or uneasy to company or conversation. It refines and tunes the language, modulates the tone and accents; not admitting the intrusion of unhandsome, earnest, or loud discourse. So that the modest tongue is like the imaginable music of the spheres, sweet and charming, but not to be heard at a distance.

As modesty prescribes the manner, so it also does the measure of speaking. It restrains all excessive talkativeness, for that indeed is one of the greatest assumings imaginable; and so rude an imposing on company, that there can scarce be a greater indecency in conversation.

Modesty therefore ought, if you have respect to virtue and a good name, to appear in its highest elevation. Your looks, your speech, and the course of your whole behaviour, should own an humble distrust of your selves; rather being willing to learn and observe, than to dictate and prescribe, unless upon very emergent occasions, and that to those that are rambling in the paths of looseness. And therefore, as you value your reputation, keep up to the strictness of this virtue, lest when you conceive it not amiss, in trivial matters, to launch beyond the bounds of modesty, you are violently carried too far to retreat before you are aware; as I shall show you in the contrary on this excellent adornment of our sex.

Immodesty is held, even in heathen nations, a great reproach and scandal, especially where it is found in women; and St. Paul, who spoke by an excellent spirit, commands, *That women adorn themselves in modest apparel, with shamefacedness, and sobriety; not with broidered hair, or gold, or pearl, or costly array, but (which becometh women professing Godliness) with God's works*, I Tim. 2.9. So that when those that are not well affected to modesty, have strained their art to the highest pitch, an innocent modesty and native simplicity of looks, will eclipse their imaginary splendour, and triumph over their artificial beauties. And indeed, if a woman be adorned with all the embellishments of art, and care of nature to boot, yet, if boldness, scorn, and haughty looks be imprinted in her face, they blot out all the lines of comeliness, and like a dark cloud over the sun, shade the view of all that was otherwise amiable; and renders its blackness but the more observable, by being placed nearer somewhat that was apt to attract the eyes, and leave a stain on their names and reputations.

There is scarce any thing to be found that appears more indecent, than to be proud, or too forward in overmuch talk, or indecent behaviour. Yet now we too sadly see, that which the former ages called pride and boldness, is called, the sign of a great spirit, gentle breeding, and assurance. Yet I have seen such bad superstructures built on that foundation, as I well hope will not recommend them to any considering person of our sex. . . .

The acts of chastity, in their proper offices of grace, are in general these, viz. To resist all unchaste and unclean thoughts, by no means entertaining pleasure in the unfruitful fancies, and remembrances of uncleanness, although no definite desire or resolution be entertained.

At no hand to entertain any desire, or phantastic imaginary love, though by shame, or disability, or other circumstances they be restrained from act. To have a chaste eye as well as all the other members, for if that be permitted to lust, you can no otherwise be termed chaste, than she can be called severe to her self and mortified, that sits all day seeing plays and revelings, and out of an appetite to feast her eyes neglects her convenient food.

Your heart and mind must be chaste as well as your members. They must be pure, detesting all uncleanness; disliking all ill motions, and past actions, circumstances, discourses, and likenesses. The discourse must be chaste and pure; and great care must be taken to decline all indecencies of language: chaining the tongue, and restraining it, with such graces as oppose uncleanness in the highest nature.

You must disapprove by an after act, all things of this kind, that may at any time crowd at unawares, into your imaginations: nay those temptations that Satan sometimes will be apt to intrude on your fancy in lascivious dreams; for if you with pleasure remember them, that which was innocent, becoming voluntary, is made sinful. In observing these rules, you will, in a great measure, keep your selves unspotted from the flesh. But [by] the blessings, and proper effects of chastity, you may better understand by the evils of its contraries.

[Richard Allestree,] *The Ladies Calling.* London, 1673 (reprinted 1675).

This great indecency of loquacity in women, I am willing to hope is the reason why that sex is so generally charged with it; not that they are all guilty, but that when they are, it appears so unhandsome, as makes it the more eminent and remarkable. Whether it were from that ungracefulness of the thing, or from the propension women have to it, I shall not determine, but we find the Apostle very earnest in his cautions against it. . . . He expressly enjoins women *to keep silence in the church,* where he affirms it is a shame for them to speak: and though this seems only restrained to the ecclesiastical assemblies, yet even so it reaches home to the gifted women of our age, who take upon them to be teachers. . . . But besides this, he has a more indefinite prescription of silence to women, I Tim. 2 11. *Let women learn in silence;* and again, V. 12. *to be in silence.* The Apostle seems to ground the phrase, not only on the inferiority of the woman in regard of the creation and the first sin, but also on the presumption that they needed instruction, towards which silence has always been reckoned an indispensible qualification . . . if some women of our age think they have outgone that novice state the Apostle supposes, and want no teaching, I must crave leave to believe, they want that very first principle which should set them to learn, i.e. the knowledge of their own ignorance.

Besides this assuming sort of talkativeness, there is another usually charged upon the sex—a mere chatting, prattling humour, which maintains itself at the cost of their neighbours, and can never want supplies as long as there is anybody within the reach of their observation. This I would fain hope is most the vice of the vulgar sort of women, the education of the nobler setting them above those mean entertainments. . . . But the greater the prejudice is that they lie under in this respect, the greater ought to be their caution to vindicate not only their persons but their sex, from the imputation, which is extremely reproachful: this babbling humour being a symptom of a loose, impotent soul, a kind of incontinence of the mind, that can retain nothing committed to it, but as if that also had its diabetic passion, perpetually and almost insensibly evacuating all.

The Ladies Dictionary. London, 1694.

Behaviour, in Conversation:

To say what seems to me to be at the first most necessary, I could content myself to wish in young gentlewomen those three perfections which Socrates desired in his disciples: discretion, silence and modesty. Behaviour in young ladies is a comely grace if well considered, and diligently regarded; it is that which makes them to be esteemed in the world, and fits them to go abroad in it, as they would wish to be prized and rated: it raises them a character that will embalm their names to posterity, and better the age they live in, if their examples be put in practice, and all allow examples better than presidents [sic] or precepts. Let your behaviour then strongly incline towards a reserved part, not excluding a modest freedom, being well timed and innocent, but avoid all extravagances that too much encumber and pester the age. And indeed though a generous freedom in it self be innocent and harmless, yet the too great liberty ill men upon that account have taken to encroach upon the honour of your sex, though but in their own opinions, has made such freedom in a manner unjustifiable, and involved you into a necessity of reducing it into more strictness, and although it cannot so alter the nature of things, as to render that criminal, which in itself is indifferent; yet if it make it hazardous to your reputations, that ought to be a sufficient cause for a nearer reservedness. A close behaviour is the most seemly to receive virtue for a constant guest, because it is a fortress in which it can only be secure from assaults: for proper and seemly reserves, are the outworks, and must not at any time be deserted by those that design to keep the main strength in possession; for then if you see the danger at a distance, you have more time to prepare for the repelling of it: she that will suffer things to come to the utmost extremity, by trusting too far to her strength is the more easily overcome. . . . Your eyes too must be kept within compass, their wanderings, restrained. . . . Virginity is an enclosed garden; it should not admit of any such violation, the very report may cast a blemish on it. Some have been enslaved to that passion deservedly, which at first they entertained disdainfully. Presumption is a daring sin, and always brings forth an untimely birth. The way to prevent this is in the behaviour, to give not the least occasion to the tempter that shall endeavour to ensnare them, nor to give way to the weakness of their own desires. How excellent had many ladies been, and how inpregnable had been their chastities, if they had not been possessed with such a dangerous security, when they let open their windows to betray themselves, when they leave their chamber to walk, and on purpose to be seen in public.

Gate or Gesture to Be Observed by Ladies:

Great notice is taken of the gate and gesture of young ladies, and observations made thereon by the nice and censorious: they guess at the disposition of her heart by the dimension of her motion, concluding a light carriage most commonly discovers a loose inclination, and that jetting, tossing the head, bridling up the chin, and walking stately, shows a haughtiness and self-conceit. They will say, were a lady's body transparent, she could not more perspicuously display her levity of mind than by wanton gesticulations. This then must be avoided, to avoid offence and scandal. . . . If a virtuous lady seriously considers the apish gestures of light and loose women, they must needs not only make her detest an imitation, but utterly put her out of conceit with any that shall be so vain to imitate them. A swimming gate, or an affected pace, as if you were treading out, or measuring the ground by the foot as you pass along, and that your mind kept pace with every step, is to be avoided, lest it be looked upon as a studied measure to be singular in your walking, and consequently draw more eyes upon you than others. A shuffling or [wriggling] motion is likewise discommendable; it gives a suspicion that you are crook-legged, or have received some hurt in your limbs that has distorted them . . . beware of taking stradling steps, or running ahead, for those are indecent in a lady.

Eye, How to Govern It:

Eyes are the casements of the body, and many times by standing too much open, let in things hurtful to the mind; a wanton eye is the truest evidence of wandering and unsteadfast thoughts; we may see too much, if we be not careful in governing our eyes, and keeping them from going astray, and returning with vain objects to the fancy and imagination, which, making unhappy impressions, they cannot be easily obliterated. . . . Therefore, ladies, to prevent the malady, which like a spreading contagion disperses itself into most societies, you must keep your eyes within compass, from wandering as much as possible. . . . Consult chas-

tity and modesty, and as far as their rules allow, you may proceed with
safety but all beyond is danger, which is to be shunned and avoided. . . .
Give no occasion then ladies for any to tax your eyes with any thing that is
not modest, comely, and allowable; consider in company at home, if of the
different sex, nor in your walkings abroad to give them their wanderings,
but let your mind be upon them, to keep them in their due bounds, lest
becoming a prey to others, you are enslaved, or if you make a prey of
others, your conquest may however prove very troublesome and uneasy to
you. The eyes are not the only dangerous things about you. The tongue
many times for want of good government, betrays you into divers misfortunes. . . .

Books. Directions to Ladies About Reading Them:

It is not necessary then to read many books, but to read the best, and
especially never to be curious of such, whereby we cannot learn any thing,
without the danger of becoming vicious. . . . The reading of many wanton things do heat by little and little; it insensibly takes away the repugnancy and the horrour we have to evil; and we acquaint our selves so
thoroughly with the image of vice, as we afterwards fear it not when we do
meet with vice itself. When once shame is lost, we are in great danger to
lose that which is not preserved but by it. But this is not all; for after that
these pamphlets and songs of wantonness, have made young maidens
bold, it afterwards doth make them to practise what they read. . . .
These are but cunning lessons, to learn young maids to sin more wittily;
and there is no man can comprehend with what reason, nay with what
probability, such perilous books and sonnets may be justified.

Anger in Ladies:

Anger is unseemly and discommendable in all, but more especially in
young ladies, who like doves, should be without the gall that ferments and
stirs up these kind[s] of passions to disturb and hurt the mind, and spot
the names of those that indulge them with the epithets of rash, peevish,
revengeful and inconsiderate anger, is a professed enemy to reason, council, or sound advice; it is a storm and loudness in which none of these can
be heard, nor is it to be surpressed [sic] but by something that is as inward
as itself, and more habitual. . . . It makes a beauteous face in a little
time monstrously deformed and contemptible, rendering the voice of an
unpleasing sound, the eyes fiery and staring, and separates the lovely mix-

ture of roses and lillies, by quite removing one or the other out of the ladies' cheeks. . . . For the most part proceeding from pusillanimity or softness of spirit, which makes the fair sex frequently more subject to anger than the other, by reason the passions of their minds are sooner moved and agitated. . . . Be diligent then, ladies, to observe that it gain not too great a power over you . . . observe what we now lay down as rules to be regarded in avoiding or remedying this dangerous evil: 1) Anger arising in your breasts, instantly seal up your lips, and let it not go forth; for like fire, when it wants vent, it will suppress itself. . . . 2) Observe that humility is the most excellent natural cure for anger. . . .

The hypocrisy of this obsession with feminine "virtue" was deplored by Lady Damaris Masham, who argued that both sexes had a duty to remain chaste.

Occasional Thoughts in Reference to a Vertuous or Christian Life. London, 1705.

The other thing which I imagine faulty, does more peculiarly concern the sex, but is yet chiefly practised in regard of those of it who are of quality, and that is the insinuation into them such a notion of honour as if the praise of men ought to be the supreme object of their desires and the great motive with them to virtue: a term which, when applied to women, is rarely designed . . . to signify anything but the single virtue of chastity. . . . To persuade Ladies, then, that what they cannot want without being contemptible, is the chief merit they are capable of having, must naturally give them such low thoughts of themselves as will hinder them from aspiring after anything excellent, or else make them believe that this mean opinion of them is owing to the injustice of such men in their regard as pretend to be their masters. A belief too often endeavoured to be improved in them by others. . . .

Chastity is, according to the Gospel, a duty to both sexes, yet a transgression herein, even with the aggravation of wronging another man, and possibly a whole family thereby, is admirably talked of, as if it was but a peccadillo in a young man. A far less criminal offence against this duty in a maid shall in the opinion of the same persons brand her with perpetual infamy: the nearest relations oftentimes are hardly brought to look upon her after such a dishonour done by her to their family, whilst the fault of her more guilty brother finds but very moderate reproof from them, and in a little while, it may be, becomes the subject of their mirth and raillery.

Margaret Cavendish, the Duchess of Newcastle, however, defended the necessity for a double sexual standard, and demonstrated how the compromise of a woman's chastity could ruin her whole family and "the whole posterity."

The World's Olio. London, 1655.

Of Adulteries

In marriage it is far worse, and more inconveniencies come by the disobedience of the wife, and her adulteries, than the husband. For first, she dishonours her self, insomuch as her company is an aspersion to all honest women that frequent therein, which makes the chaste to shun her society. Next, she is a dishonour to the family from whence she sprung, and makes the world suspect the chastity of her mother; for there is an old saying, "Cat will after kind": thus we see that the world is apt to judge from the original. The third dishonour is to their children; for were they never so beautiful, and virtuous, yet families of honour refuse to match with them, unless they bring great advantage by their wealth; and then none will receive them into their stock, but those whom poverty hath eaten up; for the disgrace is like the leprosy, never to be cured; and it infects the whole posterity, and it gives spots to the family it is joined with. The fourth and last dishonour is to the husband; for let a husband of a dishonest wife be never so worthy a man, yet her follies shall lessen the esteem of his merits to the generality of the world; although he have a great valour, a flowing generosity, a sound judgement, a fine wit, and an honest mind; well bred, beautiful, rich, honourable, yet the vulgar part of the world will point at him, as a fool, a coward; and all they can think to be bad in a man; nay those excellent virtues of nature and education, shall be dimmed, and lose their gloss even to the wife, although it be unjust to misprize one for the fault of the other. . . .

This is the reason that gallant, worthy, and wise men are dishonoured by their dishonest wives. Besides the dishonour, the inconveniencies are many; first, it abolisheth all lawful and right inheritance; for the child that is born in wedlock, although begot by another man, shall inherit the husband's estate, although it be known to be another man's, by our laws.

Next, for the abuses of industry; as for the profit and pain of his labour to go to a stranger. Thirdly, for the weakening of natural affection; for a man that mistrusts that all are not his own, makes him not love any, because he cannot guess which are his; rather, he hates all, for fear he should love him that brings him dishonour, and discontent; or at least set the parents upon the rack, with fear and grief, as afraid to mistake their own, and grieve that their own may have too little affection from them. Thence it takes away the tenderness of affection from the parents, and [adds] neglects and rigour to their children; it makes disobedience from children to their parents, for the disgrace and wrong they receive; so that suspicion is become the master of the house, and shame the mistress, unthankfulness the steward, and nothing is entertained but discontents.

Adulteries of Men

The like dishonour and inconvenience comes not by adultery of the husband, as the wife; for the children receive no dishonour by the father's liberty, nor the wife very much; for the worst that can be thought, is, that she is not so pleasing to her husband, either in her person, or in her humour. Nay, it begets rather a greater luster to her merits, and sets off her virtues more to her advantage; as, to show her fortitude in patience, her constancy in chastity, her love in her obedience; which the world taking notice of, pities her hard fortune in an unkind husband. . . .

The agonies a young woman whose reputation was compromised might suffer are eloquently testified to in a letter a young woman wrote to her lover before the Civil War.

A letter from Dorothy Denne, a gentlewoman, to her lover, William Taylor, who was her father's servingman:*

I think there lives not a sadder heart than mine in the world, neither have I enjoyed scarce one hour of contentment since we happened to be discovered at our last meeting. . . . If you had borne any true and real affection to me and valued my reputation you would never have run that hazard, knowing that that woman which has lost her good name is dead while she lives . . . do you not think it a sin of a high nature for me to be disobedient and rebellious to my father and run away with you, or can I expect to have the blessing of God if I should do so. . . . You wrote me word of a gentlewoman that you might have, worth a thousand pounds; for the Lord's sake take her or any other and make not yourself and me forever miserable. You speak of having me without any clothes or one penny in my purse; people would think me either stark mad or a fool, now I have the possibility of a fortune and may live happily, to bring myself to beggery and contempt of all that know me. . . .

* B.L., Additional Mss. 28,003, fol. 173.

The ultimate compromise of "modesty," though unthinkable, occasionally did happen. The legal penalty for this transgression was described by the author of this text as "gentle and easy."

George Meriton, *Immorality, Debauchery, and Profaneness Exposed . . . Containing a Compendium of the Penal Laws Now in Force Against . . . Debauched, Incontinency, and Bastard-getting.* London, 1698.

Every lewd woman which shall have any bastard child, which may be chargeable to the parish, the Justice of Peace shall commit such lewd women to the House of Correction, there to be punished, and set on work during the term of one whole year, and if afterwards she offend again, then to be committed to the House of Correction as aforesaid, and to remain there until she can put in good sureties for her good behaviour, not to offend so again.

II
The Women's Sharpe Revenge

In Lady Elizabeth Carey's time, there were two important sources of inspiration that provided the necessary impetus for overcoming women's reluctance to compromise their "modesty" through publication. The first was religion and the second was the debate over women. An increasing number of women entered into the passionate controversies over religion that ultimately led to the Puritan revolution, but most of the women who wrote these tracts viewed themselves as the passive vehicles for divine voices—an attitude commonly shared by their male coreligionists. One exception is the Quaker sect, whose women were more than usually conscious of the difficulties created by women's preaching.

The women who contributed to the debate over women, however, have much more in common with women who later wrote literary works. Often they overlapped, since a great number of women who published felt compelled to justify their "transgression" and were often drawn into argument concerning woman's nature in the course of doing so. The repeated attacks on women, conversely, provided a great source of anger that pushed women to answer in print.

After the death of Queen Elizabeth, the misogynistic diatribes that had appeared off and on throughout the sixteenth century accelerated noticeably in frequency—and ferocity. The most famous was a tract published in 1615 by one Joseph Swetnam, a man of the middling class who kept a fencing school in Bristol. Under the title *The Arraignment of Lewd, Idle, Froward, and Unconstant Women; or the Vanity of Them, Choose You Whether. With a Commendation of Wise, Virtuous, and Honest Women,* Swetnam brought out all the medieval arguments about woman's sinful and wayward nature, based on biblical sources. In an almost hysterical tone, Swetnam excoriated the extravagance, lust, and arrogance of women, and especially warned his contemporaries about the dangers of a woman's chief strength—her tongue. The book was enormously popular, and went into ten more editions before 1634. It was reprinted again and again during the next century; the last edition appeared in 1807.

In what was probably an unprecedented response, four (possibly five) women answered Swetnam's attack in print. The first was Rachel Speght, a young woman who published *A Mouzell for Melastomus, the Cynicall Baiter of, and Foule Mouthed Barker Against Evahs Sex. Or an Apologeticall Answere to That Irreligious and Illiterate Pamphlet Made by Io. Sw.* Despite the spirited nature of her title, Rachel Speght's defense of women was an unfortunately inept jumble of quoted Scripture, practically unintelligible for a modern reader. Speght was the daughter of a minister, and not yet twenty: clearly her education was inadequate to the task she had set herself. Much more articulate and, on occasion, savagely funny attacks on Swetnam were published by three women who wrote under pseudonyms: "Ester Sowerman" (a joke on Swetnam) published *Ester Hath Hanged Haman: or, An Answere To a Lewd Pamphlet, Entituled, The Arraignment of Women* (1617); a woman who called herself "Joane Sharpe" appended "A Defence of Women, Against the Author of the Arraignment of Women" to Sowerman's text; "Constantia Munda" wrote *The Worming of a Mad Dogge: or, A Soppe for Cerberus the Jaylor of Hell. No Confutation but a Sharp Redargution of the Bayter of Women* (1617); and finally, an author who does not specify his or her sex produced a popular play called *Swetnam, the Woman-hater, Arraigned by Women* (1620).

This outpouring of protest may well be the first time in English history that an attack on women elicited a response from women themselves in print and in multiple force. A comment made by "Esther Sowerman" indicates that the feminist discontent expressed by these writers was far from an isolated phenomenon: she begins her pamphlet by recounting that she was at a dinner party in London, among friends, when "as nothing is more usual for table-talk, there fell out a discourse concerning women, some defending, others objecting against our sex. . . ."

Putting aside Rachel Speght's rather indigestible text, I have excerpted sections from the other women's responses, as well as some of Swetnam's original attack.

Joseph Swetnam, *The Arraignment of Lewd, Idle, Froward, and Unconstant Women; or the Vanity of Them, Choose You Whether. With a Commendation of Wise, Virtuous, and Honest Women.* London, 1615.

To the Reader:

If you desire to see the bear-baiting of women, then come to the bear-garden apace, and get in betimes, and view every room, where thou mayest best sit for thy own pleasure, profit, and heart's ease, and bear with my rudeness, if I chance to offend thee. But before I open this trunk full of torments against women, I think it were not amiss to resemble those which in old time did sacrifice to Hercules, for they used continually first to whip all the dogs out of their city; and so I think it were not amiss to drive all the women out of my hearing; for doubtless this little spark will kindle into such a flame, and raise so many stinking hornets humming about my ears, that all the wit I have will not quench the one, nor quiet the other; for I fear that I have set down more than they will like of, and yet a great deal less than they deserve; and for better proof, I refer myself to the judgement of men, which have more experience than myself, for I esteem little of the malice of women; for men will be persuaded with reason, but women must be answered with silence; for I know women will bark more at me, than Cerberus's three-headed dog did at Hercules, when he came into Hell to fetch out the fair Proserpina. . . .

This first chapter showeth to what use women were made: it also showeth, that most of them degenerate from the use they were framed unto, by leading a proud, lazy, and idle life, to the great hindrance of their poor husbands.

Moses describeth a woman thus: at the first beginning (saith he) a woman was made to be a helper unto man; and so they are indeed, for she helpeth to spend and consume that which man painfully getteth. He also saith, that they were made of the rib of a man; and that their froward nature showeth, for a rib is a crooked thing, good for nothing else; and women are crooked by nature, for a small occasion will cause them to be angry.

Again, in a manner, she was no sooner made but straight away her mind was set upon mischief; for by her aspiring mind, and wanton will, she quickly procured man's fall: and therefore ever since they are, and have been, a woe unto man, and follow the line of their first leader.

For, I pray you, let us consider the times past, with the time present: first, that of David and Solomon's, if they had occasion so many hundred years ago to exclaim so bitterly against women; for one of them said, that it was better to be a door keeper, and better dwell in a den amongst lions, than to be in the house of a froward and wicked woman. And the other said, that the climbing up of a sandy hill to an aged man, was nothing so wearisome, as to be troubled with a froward woman: and further, he said, that the malice of a beast is not like the malice of a wicked woman, nor that there is any thing more dangerous than a woman in her fury. . . .

There is an old saying going thus; that he which hath a fair wife and a white horse, shall never be without troubles; for a woman that hath a fair face, it is ever matched with a cruel heart, and the heavenly looks, with hellish thoughts: their modest countenance with merciless minds; for women can both smooth and soothe; they are so cunning in their art of flattery, as if they had been bound prentice to the trade: they have Siren's songs to allure thee, and Circe's cunning to enchant thee: they bear two tongues in one mouth, like Judas; and two hearts in one breast, like Magus; the one full of smiles, and the other full of frowns: and all to deceive the simple and plain meaning man; they can with the satire out of the mouth blow both hot and cold.

And what of all this? Why nothing, but to tell thee, that a woman is better lost than found, better forsaken, than taken. Saint Paul saith, that they which marry, do well, but he also saith, that they which marry not do better: and he (no doubt) was well advised what he spake. Then, if thou be wise, keep they head out of the halter, and take heed before thou have cause to curse thy hard penny worth, or wish the priest speechless which knit the knot. . . .

It is said, that an old dog, and a hungry flea, bite sore; but, in my mind, a froward woman biteth more sorer: and if thou go about to master a woman, hoping to bring her to humility, there is no way to make her good with stripes, except thou beat her to death: for, do what thou wilt, yet a froward woman, in her frantic mood will pull, hale, swear, scratch, and tear, all that stands in her way.

What wilt thou that I say more, oh thou poor married man? If women do not feel the rain, yet here is a shower coming, which will wet them to the skins. A woman which is fair in show, is foul in condition; she is like

unto a glow-worm, which is bright in the hedge, and black in the hand: in
the greenest grass lieth hid the greatest serpent; painted pots commonly
hold deadly poison; and, in the clearest water, the ugliest toad; and the
fairest woman hath some filthiness in her. All is not gold that glittereth: a
smiling countenance is no certain testimonial of a merry heart, nor costly
garments of a rich purse. Men do not commend a judge for that he
weareth a scarlet gown, but for his just dealing; no more are women to be
esteemed of by the ornament of their bravery, but for their good behaviour; yet there is no river so clear, but there is some dirt in the bottom.
But many a man in this land, we need not go any further for examples, but
here we may see many fools in every place snared in women's nets, after a
little familiarity and acquaintance with them. I think if they were num-
bered, the number would pass infinite, if it were possible, which for the
love of wantons have lost their voyages at sea, to their great hindrances:
and many other have never regarded the far distance which they have
been from their country and friends, until they had consumed their substance; and then being ashamed to return home again in such bad sort, I
mean by weeping cross, and penniless bench, many of them rather choose
to deserve Newgate, and so come to Tyburn, far contrary to the expectation of their friends and parents, which had otherwise provided for them,
if they had had grace, or would have been ruled. . . .

Man must be at all cost, and yet live by the loss; a man must take all the
pains, and women will spend all the gains: a man must watch and ward,
fight and defend, till the ground, labour in the vineyard, and look what he
getteth in seven years, a woman will spread it abroad with a fork in one
year, and yet little enough to serve her turn, but a great deal too little to
get her good will. Nay, if thou give her never so much, and yet if thy
personage please not her humour, then will I not give a half penny for her
honesty at the year's end: for then her breast will be the harbourer of an
envious heart, and her heart the store-house of poisoned hatred: her head
will devise villany, and her hands are ready to practise that which her heart
deviseth.

Then who can but say that women sprung from the Devil, whose heads,
hands, hearts, minds and souls are evil: for women are called the hook of
all evil, because men are taken with them, as a fish is taken by the hook.
For women have a thousand ways to entice thee, and ten thousand ways to
deceive thee, and all such fools as are suitors unto them: some they keep in
hand with promises, and some they feed with flattery, and some they delay
with dalliance, and some they please with kisses. They lay out the folds of

their hair, to entangle men in their love, betwixt their breasts is the valley of destruction, and in their beds is hell, sorrow, and repentance. Eagles eat not men till they are dead, but women devour them alive: for a woman will pick thy pocket, and empty thy purse, laugh in thy face, and cut thy throat: they are ungrateful, perjured, full of fraud, flouting, and deceit, unconstant, waspish, toyish, light, sullen, proud, discourteous, and cruel: and yet they were by God created, and by nature formed, and therefore by policy, and wisdom to be avoided; for good things abused, are to be refused, or else for a month's pleasure, she may hap to make thee go stark naked: she will give thee roast meat, but she will beat thee with the spit. . . .

These things being wisely considered, then what a fool art thou to blind thy self in their bold behaviour, and bow at their becks, and come at their calls, and fell thy lands to make them swim in their silks, and sit in their jewels, making Jill a gentlewoman, in so much that she careth not a penny for the finest, nor a fig for the proudest. She is as good as the best, although she have no more honesty than hardly to serve her own turn, suffering every man's fingers as deep in the dish as thine are in the platter, and every man to angle where thou castest thy hook, holding up to all that come, not much unlike a barber's chair that so soon as one knave is out, another is in; a common hackney for every one that will ride, a boat for every one to row in. Now if thy wealth do begin to fail, then she biddeth thee farewell, and gives thee the *adieu* in the Devil's name; not much unlike the knavish porters in Bristow who will cry a new master, and hang up the old. . . .

If God had not made them only to be a plague to man, he would never have called them necessary evils, and what are they better? For what do they either get or gain, save to keep? Nay, they do rather spend and consume all that which a man painfully getteth: a man must be at all the cost, and yet life *[sic]* by the loss. . . .

Therefore if thou study a thousand years, thou shalt find, a woman nothing else but a contrary unto man. Nay, if thou continue with her a hundred years, thou shalt find in her new fancies, and contrary sorts of behaviour; therefore if all the world were paper, and all the sea ink, and all the trees and plants were pens, and every man in the world were a writer, yet were they not able with all their labour and cunning to set down all the crafty deceits of women. . . .

There is no woman, but either she hath a long tongue or a longing tooth, and they are two ill neighbours, if they dwell together: for the one will lighten the purse, if it be still pleased; and the other will waken thee from thy sleep, if it be not charmed. Is it not strange, of what kind of metal a woman's tongue is made, that neither correction can chasten, nor fair means quiet: for there is a kind of venom in it, that neither by fair means nor foul they are to be ruled. All beasts by men are made tame, but a woman's tongue will never be tame; it is but a small thing and seldom seen, but is often heard, to the terror, and utter confusion of many a man.

Therefore as a sharp bit curbs a froward horse, ever so a cursed woman must be roughly used; but if women could hold their tongues, then many times men would hold their hands: as best metaled blade is mixed with iron, even so the best woman that is, is not free from faults, the goodliest gardens are not free from weeds, no more is the best, nor fairest women from ill deeds. . . .

Divers beasts and fowls by nature have more strength in one part of the body than the other; as, the eagle, in the beak; the unicorn, in the horn; the bull, in the head; the bear, in the arms; the horse, in the breast; the dog, in his teeth; the serpent, in his tail; but a woman's chief strength, is in her tongue. The serpent hath not so much venom in his tail, as she hath in her tongue; and as the serpent never leaveth hissing and stinging, and seeking to do mischief, even so, some women are never well, except they be casting out venom with their tongues, to the hurt of their husbands, or of their neighbours. Therefore he that will disclose his secrets to a woman, is worthy to have his hair cut with Sampson: for, if thou unfoldest any of a secret unto a woman, the more thou chargest her to keep it close, the more she will seem, as it were, to be with child, till she have revealed it amongst her gossips; yet, if one should make a doubt of her secrecy, she would seem angry, and say, I am no such a light housewife of my tongue, as they whose secrets lie at their tongues' ends; which flys abroad so soon as they open their mouths; therefore fear not to disclose your secrets to me, for I was never touched with any strain of my tongue in my life; nay, she will not stick to swear that she will tread it underfoot, or bury it under a stone; yet, for all this, believe her not, for every woman hath one especial gossip at the least, which she doth love and affect above all the rest, and unto her she runneth with all the secrets she knoweth.

There is a history maketh mention of one Lyas, whom King Amasis commanded to go into the market, and to buy the best and profitablest meat he could get; and he bought nothing but tongues; the King asked him the reason why he bought no other meat: who made this answer: I was commanded to buy the best meat, and from the tongue comes many good and profitable speeches. Then the King sent him again, and bad him buy the worst and unprofitablest meat, and he likewise bought nothing but tongues. The King asked him the reason: from nothing (saith he) cometh worse venom than from the tongue, and such tongues most women have.

Ester Sowerman, *Ester Hath Hanged Haman: or, An Answere to a Lewd Pamphlet, Entituled, The Arraignment of Women. With the Arraignment of Lewd, Idle, Froward, and Unconstant Men, and Husbands. Written by Ester Sowerman, Neither Maid, Wife, nor Widow, Yet Really All, and Therefore Experienced to Defend All.* London, 1617.

To all right honourable, noble, and worthy ladies, gentlewomen, and others, virtuously disposed, of the feminine sex:

Right honourable, and all others of our sex, upon my repair to London this last Michelmas term, being at supper amongst friends, where the number of each sex [was] equal, as nothing is more usual for table-talk, there fell out a discourse concerning women, some defending, others objecting against our sex: upon which occasion, there happened a mention of a pamphlet entitled *The Arraignment of Women*, which I was desirous to see. The next day a gentleman brought me the book, which when I had superficially run over, I found the discourse as far off from performing what the title promised, as I found it scandalous and blasphemous: for where the author pretended to write against lewd, idle, and unconstant women, he doth most impudently rage, and rail generally against all the whole sex of women. Whereupon, I, in defence of our sex, began an answer to that shameful pamphlet. In which, after I had spent some small time, word was brought to me that an apology for women was already undertaken, and ready for the press, by a minister's daughter: upon this news I stayed my pen, being as glad to be eased of my intended labour, as I did expect some fitting performance of what was undertaken. At last the maiden's book was brought me, which when I had likewise run over, I did observe, that whereas the maid doth many times excuse her slenderness of years, I found it to be true in the slenderness of her answer, for the undertaking to defend women doth rather charge and condemn women, as in the ensuing discourse shall appear: so that, whereas I expected to be eased of what I began, I do now find my self double charged, as well to make reply to the one, as to add supply to the other. . . .

The argument of the first chapter is, to show to what use women were made; it also sheweth, that most of them degenerate from the use they were framed unto; &c.

Now, to shew to what use woman was made, he beginneth thus. "At the first beginning a woman was made to be a helper to man: and so they are indeed, for they help to consume and spend," &c. This is all the use, and all the end which the author setteth down in all his discourse for the creation of woman. Mark a ridiculous jest in this: spending and consuming of that which man painfully getteth, is by this authour the use for which women were made. And yet (saith he in the argument) most of them degenerate from the use they were framed unto. Woman was made to spend and consume at the first: but women do degenerate from this use, ergo, Midasse doth contradict himself. Besides this egregious folly, he runneth into horrible blasphemy. Was the end of God's creation in woman to spend and consume? Is "helper" to be taken in that sense, to help to spend? Is spending and consuming, helping? . . .

At What Estimate Women Were Valued in Ancient and Former Times.

Plato, in his books, de Legibus, estimateth of women, which do equal men in all respects, only in body they are weaker, but in wit and disposition of mind nothing inferiour, if not superiour. Whereupon he doth in his so absolute a Commonwealth, admit them to government of Kingdoms and Commonweales, if they be either born thereunto by nature, or seated in government by election.

It is apparent, that in the prime of antiquity, women were valued at highest estimate, in that all those most inestimable and incomparable benefits which might either honour or preserve mankind, are all generally attributed to the invention of women, as may appear in these few examples following.

When meum & teum, mine and thine, when right and wrong were decided by wars, and their weapons then were the furniture of nature, as fists, teeth, stones, stakes, or what came next to hand: a lady of an heroical disposition, called Bellona, did first invent a more man-like and honourable weapon for war, which was the sword, with other armour correspondent, for which she was at first (and so ever since) honored, as the goddess of war.

When at the first the finest manchet* and best bread in use was of acorns, by the singular and practical wit of a lady called Ceres, the sowing of corn, and tillage was invented.

The invention of the seven liberal sciences, of all arts, of all learning,

* The finest kind of wheaten bread.

hath been generally with one consent ascribed to the invention of Jupiter's daughters, the nine Muses, whose mother was a royal lady, Mneneosum [Mnemosyne].

Carmentis, a lady, first invented letters, and the use of them by reading and writing.

The royal and most delightful exercise of hunting was first found out and practised by Diana, who thereupon is celebrated for the goddess of hunting.

The three graces, which add a decorum, and yield favour to persons, actions, and speeches, are three ladies, Aglaia, Thalia, and Enphrosune [Euphrosyne].

The heroical exercises of Olympus were first found and put in practice by Palestra, a woman.

The whole world being divided into three parts in more ancient times, every division to this day keepeth the name in honour of a woman.

The feminine sex is exceedingly honoured by poets in their writings. . . .

Daily experience, and the common course of nature, doth tell us that women were by men in those [ancient] times highly valued, and in worth by men themselves preferred, and held better than themselves.

I will not say that women are better than men, but I will say, men are not so wise as I would wish them to be, to woo us in such fashion as they do, except they should hold and account of us as their betters.

What travail, what charge, what study do not men undertake to gain our good-will, love, and liking? What vehement suits do they make unto us? With what solemn vows and protestations do they solicit us? They write, they speak, they send, to make known what entire affection they bear unto us, that they are so deeply engaged in love, except we do compassion them with our love and favour, they are men utterly cast away. One he will starve himself, another will hang, another drown, another stab, another will exile himself from kindred and country, except they may obtain our loves. What? Will they say that we are baser than themselves? Then they wrong themselves exceedingly, to prefer such vehement suits to creatures inferiour to themselves: suitors do ever in their suits confess a more worthiness in the persons to whom they sue. These kind of suits are from nature, which cannot deceive them: nature doth tell them what women are, and custom doth approve what nature doth direct. . . .

Likewise, if a man abuse a maid and get her with child, no matter is made of it, but as a trick of youth; but it is made so heinous an offence in the maid, that she is disparaged and utterly undone by it. So in all offences, those which men commit, are made light and as nothing, slighted over; but those which women do commit, those are made grievous and shameful, and not without just cause: for where God hath put hatred betwixt the woman and the serpent, it is a foul shame in a woman to curry favour with the Devil, to stain her womanhood with any of his damnable qualities, that she will shake hands where God hath planted hate.

Let there be a fair maid, wife, or woman, in country, town or city, she shall want no resort of serpents, nor any variety of tempter: let there be in like sort, a beautiful or personable man, he may sit long enough before a woman will solicit him. For where the Devil hath good acquaintance, he is sure of entertainment there, without resistance: the Serpent at first tempted woman, he dare assault her no more in that shape, now he employeth men to supply his part; and so they do: for as the Serpent began with Eve to delight her taste, so do his instruments draw to wine and banqueting; the next, the Serpent enticed her by pride, and told her she should be like to God; so do his instruments. First, they will extoll her beauty; what a paragon she is in their eyes; next, they will promise her such maintenance, as the best woman in the parish or country shall not have better: what care they, if they make a thousand oaths, and commit ten thousand perjuries, so they may deceive a woman? When they have done all and gotten their purpose, then they discover all the woman's shame, and employ such an author as this (to whose *Arraignment* I do make haste) to rail upon her and the whole sex. . . .

The Arraignment of Joseph Swetnam, Who Was the Author of the Arraignment of Women, and under His Person, the Arraignment of All Idle, Frantic, Froward and Lewd Men.

Joseph Swetnam having written his rash, idle, furious and shameful discourse against women, it was at last delivered into my hands, presently I did acquaint some of our sex with the accident, with whom I did advise what course we should take with him. It was concluded (that his unworthiness being much like to that of Thersites, whom I have formerly mentioned) we would not answer him with Achilles' fist, or Stafford-law; neither pluck him in pieces as the Thracian woman did Orpheus, for his intemperate railing against women. But as he had arraigned women at the bar where he did us the wrong, to arraign him, that thereby we might defend our assured right. . . .

Joseph Swetnam His Indictment.

Joseph Swetnam, thou art indicted by the name of Joseph Swetnam of Bedlemmore, in the county of Onopolie:* for that thou the twentieth day of December, in the year of ———— diddest most wickedly, blasphemously, falsly, and scandalously publish a lewd pamphlet, entitled the *Arraignment of Women;* in which, albeit thou diddest honestly pretend to arraign lewd, idle, froward and unconstant women, yet contrary to thy pretended promise thou diddest rashly, and maliciously rail and rage against all women, generally writing and publishing most blasphemously that women by their Creator were made for helpers, for helpers (thou sayest) to spend and consume that which man painfully getteth. Furthermore, thou dost write, that "being made of a rib which was crooked, they are therefore crooked and froward in conditions, and that woman was no sooner made, but her heart was set upon mischief"; which thou doest derive to all the sex generally, in these words, and "therefore ever since they have been a woe unto man, and follow the line of their first leader." Further than all this, thou dost affirm an impudent lie upon Almighty God, in saying that God calleth them "necessary evils, and that they were created to be a plague unto man." Thou writest also, "that women are proud, lascivious, froward, cursed, unconstant, idle, impudent, shameless, and that they deck and dress themselves to tempt and allure men to lewdness," with much and many more foul, intemperate, and scandalous speeches, &c. . . .

The Answer to All Objections Which Are Material, Made Against Women.

Right honourable and worshipful, and you of all degrees; it hath ever been a common custom amongst idle, and humourous poets, pamphleteers, and rhymers, out of passionate discontents, or having little otherwise to employ themselves about, to write some bitter satire-pamphlet, or rhyme, against women: in which argument he who could devise anything more bitterly, or spitefully against our sex, hath never wanted the liking, allowance, and applause of giddy-headed people. Amongst the rabble of scurill writers, this prisoner now present hath acted his part, whom albeit women could more willingly let pass, than bring him to trial,

* Pamphlet-maker.

and as ever heretofore, rather condemn such authors [than] deign them any answer, yet seeing his book so commonly bought up, which argueth a general applause, we are therefore enforced to make in defence of our selves, who are by such an author so extremely wronged in public view.

You all see he will not put himself upon trial; if we should let it pass, our silence might implead us for guilty, so would his pamphlet be received with a greater current and credit than formerly it hath been: so that as well in respect of our sex, as for a general satisfaction of the world, I will take this course with our prisoner, I will at this present examine all the objections which are most material, which our adversary hath vomited out against woman, and not only what he hath objected, but what other authors of more import than Joseph Swetnam have charged upon women: alas, silly man he objecteth nothing but what he hath stolen out of English writers, as Euphues, the *Palace of Pleasure* with the like, which are as easily answered as vainly objected. He never read the vehement and pro-fessed enemies against our sex, as for Grecians, Euripides, Menander, Simonides, Sophocles, with the like, amongst Latin writers, Juvenal, Plautus, &c. . . .

You challenge women for untamed and unbridled tongues; there was never woman was ever noted for so shameless, so brutish, so beastly a scold as you prove yourself in this base and odious pamphlet. . . .

Let not your impudency, nor your consort's dishonesty, charge our sex hereafter, with those sins of which you yourselves were the first procurers. I have, in my discourse, touched you, and all yours, to the quick. I have taxed you with bitter speeches; you will (perhaps) say I am a railing scold. In this objection, Joseph Swetnam, I will teach you both wit and honesty: the difference between a railing scold and an honest accuser, is this, the first rageth upon passionate fury, without bringing cause or proof; the other bringeth direct proof for what she alleges: you charge women with clamourous words, and bring no proof; I charge you with blasphemy, with impudency, scurility, foolery, and the like. I show just and direct proof for what I say; it is not my desire to speak so much, it is your desert to provoke me upon just cause so far. . . .

Joane Sharpe, "A Defence of Women, Against the Author of the Arraignment of Women." Appended to Ester Sowerman's text.

An idle companion was raging of late
Who in fury 'gainst women expresseth his hate:
He writeth a book, an *Arraignment* he calleth,
In which against women he currishly bawleth.
He deserveth no answer but in ballad or rhyme,
Upon idle fantastics who would cast away time:
Any answer may serve an impudent liar,
Any mangy scabbed horse doth fit a scold Squire:
In the ruff of his fury, for so himself saith,
The blasphemous companion he shamefully playeth.
The woman for an helper, God did make he doth say,
But to help to consume and spend all away.
Thus, at God's creation to flout and to jest,
Who but an atheist would so play the beast?
The scriptures do prove that when Adam did fall,
And to death and damnation was thereby a thrall.
Then woman was an helper, for by her blessed seed,
From Hell and damnation all mankind was freed.
He saith, women are froward, which the rib doth declare,
For like as the rib, so they crooked are:
The rib was her subject for body we find,
But from God came her soul, and dispose of her mind.
Let no man think much if women compare,
That in their creation they much better are:
More blessings therein to woman do fall,
Than unto mankind have been given at all.
Women were the last work, and therefore the best,
For what was the end, excelleth the rest.
For woman's more honour, it was so assigned,
She was made of the rib of metal refined:
The country doth also the woman more grace,
For paradise is far the more excellent place.
Yet women are mischevous, this author doth say,
But Scriptures to that directly say nay:

God said, 'twixt the woman and serpent for ever,
Strong hatred he would put, to be qualified never.
The woman being hateful to the serpent's condition,
How excellent is she in her disposition?
The serpent with men in their works may agree,
But the serpent with women that never may be.
If you ask how it happens some women prove naught,
By men turned to serpents they are over-wrought.
What the serpent began, men follow that still,
They tempt what they may to make women do ill.
They will tempt, and provoke, and follow us long:
They deceive us with oaths, and a faltering tongue.
To make a poor maiden or woman a whore,
They care not how much they spend of their store.
But where is there a man that will anything give
That woman or maid may with honesty live?
If they yield to lewd counsel they nothing shall want,
But for to be honest, then all things are scant.
It proves a bad nature in men doth remain.
To make women lewd their purses they strain.
For a woman that's honest they care not a whit,
They'll say she is honest because she lacks wit.
They'll call women whores, but their stakes they might save,
There can be no whore, but there must be a knave.
They say that our dressings, and that our attire
Are causes to move them to lustful fire.
Of all things which are we evermore find,
Such thoughts do arise as are like to the mind.
Men's thoughts being wicked they wrack on us thus,
That scandal is taken, not given by us.
If their sight to be so weak, and their frailty be such,
Why do they then gaze at our beauty so much?
Pluck away those ill roots whence sin doth arise,
Amend wicked thoughts, or pluck out the eyes.
The humours of men, see how froward they be;
We know not to please them in any degree:
For if we go plain we are sluts they do say,
They doubt of our honesty if we go gay;

If we be honest and merry, for giglots*they take us,
If modest and sober, than proud they make us:
Be we housewifty *[sic]* quick, then a shrew he doth keep,
If patient and mild, then he scorneth a sheep.
What can we devise to do or to say,
But men do wrest all things the contrary way.
'Tis not so uncertain to follow the wind,
As to seek to please men of so numerous mind.
Their humours are giddy, and never long lasting,
We know not to please them, neither full nor yet fasting.
Either we do too little, or they do too much:
They strain our poor wits, their humours are such.
They say, women are proud, wherein made they trial?
They moved some lewd suit, and had the denial:
To be crossed in such suits, men cannot abide,
And thereupon we are entitled with pride.
They say we are cursed and froward by kind,
Our mildness is changed, where raging we find,
A good Jack says the proverb, doth make a good Jill,
A curst froward husband doth change woman's will.
They use us (they say) as necessary evils,
We have it from them, for they are our devils.
When they are in their rages and numerous fits,
They put us poor women half out of our wits.
Of all naughty women name one if you can,
If she proved bad, it came by a man.
Fair Helen forsook her husband of Greece,
A man called Paris, betrayed that peace.
Medea did rage, and did shamefully murder,
A Jason was cause, which her mischief did further.
A Cressid was false, and changed her love,
Diomedes her heart by constraint did remove.
In all like examples the world may see,
Where women prove bad, there men are not free.
But in those offences they have the most share,
Women would be good, if serpents would spare.
Let women and maids whatsoever they be,
Come follow my counsel, be warned by me.

* A lewd woman

Trust no men's suits, their love proveth lust,
Both hearts, tongues, and pens, do all prove unjust.
How fair they will speak and write in their love,
But put them to trial how false do they prove?
They love hot at first, when the love is a stranger,
But they will not be tied to rack and to manger.
What call you that when men are a wooing,
And seek nothing else but shame and undoing.
As women in their faults I do not commend,
So wish I all men their lewd suits they would end.
Let women alone, and seek not their shame,
You shall have no cause then women to blame.
'Tis like that this author against such doth bawl,
Who by his temptations have gotten a fall.
For he who of women so wickedly deemeth,
Hath made them dishonest, is probably seemeth.
He hath been a traveller, it may be well so,
By his tales and reports as much we do know.
He promiseth more poison against women to trust,
He doth it for physic, or else he would bust.
Thus I bid him farewell till next we do meet,
And then as cause moveth, so shall we greet.

Joane Sharpe

Constantia Munda, *The Worming of a Mad Dogge: or, A Soppe for Cerberus the Jaylor of Hell. No Confutation but a Sharp Redargution of the Bayter of Women.* London, 1617.

The itching desire of oppressing the press with many sottish and illiterate libels, stuffed with all manner of ribaldry and sordid inventions, when every foul-mouthed male-content *[sic]* may disgorge his Licambean poison in the face of all the world, hath broken out into such a dismal contagion in these our days, that every scandalous tongue and opprobrious wit, like the Italian mountebanks will advance their pedalling wares of detracting virulence in the public piazza of every stationer's shop. . . .

Though feminine modesty hath confined our rarest and ripest wits to silence, we acknowledge it our greatest ornament, but when necessity compels us, tis as great a fault and folly *loquenda tacere, ut contra gravis est culpa tacenda loqui,* being too much provoked by arraignments, baitings, and rancorous impeachments of the reputation of our whole sex, *stulta est clementia—periturae parcere curtae,* opportunity of speaking slipped by silence, is as bad as importunity upheld by babbling. . . . Know therefore that we will cancel your accusations, traverse your bills, and come upon you for a false inditement, and think not 'tis our waspishness that shall sting you; no sir, until we see your malepert sauciness reformed, which will not be till you make a long letter to us, we will continue. . . .

'Tis a poor achievement to overcome a woman, you would never have been so grievously troubled with the over-flowing of the gall, neither would the relish of your furr'd palate have been so bitter, as what delicates soever you tasted should become unpleasing. I read of a mad fellow, which had lost his goods by sea, that whatsoever ships had come into the port at Athens, he would take a catalogue of them, and very busy would he be in making an inventory of the goods they brought in and received, thinking all to be his. So you having peradventure had some cursed wife that has given you as good as you brought, whatsoever faults you espy in others, you take that to heart: you run a madding up and down to make a scroll of female frailties, and an inventory of meretricial behaviours, ascribing them to those that are joined in the sacred bands of matrimony. Because you have been gulled with brass money, will you think no coin current? . . .

Your ill-favored countenance, your wayward conditions, your peevish and pettish nature is such, that none of our sex with whom you have obtained some partial conference, could ever brook your dogged frompard [sic] forwardness, upon which male-contented [sic] desperation, you hanged out your flag of defiance against the whole world, as a prodigious monstrous rebel against nature. Besides, if your currish disposition had dealt with men, you were afraid that *lex talionis* (like for like) would meet with you. Wherefore you surmised that, inveighing against poor, illiterate women, we might fret and bite the lip at you; we might repine to see ourselves baited and tossed in a blanket, but never durst in open view of the vulgar either disclose your blasphemous and derogative slanders, or maintain the untainted purity of our glorious sex. Nay, you'll put gags in our mouths, and conjure us all to silence; you will first abuse us, then bind us to the peace; we must be tongue-tied, lest in starting up to find fault, we prove our selves guilty of those horrible accusations. . . .

Indeed, I write not in hope of reclaiming thee from thy profligate absurdities, for I see what a pitch of disgrace and shame thy self-pining envy hath curried you to, for your greater vexation and more perplexed ruin. You see your black grinning mouth has been muzzled by a modest and powerful hand,* who has judiciously bewrayed,† and wisely laid open your singular ignorance, couched under incredible impudence, who hath most gravely (to speak in your own language) unfoulded every pleat, and showed every wrinkle of a profane and brutish disposition, so that 'tis a doubt whether she has showed more modesty or gravity, more learning or prudence in the religious confutation of your undecent railings. But as she hath been the first champion of our sex that would encounter with the barbarous bloodhound and wisely damned up your mouth, and sealed up your jaws, lest your venomed teeth like mad dogs' should damage the credit of many, nay all innocent damosels; so no doubt, if your scurrilous and depraving tongue break prison, and falls to licking up your vomited poison, to the end [that] you may squirt out the same with more pernicious hurt, assure yourself there shall not be wanting store of Helebore to scour the sink of your tumultuous gorge, at least we will cram you with antidotes and catapotions, [so] that if you swell not 'till you burst, yet your digested poison shall not be contagious. I hear you foam at mouth and growl against the author with another head like the triple dog of hell,

* A reference to Rachel Speght's *A Mouzell for Melastomus, the Cynicall Baiter of, and Foule Mouthed Barker Against Evahs Sex.*
† Maligned.

wherefore I have provided this sop for Cerberus, indifferent well steeped in vinegar. I know not how your palate will be pleased with it to make you secure hereafter. I'll take the pains to worm the tongue of your madness, and dash your rankling teeth down your throat: 'tis not holding up a wisp, nor threatening a ducking-stool shall charm us out of the compass of your chain; our pens shall throttle you, or like Archilochus with our tart iambics make you Lopez, his godson: we will thrust thee like Phalaris into thine own brazen bull, and bait thee at thy own stake, and beat thee at thine own weapon. . . .

I would run through all your silly discourse and anatomize your basery, but as some have partly been bolted out already, and are promised to be prosecuted, so I leave them as not worthy rehearsal or refutation. I would give a *supersedeas* to my quill, but there is a most pregnant place in your book which is worthy laughter that comes to my mind where you most graphically describe the difference and antipathy of man and woman, which being considered, you think it strange there should be any reciprocation of love, for a man, say you, delights in arms, and hearing the rattling drum, but a woman loves to hear sweet music on the lute, cittern,‡ or bandore.* I prithee, who but the long-eared animal had rather hear the cuckoo than the nightingale? Whose ears are not more delighted with the melodious tunes of sweet music, than with the harsh sounding drum? Did not Achilles delight himself with his harp as well as with the trumpet? Nay, is there not more men that rather affect the laudable use of the cittern, and the bandore, and lute for the recreation of their minds, than the clamorous noise of drums? [Is it] more agreeable to human nature to march amongst murdered carcasses, which you say men rejoyeth in, than to enjoy the fruition of peace and plenty, even to dance on silken carpets, as you say, is our pleasure? What man soever maketh wars; is it not to this end, that he might enjoy peace? Who marcheth among murdered carcasses, but to this end, that his enemies being subdued and slain, he may securely enjoy peace? Man loves to hear the threatening of his Prince's enemies, but woman weeps when she hears of wars. What man that is a true and loyal subject loves to hear his Prince's enemies threaten: is not this a sweet commendation think you? Is it not more humane to bewail the wars and loss of our countrymen, than to rejoice in the threats of an adversary?

‡ A guitar with a pear-shaped, flat-backed body, popular in Renaissance England.
* A bass stringed instrument.

Swetnam, the Woman-hater, Arraigned by Women. London, 1620.

Misogynos [Swetnam] enters:

My thundering book is pressed abroad;
I long to hear what a report it bears:
I know 't will startle all our City Dames,
Worse than the roaring lions, or the sound
Of a huge double canon; Swetnam's name,
Will be more terrible in women's ears,
Than ever yet misogynists have been.

Enter Clown.

Clown: Puff-e, give me some air—
[I'm] almost stifled, puff. Oh, my sides!
Mysogynos: From whence comm'st thou in such a puffing heat?
Hast thou been running for a wager, Swash?
Thou art horribly embossed. Where hast thou been?
My life, he was haunted with some spirit.
Clown: A spirit? I think all the Devils in hell,
Have had a pinch at my haunches;
I have been among the Furies, the Furies.
A pox on your book: I have been paid, i'faith:
You have set all the women in the town in an uproar.
Misogynos: Why, what's the matter, Swash?
Clown: Ne'r was poor Swash, so lashed, and pashed,
And crashed, and dashed, as I have been;
Look to your self, they're up in arms for you.
Misogynos: Why, have they weapons, Swash?
Clown: Weapons, Sir, I, I'll be sworn they have;
And cutting ones: I felt the smart of 'em;
From the loins to the legs, from the head to the hams,
From the front to the foot, I have not one free spot:
Oh, I can show you, Sir, such characters. *(Begins to strip)*
Misogynos: What dost thou mean, man, wilt shame thy self?
Clown: Why, here's none but you and I, Sir, is there?
Misogynos: Good, good, i'faith. This was a brave revenge.

Clown: If't be so good, would had had't for me.
Misogynos: And if I live, I will make all the world
To hate, as I do, this affliction, woman.
Clown: But we shall be afflicted in the meantime.
Pray let's leave this land: if we stay here,
We shall be torn a-pieces: would we had kept
In our own country [Sicily]; There we're safe enough:
You might have writ and railed your bellyfull,
And few, or none would contradict you, Sir.
Misogynos: Oh, but for one that writ against me, Swash,
I'd had a glorious conquest in that isle;
How my books took effect! How greedily
The credulous people swallowed down my hooks!
How rife debate sprang betwixt man and wife!
The little infant that could hardly speak,
Would call his mother whore. Oh, it was rare!
Clown: Oh, damned rogue!————
I stay but here, in hope, to see him hanged,
And carry news to England; then, I know,
The women there will never see me want.
For God he knows, I love 'em with my heart,
But dare not shew it for my very ears.*
What course, Sir, shall we take to hide ourselves?
Misogynos: The same we did at Bristol, "Fencing Boy";†
Oh, 'tis a fearful name to females, Swash:
I have bought foils already; set up bills;
Hung up my two-hand sword, and changed my name:
Call me Misogynos. . . .

[Conclusion: Swetnam has been convicted of crimes against women
by the women themselves. Swash reveals all in the end, and the
females sentence the offender of their sex.]

Swash: . . . I'll tell you all:
[Swetnam/Misogynos] is no fencer, that's but for a show,
For fear of being beaten: the best clerk,
For cowardice that can be in the world,

* I.e., for fear he will have his ears cut off by Misogynos.
† Swetnam was a fencing instructor at Bristol.

To terrify the female champions:
He was in England, a poor scholar first,
And came to Medley, to eat cakes and cream,
At my old mother's house; she trusted him
At least some sixteen shillings of the score,
And he persuaded her he would make me
A scholar of the university, which she, kind fool, believed:
He never taught me any lesson, but to rail against women,
That was my morning and evening lecture.
And in one year he run away from thence,
And then he took the habit of a fencer:
And set up school at Bristol: there he lived
A year or two, till he had writ this book:
And then the women beat him out of town,
And then we came to London: there forsooth,
He put his book in the press, and published it,
And made a thousand men and wives fall out.
Till two or three good wenches, in mere spite,
Laid their heads together, and railed him out of the land.
Then we came hither: this is all forsooth.
Aurelia: 'Tis e'en enough.
Misogynos: 'Tis all as false as women.
Omnes: Stop his mouth.
Atlanta: Either be quiet, or y'are gagged again.
Aurelia: Proceed in judgement.
Atlanta: Madam, thus it is.
First, he shall wear this muzzle, to express
His barking humour against womankind.
And he shall be led, and public shown,
In every street in the city, and be bound
In certain places to a post or stake,
And baited by all the honest women in the parish. . . .

In 1620 King James himself entered into the debate over women, instructing the clergy to chastise what he saw as an increasingly rebellious temper among the women of London, and furthermore to put a stop to the new fashion of cutting off their hair and wearing the same hats and ruffs that men were accustomed to wear. A contemporary, John Chamberlain, described the unleashing of this fury against women in a series of letters. On the twenty-fifth of January, 1620, he recorded: "Yesterday the Bishop of London called together all his clergy about this town, and told them he had express commandment from the King to will them to inveigh vehemently against the insolency of our women, and their wearing of broad brimmed hats, their hair cut short or shorn, and some of them stilettoes or poinards, and such other trinkets of the moment; adding withal that if pulpit admonitions will not reform them he would proceed by another course; the truth is the world is very much out of order, but whether this will mend it God knows."

On February 12, Chamberlain wrote: "Our pulpits ring continually of the insolence and impudence of women, and to help the matter forward the players have likewise taken them to task, and so to the ballads and the ballad-singers, so that they can come nowhere but their ears tingle; and if all this will not serve, the King threatens to fall upon their husbands, parents or friends that have or should have power over them, and make them pay for it."

One of these attackers wrote a pamphlet entitled *Hic Mulier: Or, The Man-Woman: Being a Medicine to Cure the Coltish Disease of the Staggers in the Masculine-Feminines of Our Times* (1620). Within a matter of weeks, he was answered by *Haec-Vir: Or, The Womanish-Man: Being an Answere to a Late Booke Intituled Hic-Mulier.* (1620). I have here excerpted sections from both.

Hic Mulier: Or, The Man-Woman: Being a Medicine to Cure the Coltish Disease of the Staggers in the Masculine-Feminines of Our Times. London, 1620.

Since the days of Adam women were never so masculine; masculine in their genders and whole generations, from the mother, to the youngest daughter; masculine in number, from one to multitudes; masculine in case, even from head to foot; masculine in mood, from bold speech, to impudent action; and masculine in tense: for (without redress) they were, are, and will be still most masculine, most mankind, and most monstrous. Are all women then turned masculine? No, God forbid, there are a world full of holy thoughts, modest carriage, and severe chastity; to these let me fall on my knees and say, "You, O you women, you good women. . . . O do not look to find your names in this declamation, but with all honour and reverence do I speak to you. You are Seneca's Graces, women, good women, modest women, true women: ever young, because ever virtuous, ever chaste, ever glorious: when I write of you, I will write with a golden pen, on leaves of golden paper; now I write with a rough quill, and black ink, on iron sheets, the iron deeds of an iron generation.

Come then, you masculine-women, for you are my subject, you that have made admiration an ass, and fooled him with a deformity never before dreamed of, that have made your selves stranger things than ever Noah's Ark unladed, or Nile engendered, whom to name, he that named all things might study an age to give you a right attribute, whose like are not to be found in any antiquary's study, in any sea-man's travel, nor in any painter's cunning, you that are stranger than strangeness itself, whom wisemen wonder at, boys shout at, and goblins themselves start at . . . 'tis of you that I entreat, and of your monstrous deformity; you that have made your bodies like antic boscage, or crotesco work, not half man, half woman, half fish, half flesh, half beast, half monster, but all odious, all devil, that have cast off the ornaments of your sex, to put on the garments of shame, that have laid by the bashfulness of your natures, to gather the impudence of harlots; that have buried silence, to revive slander; that are all things but that which you should be, and nothing less than friends to virtue and goodness; that have made the foundation of your highest detested work, from the lowest despised creatures that record can give testimony of; the one cut from the Common-wealth at the gallows; the other is well known. From the first you got the false armory of yellow starch (for to wear yellow on white, or white upon yellow is by the rules of heraldry baseness, bastardy, and indignity), the folly of imitation, the deceitfulness of flattery, and the grossest baseness of all baseness, do to whatsoever a greater power will command you. From the other, you have taken the monstrousness of your deformity in apparel, exchanging the modest attire of the comely hood, cawl, coif, handsome dress or kerchief, to the cloudy ruffianly broad-brimmed hat, and wanton feather, the modest upper parts of a concealing straight gown, to the loose, lascivious civil embracement of a French doublet, being all unbuttoned to entice, all of one shape to hide deformity, and extreme short waisted to give a most easy way to every luxurious action: the glory of a fair large hair, to the shame of most ruffianly short locks; the side, thick gathered, and close guarding safe-guards, to the short, weak, thin, loose, and every hand-entertaining short basses; for needles, swords; for Prayer books, bawdy ligs;* for modest ges-tures, giant-like behaviours, and for women's modesty, all mimic and apish incivility: these are your founders, from these you took your copies, and (without amendment) with these you shall come to perdition. . . .

What can be more barbarous, than with the gloss of mumming art, to disguise the beauty of their creation? To mould their bodies to every deformed fashion; their tongues to vile and horrible profanations, and their hands to ruffianly and uncivil actions; to have their gestures as pie-bald, and as motley-various as their disguises; their souls fuller of infirmi-ties than a horse or a prostitute, and their minds languishing in those infirmities. . . .

It is an infection that emulates the plague, and throws it self amongst women of all degrees, all deserts, and all ages; from the capitol to the cottage, are some spots or swellings of this disease, yet evermore the greater the person is, the greater is the rage of this sickness, and the more they have to support the eminence of their fortunes, the more they bestow in the augmentation of their deformities: not only such as will not work to get bread, will find time to weave her self points to truss her loose breeches: and she that hath pawned her credit to get a hat, will sell her smock to buy a feather: she that hath given kisses to have her hair shorn, will give her honesty to have her upper parts put into a French doublet: to

* Bands or stripes.

conclude, she that will give her body to have her body deformed, will not stick to give her soul to have her mind satisfied.

But such as are able to buy all at their own charges, they swim in the excess of these vanities, and will be man-like not only from head to waist, but to the very foot, and in every condition: man in body by attire, man in behaviour by rude compliment, man in nature by aptness to anger, man in action by pursuing revenge, man in wearing weapons, man in using weapons: and in brief, so much man in all things, that they are neither man, nor women, but just good for nothing.

Haec-Vir: Or, The Womanish-Man: Being an Answere to a Late Booke Intituled Hic-Mulier. Exprest in a Brief Dialogue Between Haec-Vir, the Womanish-Man, and Hic-Mulier, the Man-Woman. London, 1620.

Haec-Vir: What, Hic-Mulier, the Man-Woman? She that like a larum-bell at midnight hath raised the whole kingdom in arms against her? Good, stand, and let me take a full survey both of thee, and all thy dependents.

Hic-Mulier: Do freely: and when thou hast daubed me over, with the worst colours thy malice can grind, then give me leave to answer for my self, and I will say thou art an accuser just and indifferent. Which done, I must entreat you to sit as many minutes, that I may likewise take your picture, and then refer to censure, whether of our deformities is most injurious to nature, or most effeminine *[sic]* to good men, in the notoriousness of the example.

Haec-Vir: With like condition of freedom to answer. The articles are agreed on: therefore stand forth, half Birchen-lane, half St. Thomas Apostles: the first lent thee a doublet, the latter a nether-skirt: half Bridewell, half Black-Friars; the one for a scurvy block, the other for a most prophane feather; half Mull'd-Sack the chimney sweeper, half Garrat the fool at a tilting; the one for a yellow ruff, the other for a scarf able to put a soldier out of countenance; half Bedlam, half Brimendgham *[sic]*, the one for a base sale boot, the other for a beastly leaden gilt spur: and to conclude, all Hell, all damnation. For a shorn, powdered, borrowed hair, a naked, lascivious, bawdy bosom, a Leaden-Hall dagger, a high-way pistol, and a mind and behaviour suitable or exceeding every repeated deformity. To be brief, I can but in those few lines delineate your proportion, for the paraphrase or compartment, to set out your ugliness to the greatest extent of wonder. I can but refer you to your god-child that carries your own name, I mean the book of *Hic-Mulier*, there you shall see your character, and feel your shame, with that palpable plainess *[sic]*, that no Egyptian darkness can be more gross and terrible.

Hic-Mulier: My most tender piece of man's flesh, leave this lightening and thunder, and come roundly to the matter, draw mine accusation into heads, and then let me answer.

Haec-Vir: Then thus. In that book you are arraigned, and found guilty.

First of baseness, in making your self a slave to novelty, and the poor invention of every weak brain that hath but an embroidered outside. Next, of unnaturalness, to forsake the creation of God, and customs of the kingdom, to be pieced and patched up by a French tailor, an Italian baby-maker, and a Dutch soldier (beat from the army for the ill example of ruffianly behaviour) then of shamelessness, in casting off all modest soft-ness, and civility, to run through every desert and wilderness of men's opinions, like careless untamed hiefers, or wild savages. Lastly, of foolish-ness, in having no moderation or temper, either in passions or affections: but turning all into perturbations and fullnesses of the soul, laugh away the preciousness of your time, and at last die with the flattering sweet malice of an incurable consumption. Thus baseness, unnaturalness, shame-lessness, foolishness, are the main hatch-ments, or coat-armours, which you have tane* as rich spoils to adorn you in the deformity of your appar-rel: which if you can excuse, I can pity, and thank Proserpina for thy wit; though no good man can allow of the reasons.

Hic-Mulier: Well, then to the purpose: first, you say, I am base, in being a slave to novelty. What slavery can there be in freedom of election? Or what baseness, to crown my delights with those pleasures which are most suitable to mine affections? Bondage or slavery, is a restraint from those actions, which the mind (of its own accord) doth most willingly desire: to perform the intents and purposes of another's disposition, and that not but by mansuetude or sweetness of intreaty; but by the force of authority and strength of compulsion. Now for me to follow change, according to the limitation of mine own will and pleasure, there cannot be a greater freedom. Nor do I in my delight of change otherwise than as the whole world doth, or as becommeth a daughter of the world to do. For what is the world, but a very shop or ware-house of change? Sometimes winter, sometimes summer; day and night; they hold sometimes riches, sometimes poverty, sometimes health, sometimes sickness: now pleasure; presently anguish; now honour; then contempt: and to conclude, there is nothing but change, which doth surround and mix with all our fortunes. And will you have poor woman such a fixed star, that she shall not so much as move or twinkle in her own sphere? That were true slavery indeed, and a base-ness beyond the chains of the worst servitude. Nature to everything she hath created, hath given a singular delight in change, as to herbs, plants and trees a time to wither and shed their leaves, a time to bud and bring

* Taken.

forth their leaves, and a time for their fruits and flowers: to worms and creeping things a time to hide themselves in the pores and hollows of the earth, and a time to come abroad and suck the dew; to beasts liberty to choose their food, liberty to delight in their food, and liberty to feed and grow fat with their food. The birds have the air to fly in, the waters to bathe in, and the earth to feed on. But to man, both these and all things else, so alter, frame and fashion, according to his will and delight shall rule him. Again, who will rob the eye of the variety of objects, and the care of the delight of sounds, the nose of smells, the tongue of tastes, and the hand of feeling? And shall only woman, excellent woman; so much better in that she is something purer, be only deprived of this benefit? Shall she be the bondslave of time, the hand-maid of opinion, or the strict observer of every frosty or cold benumbed imagination? It were a cruelty beyond the rack or strapado. . . .

Next, you condemn me of unnaturalness, in forsaking my creation, and condemning custom. How do I forsake my creation, that do all the rights and offices due to my creation? I was created free, born free, and live free: what lets me then so to spin out my time, that I may die free?

To alter creation, were to walk on my hands with my heels upward, to feed my self with my feet, or to forsake the sweet sound of sweet words, for the hissing noise of the serpent: but I walk with a face erected, with a body clothed, with a mind busied, and with a heart full of reasonable and devout cogitations; only offensive in attire, in as much as it is a stranger to the curiosity of the present times, and an enemy to custom. Are we then bound to be the flatterers of time, or the dependents on custom? O miserable servitude chained only to baseness and folly! For than custom, nothing is more absurd, nothing more foolish. . . .

But you say we are barbarous and shameless and cast off all softness, to run wild through a wilderness of opinions. In this you express more cruelty than in all the rest, because I stand not with my hands on my belly like a baby in Bartholomew-Fair, that move not my whole body when I should but only stir my head like Jack of the cloche house which hath no joints, that am not dumb when wantons court me, as if ass-like I were ready for all burdens, or because I weep not when injury gripes me, like a worried deer in the fangs of many curs: am I therefore barbarous or shameless? He is much injurious that so baptized us: we are as free-born as men, have as free election, and as free spirits, we are compounded of like parts, and may with like liberty make benefit of our creations: my countenance shall smile on the worthy, and frown on the ignoble, I will hear the wise, and be deaf to idiots, give counsel to my friend, but be dumb to flatterers, I have hands that shall be liberal to reward desert, feet that shall move swiftly to do good offices, and thoughts that shall ever accompany freedom and severity. If this be barbarous, let me leave the city, and line with creatures of like simplicity.

Vituperation and mockery of women were kept alive in the broadsides and ballads of the 1620s, but in the 1630s the polemical debate was renewed once more with the publication of John Taylor's *A Juniper Lecture* and *Divers Crab-Tree Lectures*. Richard Brathwaite joined in shortly afterward with *Art Asleep Husband? A Boulster Lecture*. Sharply satirical in tone, each "lecture" portrayed another aspect of woman's shrewishness, interlarded with verses and mock-scholarly argument demonstrating the innate inferiority of the female sex by historical example and biblical citation.

A woman (or women) replied to Taylor's burlesque with *The Women's Sharpe Revenge; or, An Answer to Sir Seldom Sober, That Writ Those Railing Pamphlets Called the Juniper and Crab-Tree Lectures, Being a Sound Reply and a Full Confutation of Those Books, with an Apology in This Case for the Defence of Us Women, Performed by Mary Tattlewell and Joan Hit-Him-Home, Spinsters*. The authors begin by ridiculing Taylor as Sir Seldom Sober, but then turn to a more serious argument and in the course of the attack set out an articulate protest against the slight attention given to women's education and criticize the sexual double standard. It has been speculated that Taylor himself wrote *The Women's Sharpe Revenge* in order to sell more books, but the differences in style as well as the content and tone of the two texts argue strongly against this thesis. As many of the "words to the reader" written by female authors complained, it was also common to assert that a text by a woman was in fact the work of a man.

John Taylor, *A Juniper Lecture*. London, 1639.

A Lecture of a Wife to her Husband, That Hath Been Married Three or Four Years.

In troth husband I can hold no longer, but I must speak: I see you still follow this vein of ill-husbandry, never keep at home; is the house a wild-cat to you? Here I sit all the day long with the children, sighing, and looking every minute when you will return home: y'faith this course of life must be left; do you think I can sell your wares, or know the prizes *[sic]* of them when your customers come? . . .

A man, if he had or bore any love to his wife at all, which hath brought him so many children, would sometime remember her . . . but your children and I must be content with any thing: I would I were dead, that you might have another wife, and then you should see it, she would not be made such a fool as I am by you. . . . I would I had been made a man, for women are nothing but your drudges and your slaves, to make you clean, and to wash and starch your cloaths, when you go whither you please, and take no care at all for any thing. A woman's work is never at an end, and never done, but like a wheel, still turning round, and hath no end. I am forced as soon as I rise in the morning, to make a fire, sweep the house, and get the children's and your servant's breakfast; no sooner that done, and they out of the way, think upon dinner; then no sooner dinner eaten, then I must make all the dishes clean again, and sweep the house. Then because I would be thought a good housewife, I sit me down to spin, then think upon your supper, and study what will please your dainty chops; I make it ready against you come home, when you are half fox't; and then the children must be straightaway thought upon, or else there's nothing but crying and bawling, which makes my brains ache again. Then all being satisfied, put the children to sleep, then to bed my self, and thus a woman's work is never done. . . .

On a Woman's Tongue.

Things that be bitter,
    bitterer than gall
Physicians say are always
    physical:
Than women's tongues, if
    into a powder beaten,
And in a potion or a pill
    be eaten,
Nothing more bitter is.
    I therefore muse,
That women's tongues in
    physic they ne're use:
There's many men who
    live unquiet lives,
Would spare that bitter
    member of their wives.
Then prove them doctor,
    use them in a pill,
Things oft help sick men,
    that doth sound men kill.

The Author's Advice How to Tame a Shrew.

If you perceive her to increase her language, be sure you give her not a word, good nor bad, but rather seem to slight her, by doing some action or other, as singing, dancing, whistling, or clapping thy hands on thy sides; for this will make her vex extremely, because you give her not word for word: and be sure you do not offer to go away, but walk still before her, or in her hearing; for if you do think to avoid her clamour by going abroad, you are deceived; for then you do but give her breath, and so by that means will have another sling at your jacket: and if you must needs go forth about your occasions, beware that she doth not meet you as Xantippe, the wife of Socrates, did meet with him: for after he had endured her railing and bitter words for two or three hours together, and slighted her by his merry conceits, she studying how to be revenged of him, as he went out of his house she poured a chamber-pot on his head, which wet him exceedingly; whereupon he presently said, "I did think that after so great a clap of thunder, we should have some shower of rain," and so passed it off merrily; but if all will not serve that you can do, to stop her rage, but she will thus every day clamour, then I wish you to buy a drum into your house, and lock it up in some private room or study, that she may not come at it, and when she doth begin to talk aloft, do then begin to beat aloud, which she hearing, will presently be amazed, hearing a louder voice than her own, and make her forbear scolding any more for that time. And at any time if she do talk or scold, then sing this catch,

> He that marries a scold,
> He hath most cause to be merry,
> For when she's in her fits,
> He may cherish his wits
> With singing *Hey downe dery*, with a cup of sherry.

or thus:

> What hap had I to marry a
>   shrew,
> For she hath given me many
>   a blow,
> And how to please her, alas,
>   I do not know.

Another:

> Dub a dub, kill her with a
>   club,
> Be thy wife's master:
> Each one can tame a shrew,
>   but he that hath her. . . .

The Women's Sharpe Revenge; or, An Answer to Sir Seldom Sober, That Writ Those Railing Pamphlets Called the Juniper and Crab-Tree Lectures, Being a Sound Reply and a Full Confutation of Those Books, with an Apology in This Case for the Defence of Us Women, Performed by Mary Tattlewell and Joan Hit-Him-Home, Spinsters. London, 1640.

The Epistle of the Female Frailty, To the Male Gender, in General:

Reader, if thou beest of the masculine sex, we mean thee, and thee only, and therefore greet thee with these attributes following: affable, loving, kind, and curteous: affable, we call thee, because so apt (I will not say to prate, but) to prattle with us; loving, in regard that the least grace, being from us granted, you not only avow to love us, but are loathe to leave us; kind, that you will not meet with us, without congies,* not part with us without kisses; and curteous, because so willing to bring yourselves upon your knees before us . . . and therefore our hope is that what you used to protest in private, you will not now blush to profess in public: otherwise, in clearing our cause, and vindicating our own virtues, we shall not doubt to divulge you, for the only dissemblers. And in this case we appeal to your own consciences, even to the most crabbed and censorious, and the most sour and supercilious. Which of you all hath not solicited our sex? Petitioned to our persons? Praised our perfections? And which of you hath not met us coming, followed us flying, guarded us going, stood for us standing, waited on us walking, and ambushed us lying? Use women to court men? Or have we at any time complained of their coyness? Have we bribed them with our bounties? Troubled them with our tokens, palatized *[sic]* in their praises, prayed and protested, sued and solicited, voted and vowed unto them? Or rather they to us? Would you apprehend a new antipodes, to make all things to be carried by contrary course and run retrograde? Then let the radish root pluck the gardner up by the heels, and the shoulder of mutton put the cook upon the spit: for you as well may prove the one, as produce the other. You suffer us to be reviled and railed at, taunted and terrified, undervalued and even vilified, when among you all we cannot find one champion to oppose so obstinate a challenger,

---

* A courteous bow.

but that we are compelled to call a ghost from her grave, to stand up in the defence of a proud defiance. Since then you will not be combattants for us in so just a cause, we entreat you to be competent judges, to censor indifferently betwixt the accuser and the accused, to punish his petulancy, and not to favour us if we be found the sole faulty. So, if you shall give our defamer his due, and that we gain the honour of the day, if you be young men, we wish you modest maids in marriage; if bachelors, beautiful mistresses; if husbands, handsome wives and good housewives; if widowers, wise and wealthy widows; if young, those that may delight you; if old, such as may comfort you; and so we women bequeath unto you all our best wishes.

—Mary Tattlewell and Joan Hit-Him-Home,
spinsters. . . .

Some are raised [to honors and titles] for their wealth, others for their worth, some by the law, others by their learning, some by marital discipline, and others for malicious detraction, as thinking to rise by others' ruins, and by supplanting others, to support themselves. In which number we must rank you, master satirist, the passionate author of those most pitiful pamphlets called the *Juniper Lectures* and *Crab Tree Lectures*, who by your knavery, ambitious to purchase knighthood, and to add a reverence to your name, are now arrived at the height of your aim, and from plain Seldom Sober, are now come to the title of *Sir* Seldom Sober, who we term so, for he is ashamed to set his name to books; a name fitting his nature, and well complying with his condition. And as there have been formerly, by your means, Sir Seldom Sober, many railing, bitter, invective pasquils and scurrilous libels, some written, some printed, and all dispersed and scattered abroad, all of them made and forged on purpose to caluminate, revile, despite, and flout women; and now lately one or two of the sons of ignorance have penned three several, sweet, filthy, fine, ill-favoured pamphlets, which were printed, and (out of the most deep shallowness of the author's abundant want of wisdom) are called lectures, as *The Juniper Lecture, The Crab Lecture,* and *The Wormwood Lecture,* wherein they have laid most false aspersions on all women generally; some they have taxed with incontinency, some with incivility, some with scolding, some with drinking, some with backbiting, and slandering their neighbours, some with a continual delight in lying, some with an extraordinary desire of perpetual gossiping; in a word, we are each of us accused and blazed to be addicted and frequently delighted with one grievous enormity or another, wherein, although it be true that we are all daughters of Eve in frailty, yet they might have remembered that they likewise are all sons of Adam, in failing, falling, and offending. We are not so partially in defence of all women's virtues, that we thereby do hold none to be vicious. Some women are incontinent by nature (or inheritance) from their mothers; some, through extreme want and poverty have been forced to make more bold with that which is their own, than to beg, steal, or borrow from others: some (by a harsh usage of their too unkind husbands) have been driven to their shifts hardly; some, having had the hard fortune to match with such coxcombs, as were jealous without a cause . . . dogged and crabbed-dealing with their wives, [who are] given too often too much cause to make their [husband's] jealousy true. And whereas a woman's reputation is so poor, that if it be but so much as suspected, it will be long before the suspicion will be cleared: but if it be once blemished or tainted, the stains and spots [are of] such a tincture, that the dye of the blemishes will stick to her all her life, and to her children after her. But for the man, he takes or assumes to himself such loose liberty, or liberty of licentious looseness, that only he be (as they call it) the common town ball, or a runner at sheep, though he pass the censures of spiritual courses or high conditions, yet, by custom, his disgrace will be quickly worn out, and [said] it was but a trick of youth; for the shame or scandals of a whoremaster is like a nine-day's wonder, or a record written in the sand . . . but the faults of a weak woman, are a continual alarm against her, they are engraven in brass, and like a suit of buff,† it may be turned, and scoured and scraped and made a little cleanly, but it lasts the whole lifetime of the wearer. . . .

But first, touching the person who put these foul and calumnious aspersions upon us: if he were a tailor, [surely] he was [not] a woman's tailor, or (if so) no good artist, because not being able to take the measure of a woman's body, much less was he powerful to make a true dimension of her mind (and therein you are gone, Master Taylor) nay, what artist soever you were, (for in one I include all) most of you have wives and children and love them, and are indulgent over them, and wherefore then do you encourage such invectives against us? If you being of yourselves lewd, we be loving, we untutored, you untoword, we familiar, you forward, we doting, and you dogged, and what we get by spinning in the day, you spend in

† Buff leather.

the night, and come reeling from the tavern or the alehouse: is the fault ours? Are we worthy any to be blamed for this. . . .

We find you moreover to be no scholar at all, as neither understanding us in our gender, number, or case. . . .

And this is an argument which we might amplify even from the original of all of history, and would not spare to do it, had we but the benefit of your breeding. But it hath been the policy of all parents, even from the beginning, to curb us of that benefit by striving to keep us under, and to make us men's mere vassals even unto all posterity. How else comes it to pass, that when a father has a numerous issue of sons and daughters, the sons forsooth they must be first put to the grammar school, and after perchance sent to the university, and trained up in the liberal arts and sciences, and there (if they prove not blockheads), they may in time be booklearned: and what do they then? Read the poets perhaps, out of which, if they can pick out anything maliciously devised, or malignantly divulged by some mad muse, discontented with his coy, disdainful mistress, that in imitation of them, he must devise some passionate elegy . . . and in the stead of picking out the best poets, who have strived to write us (that is to say, women) follow the others, who do nothing but rail at us, thinking he has done his mistress praise, when it may be he has no mistress at all, but only feigns to himself some counterfeit Phyllis or Amaryllis, such as never had any person, but a mere airy name: and against them he must vie out his vain enthusiasms and raptures, to the disgrace and prejudice of our whole sex. When we, who may style by a name of weaker vessels, though of a more delicate, fine, soft and more pliant flesh, and therefore of a temper most capable of the best impression, have not that generous and liberal education, lest we should be made able to vindicate our own injuries. We are set only to the needle, to prick our fingers: or else to the wheel to spin a fair thread for our own undoings, or perchance to some dirty and debased drudgery; if we be taught to read, they then confine us within the compass of our mother tongue, and that limit we are not suffered to pass; or if (which sometimes happens) we be brought up to music, to singing, and to dancing, it is not for any benefit that thereby we can engross unto ourselves, but for their own particular ends, the better to please and content their licentious appetites, when we come to our maturity and ripeness; and thus if we are weak by nature, they strive to make us more weak by our nurture. And if in degree of place low, they strive by their policy to keep us more under.

Now to show we are no such despised matter as you would seem to make us, come to our first creation, when man was made of the mere dust of the earth, the woman had her being from the best part of his body, the rib next to his heart: which difference even in our complexions, may be easily decided. Man is of a dull, earthy, and melancholy aspect, having furrows in his face, and a very forest upon his chin, [while] our soft and smooth cheeks are a true representation of a garden of intermixed roses and lilies.

Others have said, the closets of women's thoughts are always open; and the depth of their hearts have a string that reaches to their tongues: and say this be granted, may we not also say of men's breasts that [they] lie unveiled to entertain all vices: and whatsoever they cannot sufficiently twaddle with their tongues, they cannot contain themselves there, but must publish it with their pens (one of the grand faults of which our arch adversary at this present stand is convicted).

During the Civil War many women began to preach and prophesy. The spread of doctrines of divine inspiration and the emergence of dissenting groups like the Ranters, Baptists, Seekers, and Quakers, whose advocacy of the priesthood of all believers encouraged lay preaching, all contributed to the enthusiasm for "women's speaking." Numbers of women wrote ecstatic religious verse, polemics on church doctrine, and books of prophesy. Mary Cary, a believer in the Fifth Monarchy, or millennium, prophesied in 1651 that "the time is coming when this promise shall be fulfilled, and the Saints shall be abundantly filled with the spirit; and not only men, but women shall prophesie. . . ." *(A New and More Exact Map or Description of the New Jerusalem's Glory)*

Though men like George Fox not only approved of but also supported women preachers, other ministers gave stern reminders of the biblical injunction against women's speaking. The anonymous text that follows illustrates the kind of effort that was made to discredit women preachers throughout the interregnum. Many women answered from the pulpit, but Margaret Fell was one of the few who had the leisure to construct an argument in writing. She composed *Women's Speaking Justified* while in prison.

A Discoverie of Six Women Preachers . . . in Middlesex, Kent, Cambridgeshire, and Salisbury. With a Relation of Their Names, Manners, Life, and Doctrine, Pleasant to Be Read, but Horrid to Be Judged of. Their Names Are These: Anne Hempstall, Mary Bilbrowe, Joan Bauford, Susan May, Elizabeth Bancroft, Arabella Thomas. London, 1641.

In ancient times have I read of prophetesses, but not until of late heard of women preachers, their only reason or cause of preaching was, that there was a deficiency of good men, wherefore it was but fit, that virtuous women should supply their places, they were (men they did mean) good for nothing, but to make their texts good by expounding the language of the Beast, but they themselves would preach nothing, but such things as the spirit should move them.

The first and chief of this female and sacerdotical function, was one Anne Hempstall, living in the parish of Saint Andrews, Holborne, near London, and in the county of Middlesex, upon a certain time, she having made a mind, said she was moved to be zealously affected, called an assembly of her bibbing gossips together, whose thoughts were bent more upon the strong water bottle, than upon the uses or doctrines which their holy sister intended to expound unto them, but being come to the house of this Anne Hempstall, zealous Nan spoke to them after this manner.

"Beloved sisters, this last night I dreamed a strange dream, moreover me thought I saw a vision, in which Anna the Prophetess was presented unto my view, the splendour of whose countenance did cast me into a trance, wherein I lay until the next morning, and the morning being come, I could conceive no interpretation of my dream but this, that I should imitate godly Anna, by preaching unto you, as she prophesied to others." Her speech struck them all into an astonishment, at which, this prophane Anne cried out, "Now does the holy ghost descend down upon you, wherefore give ear unto me." Then did she begin to talk, and speak unto them that which first came into her mind, but the chief matter of her text was this, that woman's hair was an adorning to her, but for a man to have long hair, it was a shame unto him, which the Scripture itself cried fie upon; long did she preach, and longer I dare avouch than some of the audience were willing, for some of them had as far home as White Chapel, wherefore her longitude might cause a brevitude of her sucking the aquavit bottle; two hours being expired, and the bottom of the stool beginning to look open-mouthed with her furious stamps, she gave them as much peace as in her lay, and so concluded.

Mary Bilbrowe, one of the audience, being of the parish of Saint Giles in the Fields, desired them to be all with her the next morning, and after sermon, they should have a good fat pig to breakfast, besides a cup of sack or claret to wash it down. They all agreed unto it, and making use of all the rhetoric which they were born unto, they gave her thanks, and so for that time a bottle of ale or two being devoured, they departed every one to their own houses. The next morning, they met altogether at the house of Mary Bilbrowe, whose husband was a good honest bricklayer, and so soon as they came within the doors of her house, she brought them all into her parlour as she called it, and instead of stools and cushions, she had provided before hand, three bricks a piece for them to sit upon. Her reason was this: she thought they would not sit much, because women to good instructions love standing. Her pulpit was framed very substantially of brick, so high, that scarce anything, but her standing up tippet could be seen. She began there very devoutly to make an *ex tempore* prayer, but before she had scarce spoke twenty words, her daughter came running in very hastily, telling her a gentleman at Bloomsbury stayed to speak with her about urgent occasions, which hearing, she leapt out of her prayer into this serious meditation, "I think it be the gentleman I was withall at Salisbury Court, whom I promised this day to meet withall." Whereupon she left her pulpit, spread the cloth, and brought her gossips in a pig according to her promise, who fed heartily, and so departed; so much at this time for Middlesex female teachers.

Now give me leave to take water, and go to Gravesend, and so further into Kent, where I shall tell you of one Joan Bauford in the town of Faversham, who taught in Faversham, that husbands being such as crossed their wives' wills might lawfully be forsaken.

Then was there one Susan May of Ashford in the county of Kent also which preached in a barn there, that the Devil was the father of the Pope, the Pope the father of those which did wear surplices, wherefore consequently the Devil was the father of all those which did not love Puritans.

There was likewise one Elizabeth Bancroft in Ely in Cambridgeshire, where Bishop Wren first going to place altars there, preached behind the minister upon a Saturday, that it was fit upon Sunday to sacrifice the Pope's bird upon his own altar.

Then lastly there was one Arabella Thomas, a Welch woman, which lived in the city of Salisbury, which preached, and in her sermon said that none but such painful creatures as her self should go to heaven, so those ministers which did not preach twice upon every Sabbath day, she said that very shortly the black raven by day, and the white owl by night should scratch out their eyes.

Thus have I declared some of the female academies, but where their university is I cannot tell, but I suppose that Bedlam or Bridewell would be two convenient places for them. Is it not sufficient that they may have the gospel truly and sincerely preached unto them, but that they must take their ministers' office from them? If there had been such a dearth of the gospel as there was in the reign of Queen Mary it had been an occasion somewhat urgent, but God be praised it was not so, but that they seemed to be ambitious, and because they would have superiority they would get upon a stool, or in a tub instead of a pulpit. At this time I have described but six of them, 'ere long I fear I shall relate more, I pray God I have not cause, and so for this time I conclude.

FINIS

Margaret Fell, *Women's Speaking Justified; Proved and allowed of by the scriptures, all such as speak by the spirit and power of the Lord Jesus, and how women were the first that preached the tidings of the resurrection of Jesus, and were sent by Christ's own command, before he ascended to the Father, John 20.17.* London, 1666 (reprinted 1667).

Whereas it hath been an objection in the minds of many, and several times hath been objected by the clergy, or ministers, and others, against women's speaking in the church; and so consequently may be taken, that they are condamned [sic] for meddling in the things of God; the ground of which objection, is taken from the Apostle's words, which he writ in his First Epistle to the Corinthians, chap. 14 vers. 34, 35., and also what he writ to Timothy in the First Epistle; chap. 2. vers. 11, 12. But how far they wrong the Apostle's intentions in these Scriptures, we shall show clearly when we come to them in their course and order. But first let me lay down how God himself hath manifested his will and mind concerning women, and unto women.

And first, when *God created man in his own image: in the image of God created he them, male and female: and God blessed them, and God said unto them, be fruitful and multiply: and God said, Behold, I have given you of every herb, etc.* Gen 1. Here God joins them together in his own image, and makes no such distinctions and differences as men do, for though they be weak, he is strong, and as he said to the Apostle, *his grace is sufficent* and *his strength is made manifest in weakness,* 2 Cor. 12.g. [sic] And such hath the Lord chosen, even *the weak things of the world to confound the things which are mighty; and things which are despised, hath God chosen to bring to nought things that are,* 1 Cor. 1. And God hath put no such difference between the male and female as men would make.

It is true, the serpent was more subtle than any other beast of the field, came unto the woman, with his temptations, and with a lie; his subtlety discerning her to be more inclinable to hearken to him, when he said, *If ye eat, your eyes shall be opened.* And the woman saw that the fruit was good to make one wise, there the temptation got into her, and she did eat, and gave to her husband, and he did eat also, and so they were both tempted into the transgression and disobedience; and therefore God said unto

Adam, when that he hid himself when he heard his voice, *Hast thou eaten of the tree which I commanded thee that thou shouldest not eat?* And Adam said, *The woman which thou gavest me, she gave me of the tree, and I did eat.* And the Lord said unto the woman, *What is this that thou hast done?* and the woman said, *The serpent beguiled me, and I did eat.* [Here] the woman spoke the truth unto the Lord: see what the Lord said, vers. 15. after he had pronounced sentence on the serpent; *I will put enmity between thee and the woman, and between thy seed and her seed; it shall bruise thy head, and thou shalt bruise his heel,* Gen. 3.

Let this word of the Lord, which was from the beginning, stop the mouths of all that oppose women's speaking in the power of the Lord; for he hath put enmity between the woman and the serpent; and if the seed of the woman speak not, the seed of the serpent speaks; for God hath put enmity between the two seeds, and it is manifest that those that speak against the woman and her seeds' speaking speak out of the enmity of the old serpent's seed; and God hath fulfilled his word and his promise: *When the fullness of time was come, he hath sent forth his son, made of a woman, made under the Law, that we might receive the adoption of sons,* Gal. 4.4,5.

Moreover, the Lord is pleased, when he mentions his Church, to call her by the name of woman, by his prophets, saying, *I have called thee as a woman forsaken, and grieved in spirit, and as a wife of youth,* Isa. 54.6 Again, *How long wilt thou go about, thou back-sliding daughter? For the Lord hath created a new thing in the earth, a woman shall compass a man,* Jer. 31.22. And David, when he was speaking of Christ and his Church, he saith, *The King's daughter is all glorious within, her clothing is of wrought gold; she shall be brought unto the King: with gladness and rejoicing shall they be brought; they shall enter into the King's palace,* Psal. 45. And also King Solomon in his Song, where he speaks of Christ and his Church, where she is complaining and calling for Christ, he saith, *If thou knowest not, O thou fairest among women, go thy way by the footsteps of the flock,* Cant. 1.8. And John, when saw the wonder that was in Heaven, he saw a woman clothed with the sun, and the moon under her feet, and upon her head a crown of twelve stars; and there appeared another wonder in Heaven, a great red dragon stood ready to devour her child: here the enmity appears that God put between the woman and the dragon, Revelation 12.

Thus much may prove that the Church of Christ is a woman, and those that speak against the woman's speaking, speak against the Church of

Christ, and the seed of the woman, which seed is Christ; that is to say, those that speak against the power of the Lord, and the spirit of the Lord speaking in a woman, simply by reason of her sex, or because she is a woman, not regarding the seed, and spirit, and power that speaks in her; such speak against Christ, and his Church, and are of the seed of the serpent, wherein lodgeth the enmity. And as God the Father made no such difference in the first creation, nor never since between the male and the female, but always out of his mercy and loving kindness, had regard unto the weak. So also, his son, Christ Jesus, confirms the same thing: when the Pharisees came to him, and asked him, if it were lawful for a man to put away his wife, he answered and said unto them, *Have you not read that he that made them in the beginning, made them male and female,* and said, *For this cause shall a man leave father and mother, and shall cleave unto his wife, and they twain shall be one flesh, wherefore they are no more twain but one flesh; what therefore God hath joined together, let no man put asunder,* Mat. 19.4,5,6.

Again, Christ Jesus, when he came to the city of Samaria, where Jacob's Well was, where the woman of Samaria was, you may read, in John 4.25,26 how he was pleased to preach the everlasting Gospel to her; and when the woman said unto him, *I know that when the Messiah cometh* (which is called Christ) *when he cometh, he will tell us all things:* Jesus saith unto her, *I that speak unto thee am he.* This is more than ever he said in plain words to man or woman (that we read of) before he suffered. Also he said unto Martha, when she said, she knew that her brother should rise again in the last day, Jesus said unto her, *I am the Resurrection and the Life; he that believeth on [sic] me, though he were dead, yet shall he live; and whosoever liveth and believeth shall never die. Believest thou this?* She answered, *Yea Lord, I believe thou art the Christ, the son of God.* Here she manifested her true and saving faith, which few at that day believed so on him, John 11.25,26,27.

Also that woman that came unto Jesus with an alabaster box of very precious ointment and poured it in his head as he sat at meat; it is manifested that this woman knew more of the secret power and wisdom of God, than his disciples did, that were filled with indignation against her; and therefore Jesus saith, *Why do ye trouble the woman? For she hath wrought a good work upon me; Verily, I say unto you, wheresoever this Gospel shall be preached in the whole world, there shall also [be] this that this woman hath done, he told for a memorial of her.* Mat. 26.10. Mark

14.3.* saith under, she was a sinner, and that she stood at his feet behind him weeping, and began to wash his feet with her tears and did wipe them with the hair of her head, and kissed his feet, and annointed them with ointment. And when Jesus saw the heart of the Pharisee that hath bidden him to his house, he took occasion to speak unto Simon, as you may read in Luke 7. And he turned to the woman, and said, *Simon, seest thou this woman? Thou gavest me no water to my feet, but she hath washed my feet with tears, and wiped them with the hair of her head: Thou gavest me no kiss, but this woman, since I came in, hath not ceased to kiss my feet. My head with oil thou didst not anoint, but this woman hath anointed my feet with ointment: wherefore I say unto thee, her sins, which are many, are forgiven her, for she hath loved much,* Luke 7.37, to the end.

Also, there [were] many women which followed Jesus from Galilee, ministring unto him, and stood afar off when he was crucified, Mat. 28.55.† Mark 15. Yea even the women of Jerusalem wept for him, insomuch that he said unto them, *Weep not for me, ye daughters of Jerusalem, but weep for your selves, and for your children,* Luke 23.28.

And certain women which had been healed of evil spirits and infirmities, Mary Magdalen, and Joanna the wife of Chuza, Herod's steward's wife, and many others which ministered unto him of their substance, Luke 8.2,3.

Thus we see that Jesus owned the love and grace that appeared in women, and did not despite it, and by what is recorded in the Scriptures, he received as much love, kindness, compassion, and tender dealing towards him from women, as he did from any others, both in his life time, and also after they [i.e., the others] had exercised their cruelty upon him. . . .

And now to the Apostle's words, which is the ground of the great objection against women's speaking: and first, 1 Cor. 14. Let the reader seriously read that chapter, and see the end and drift of the Apostle in speaking these words: for the Apostle is [there] exhorting the Corinthians unto charity, and to desire spiritual gifts, and not to speak in an unknown tongue, and not to be children in understanding, but to be children in malice, but in understanding to be men; and that the spirits of the prophets should be subject to the prophets, for God is not the author of

* "Verily, I say unto you . . ." is in fact Mat. 26.13.

† Margaret Fell has also misidentified this passage. There is no Mat. 28.55. The text referred to is Mark 15.41.

confusion, but of peace: and then he saith, *Let your women keep silence in the church,* etc.

Where it doth plainly appear that the women, as well as others that were among them, were in confusion, for he saith, *How is it brethen, when ye came together, everyone of you hath a psalm, hath a doctrine, hath a tongue, hath a revelation, hath an interpretation? Let all things be done to edifying.* Here was no edifying, but all was in confusion speaking together: therefore he saith, *If any man speak in an unknown tongue, let it be by two, or at most by three, and that by course, and let one interpret, but if there be no interpreter, let him keep silence in the church.* Here the man is commanded to keep silence as well as the woman, when they are in confusion and out of order.

But the Apostle saith further, *They are commanded to be in obedience,* as also saith the Law; and *if they will learn anything, let them ask their husbands at home, for it is a shame for a woman to speak in the church.* Here the Apostle clearly manifests his intent; for he speaks of women that were under the Law, and in that transgression as Eve was, and such as were to learn, and not to speak publickly, but they must first ask their husbands at home, and it was a shame for such to speak in the church: and it appears clearly, that such women were speaking among the Corinthians, by the Apostle's exhorting them from malice and strife, and confusion, and he preacheth the Law unto them, and he saith, in the Law it is written, *With men of other tongues, and other lips, will I speak unto this people,* vers. 2.‡

And what is all this to women's speaking, that have the everlasting Gospel to preach, and upon whom the promise of the Lord is fulfilled, and his spirit poured upon them according to his word, Acts 2.16,17,18. And if the Apostle would have stopped such as had the spirit of the Lord poured upon them, why did he say just before, *If anything be revealed to another that sitteth by, let the first hold his peace?* and *you may all prophesie one by one?* Here he did not say that such women should not prophesy as had the revelation and spirit of God poured upon them, but their women that were under the Law, and in the transgression, and were in strife, confusion and malice in their speaking, for if he had stopped women's praying or prophesying, why doth he say: *Every man praying or prophesying having his head covered, dishonoureth his head; but every woman that prayeth or prophesieth with her head uncovered, dishonoured [sic] her head? Judge in*

‡ This is 1 Cor. 14.21.

yourselves, is it comely that a woman pray or prophesie uncovered? For the woman is not without the man, neither is the man without the woman, in the Lord, 1 Cor. 11.3,4,13.*

Also that other Scripture, in 1 Tim 2. where he is exhorting that prayer and supplication be made every where, lifting up holy hands without wrath and doubting; he saith in the like manner also, that women must adorn themselves in modest apparel, with shamefastness and sobriety, not with broidered hair, or gold, or pearl, or costly array, he saith, *Let women learn in silence will all subjection, but I suffer not a woman to teach, nor to usurp authority over the man, but to be in silence; for Adam was first formed, then Eve; and Adam was not deceived, but the woman being deceived was in the transgression.*

Here the Apostle speaks particularly to a woman in relation to her husband, to be in subjection to him, and not to teach, nor usurp authority over him, and therefore he mentions Adam and Eve: but let it be strained to the utmost, as the opposers of women's speaking would have it, that is, that they should not preach nor speak in the church, of which there is nothing here: yet the Apostle is speaking to such as he is teaching to wear their apparel, what to wear, and what not to wear; such as were not come to wear modest apparel, and such as were not come to shamefastness and sobriety, but he was exhorting them from broidered hair, gold and pearls, and costly array; and such are not to usurp authority over the man, but to learn in silence with all subjection, as it becometh women professing godliness with good works.

And what is all this to such as have the power and spirit of the Lord Jesus poured upon them, and have the message of the Lord Jesus given unto them? Must not they speak the word of the Lord because of these undecent and unreverent women that the Apostle speaks of, and to, in these two Scriptures? And how are the men of this generation blinded, that bring these scriptures, and pervert the Apostle's words, and corrupt this intent in speaking of them, and by these scriptures, endeavour to stop the message and word of the Lord God in women, by condemning and despising of them. If the Apostle would have had women's speaking stopped, and did not allow of them, why did he entreat his true yoke-fellow to help those women, who laboured with him in the gospel? Phil. 4.3 And why did the Apostles join together in prayer and supplication with the women and Mary the mother of Jesus, and with his Bethren,

* Margaret Fell is in fact quoting 1 Cor. 11.4,5,13,11.

Acts 1.14 if they had not allowed, and had union and fellowship with the spirit of God, wherever it was revealed in women as well as others? But all this opposing and gainsaying of women's speaking hath risen out of the bottomless pit, and spirit of darkness that hath spoken for these many hundred years together in this night of apostacy, since the revelations have ceased and been hid, and so that spirit hath limited and bound all up within its bond and compass, and so would suffer none to speak, but such as that spirit of darkness, approved of, man or woman. . . .

A Further Addition in Answer to the Objection Concerning Women Keeping Silent in the Church.

For it is not permitted for them to speak, but to be under obedience; as also saith the Law, *If they will learn anything, let them ask their husbands at home, for it is a shame for a woman to speak in the church:* now this as Paul writeth in 1 Cor. 14.35 is one with that of 1 Tim. 2.11., *Let women learn in silence with all subjection.*

To which I say, if you tie this to all outward women, then there were many women that were widows which had no husbands to learn of, and many were virgins which had no husbands; and Philip had four daughters that were prophets; such would be despised, which the Apostle did not forbid: and if it were to all women, that no woman might speak, then Paul would have contradicted himself; but they were such women that the Apostle mentions in Timothy, that *grew wanton, and were busy-bodies and tatlers and kicked against Christ.* For Christ in the male and in the female is one, and he is the husband, and his wife is the Church, and God hath said, that his daughters should prophesy as well as his sons: and where he hath poured forth his spirit upon them, they must prophesy, though blind priests say to the contrary, and will not permit holy women to speak.

And whereas it is said, *I permit not a woman to speak, as saith the Law:* but where women are lead by the spirit of God, they are not under the Law, for Christ in the male and in the female is one; and where he is made manifest in male and female, he may speak, for he is the end of the Law for righteousness for to all them that believe. So here you ought to make a distinction what sort of women are forbidden to speak, such as were under the Law, who were not come to Christ, nor to the spirit of prophesy: for Huldah, Miriam, and Hannah, were prophets, who were not forbidden in the time of the Law, for they all prophesied in the time of the Law: as you may read, in 2 Kings 22. . . .

Likewise you may read how Judith spoke, and what noble acts she did, and how she spoke of the elders of Israel, and said, *Dear Brethen, seeing ye*

are the honourable and elders of the People of God, call to remembrance
how our Fathers in time past were tempted, that they might be proved if
they would worship God aright; they ought also to remember how our
father Abraham, being tried through manifold tribulations, was found a
friend of God; so was Issac, Jacob and Moses, and all they pleased God,
and were steadfast in Faith through manifold troubles. And read also her
prayer in the Book of Judith, and how the elders commended her, and
said, *All that thou speakest is true, and no man reprove thy words, pray*
therefore for us, for thou art a holy woman, and fearest God. So these elders
of Israel did not forbid her speaking, as you blind priests do; yet you will
make a trade of women's words to get money by, and take texts, and
preach sermons upon women's words; and still cry out, "Women must not
speak, women must be silent"; so you are far from the minds of the elders
of Israel, who praised God for a woman's speaking. . . .

There was hardly a Restoration wit who did not write verses vilipending women. In the 1680s, however, the attacks intensified. Robert Gould's *Love Given O're: or, A Satyr Against the Pride, Lust, and Inconstancy, &c. of Woman* was one of the most prominent examples.

Love Given O're: or, A Satyr Against the Pride, Lust, and Inconstancy, &c. of Woman. London, 1682.

To the Reader.

The pious endeavours of the gown, [have] not proved more ineffectual in the reclaiming the errors of a vicious age, than satire (the better way, though less practised) the amendment of honesty, and good manners amongst us. Nor is it a wonder, when we consider that women, (as if they had the ingredient of fallen angel in their composition) the more they are lashed, are but the more hardened in impenitence: and as children in some violent distemper, commonly spit out those cherishing cordials, which if taken, might chase away the malady: so they (inspired as 'twere with a natural averseness to virtue) despise that wholesome counsel, which is religiously designed for their future good, and happiness. Judge then, if satire ever had more need of a sharper sting than now; when he can look out of his cell on no side but sees so many objects beyond the reach of indignation. Nor is it altogether unreasonable for me (while others are lashing the rebellious times into obedience) to have one fling at woman, the original of mischief. Although I'm sensible I might as well expect to see truth and honesty uppermost in the world, as think to be free from the bitterness of their resentments: but I have no reason to be concerned at that; since I'm certain my design's as far from offending the good, (if there are any amongst them that can be said to be so) as those few that are good, would be offended at their reception into the eternal inhabitations of peace, to be crowned there with the sacred reward of their labours. As for those that are ill, if it reflect on them it succeeds according to my wish; for I have no other design but the amendment of vice, which if I could but in the least accomplish, I should be well pleased; and not without reason too; for it must needs be a satisfaction to a young unskillful archer, to hit the first mark he ever aimed at.

At length from love's vile slav'ry I am free,
And have regained my ancient liberty;
I've shook those chains off which my bondage wrought,
Am free as air, and unconfined as thought;
For faithless Silvia I no more adore,
Kneel at her feet, and pray in vain no more:
No more my verse shall her fled worth proclaim,
And with soft praises celebrate her name:
Her frowns do now no awful terrors bear;
Her smiles no more can cure or cause despair.
I've banished her forever from my breast,
Banished the proud invader of my rest,
Banished the tyrant author of my woes,
That robbed my soul of all its sweet repose:
Not all her treacherous arts, bewitching wiles,
Her sighs, her tears, nor her deluding smiles,
Shall my eternal resolution move,
Or make me talk, or think, or dream of love:
The whining curse I've banished from my mind,
And with it, all the thoughts of womankind.
Come then my Muse, and since the occasion's fair,
'Gainst the lewd sex proclaim an endless war;
Which may renew as still my verse is read,
And live, when I am mingled with the dead:
Discover all their various sorts of vice,
The rules by which they ruin and entice,
Their folly, falsehood, luxury, lust and pride,
With all their numerous race of crimes beside:
Unveil 'em quite to every eye,
And in that shameful posture let 'em lie,
Till they (as they deserve) become to be
Abhorred by all mankind, as they're abhorred by me.

Woman! by heavens the very name's a crime,
Enough to blast, and to debauch my rhyme.
Sure heaven itself (entranced) like Adam lay,
Or else some banished fiend usurped the sway
When Eve was formed; and with her, ushered in
Plagues, woes, and death, and a new world of sin.

The fatal rib was crooked and uneven,
From whence they have their crab-like nature given;
Averse to all the laws of man, and heaven.
    O Lucifer, thy regions had been thin,
Were't not for woman's propagating sin:
'Tis they alone that all true vices know;
And send such throngs down to thy courts below:
More souls they've made obedient to thy reign,
Than heaven, and earth, and seas beside, contain.
True, the first woman gave the first bold blow,
And bravely sailed down to the abyss below;
But had the great deed still been left undone,
None of the daring sex, no, hardly one,
But in the very self-same path would go,
Though sure t'would lead 'em to eternal woe:
Find me ye powers, find one amongst 'em all,
That does not envy Eve the glory of the fall:
Be cautious then, and guard your empire well;
For should they once get power to rebel,
They'd surely raise a civil-war in hell,
Add to the pains you feel; and make you know,
We're here above, as cursed as you below.
    How happy had we been, had heaven designed
Some other way to propagate our kind?
For whatso'ere those all-discerning powers
Created sweet, wife! Nauseous wife! turned sour;
Debauched the innocent, ambrosial meat,
And (like Eve's apple) made it death to eat:
But cursed be the vile name, and cursed be they,
Who are so tamely dull as to obey.
The slaves they may command; is there a dog,
Who, when he may have freedom, wears a clog?
But man, base man, the more imprudent beast,
Drags the dull weight when he may be released:
May such ye Gods (too many such we see)
While they live here, just only live, to be
The marks of scorn, contempt, and infamy.
But if the tide of nature boist'rous grow,
And would rebelliously its banks o'reflow,

Then choose a wench, who (full of lewd desires)
Can meet your floods of love with equal fires;
And will, when e're you let the deluge fly,
Through an extended sluice strait drain it dry;
That whirlpool sluice which never knows a shore,
Never can be filled so full as to run o'er,
For still it gapes, and still cries—room for more!
Such only damn the soul; but a damned wife,
Damns that, and with it all the joys of life:
And what vain blockhead is so dull, but knows,
That of two ills the least is to be chose.

But now, since woman's boundless lust I name,
Woman's unbounded lust I'll first proclaim:
Trace it through all the secret various ways,
Where it still runs in an eternal maze:
And show that our lewd age has brought to view,
What impious Sodom, and Gomorrah too,
Were they what once they were, would blush to do.
True, I confess that Rome's imperial whore,
(More famed for lust, than for the crown she wore)
Aspired to deeds so impiously high,
That their immortal fame will never die:
Into the public stews (disguised) she thrust,
To quench the raging fury of her lust:
Her part against the assembly she made good,
And all the sallies of their lust withstood,
And drained them dry; exhausted all their store;
Yet all could not content the insatiate whore,
Her c—— like the dull grave, still gaped for more.
This, this she did, and bravely got her name
Bourne up forever on the wings of fame:
Yet this is poor, to what our modern age
Has hatched, brought forth, and acted on the stage:
Which for the sex's glory I'll rehearse;
And make that deathless, as that makes my verse.

Who knew not (for to whom was she unknown)
Our late illustrious Bewley?* True, she's gone

* An infamous London prostitute.

To answer for the numerous ills she's done;
Who, though in hell (in hell, if any where)
Hemmed round with all the flames and tortures there,
Finds 'em not fiercer, though she feels the worst,
Than when she lived, her own wild flames of lust.
As Albion's isle fast rooted in the main,
Does the rough billows' raging force disdain,
Which though they foam, and with loud terrors roar,
Yet they can never reach beyond their shore,
So she with lust's enthusiastic rage,
Sustained all the salt stallions of the age.
Whole legions she encountered, legions tired;
Insatiate yet, still fresh supplies desired.
Illustrious bawd! whose fame shall be displayed,
When heroes' glories are in silence laid,
In as profound a silence, as the slaves
Their conquering swords dispatched into their graves.
But bodies must decay; for 'tis too sure,
There's nothing from the jaws of time secure.
Yet, when she found that she could do no more,
When all her body was one putrid sore,
Studded with pox, and ulcers quite all o'er;
Even then, by her delusive treacherous wiles,
(Which showed most specious when they most beguiled)
She enrolled more females in the list of whore,
Than all the arts of man e're did before.
Pressed with the ponderous guilt, at length she fell;
And through the solid center sunk to hell:
The murm'ring fiends all hovered round about,
And in hoarse howls did the great bawd salute;
Amazed to see a sordid lump of clay,
Stained with more various bolder crimes than they:
Nor were her torments less; for the dire train,
Soon sent her howling through the rowling flames,
To the sad seat of everlasting pain.
Cresswold, and Stratford,† the same path do tread;
In lust's black volumes so profoundly read,

That wheresoe're they die, we well may fear,
The very tincture of the crimes they bear,
With strange infusion may inspire the dust,
And in the grave commit true acts of lust.

And now, if so much to the world's revealed,
Reflect on the vast stores that lie concealed:
How, when into their closets they retire,
Where flaming dil——s [do] inflame desire,
And gentle lap-d——s feed the amorous fire:
Lap-d——s! to whom they are more kind and free,
Than they themselves to their own husbands be.
How cursed is man! when brutes his rivals prove,
Even in the sacred business of his love.
Great was the wise man's saying, great, as true;
And we well know, than he none better knew;
Even he himself acknowledges the womb
To be as greedy as the gaping tomb:
Take men, dogs, lions, bears, all sorts of stuff,
Yet it will never cry ——— there is enough.
Nor are their consciences (which can betray
Where e're they're sworn to love) less large than they;
Consciences; so lewdly unconfined!
That every one would, could they act their mind,
To their own single share engross even all mankind.
And when the mind's corrupt, we all well know,
The actions that proceed from it must be so.
Their guilt's as great who any ills would do,
As their's who freely do those ills pursue:
That they would have it so their crime assures;
Thus if they durst, all women would be whores.

† Also well known London prostitutes.

Robert Gould's diatribe was answered, point by point, with a pamphlet entitled *The Female Advocate: or, An Answer to a Late Satyr Against the Pride, Lust and Inconstancy of Woman*. It has been speculated that the author, who identified herself only by the initials S.F., was Sarah Fyge (Egerton). While it is true that Sarah Fyge unquestionably would have agreed with the feminist point of view the author of this work expresses, the literary style of S.F. does not much resemble that of the poems Fyge published later.

The Female Advocate: or, An Answer to a Late Satyr Against the Pride, Lust and Inconstancy of Woman. Written by a Lady in Vindication of Her Sex. London, 1686.

To the Reader.

That which makes many books come abroad into the world without prefaces, is the only reason that incites me to one, viz. the smallness of them; being willing to let my reader know why this is so: for as one great commendation of our sex, is to know much, and speak little, so an intelligent modesty informs my soul, I ought to put a period to the intended length of the ensuing lines, lest censuring critics should measure my tongue by my pen, and condemn me for a talkative by the length of my poem. Though I confess the illustrious subject requires (nay commands) an enlargement from any other pen than mine, (or those under the same circumstances;) but I think it is good frugality for young beginners to send forth a small venture at first, and see how that passes the merciless ocean of critics, and what returns it makes, and so accordingly adventure the next time. I might, if I pleased, make an excuse for the publication of my book, as many others do; but then, perhaps, the world might think 'twas only a feigned unwillingess: but when I found I could not hinder the publication, I set a resolution to bear patiently the censures of the world, for I expected its severity, the first copy being so ill writ, and so much blotted, that it could scarce be read; and they that had the charge of it, in the room of lots, writ what they pleased, and much different from my intention. I find the main objection is, that I should answer so rude a book, when, if it had not been against our sex, I should not have read it, much less have answered it; but I think it's being so, required the sharper answer, and severer contradictions. I suppose some will think the alterations occasioned by their dislike of the former: if that had been intended for the press, some things there inserted, had been left out; which I have now done, though they might pass well enough in private, they were not fit to be exposed to every eye; but I think, when a man is so extravagant as to damn all womankind for the crimes of a few, he ought to be corrected: but in his second edition he hath been more favourable, yet there he goes beyond the bounds of modesty and civility, and exclaims not only against virtue, but moral honesty too, and supposes he hath banished all goodness out of them; but it will be an impossible thing, because they are more essentially good than men; for 'tis observed in all religions, that women are the truest devotionists, and the most pious, and more heavenly than those who pretend to be the most perfect and rational creatures; for many men, with conceit of their own perfections, neglect that which should make them so; as some mistaken persons, who think if they are of the right church they shall be infallibly saved, when they never follow the rules which lead to salvation: and when persons with this inscription pass current in heaven, then should it be according to my antagonist's fancy, that all men are good, and fitting for heaven, because they are men; and women irreversibly damned, because they are women: but that heaven should make a male and female, both of the same species, both endued with the like rational souls, for two such differing ends, is the most notorious principle, and the most unlikely of any that ever was maintained by any rational man; and I shall never take it for an article of my faith, being assured that heaven is for all those whose purity and obedience to its law, qualifies them for it, whether male or female; to which place the latter seem to have the justest claim, is the opinion of one of its votaries.

S.F.

Blasphemous wretch! How canst thou think or say
Some cursed or banished fiend usurpt the sway
When Eve was formed? For then's denied by you
God's omnipresence and omniscience too:
Without which attributes he could not be
The greatest and supremest deity:
Nor can heaven sleep, though it may mourn to see
Degenerate man speak such vile blasphemy.

When from dark chaos heaven the world did make,
And all was glorious it did undertake;
Then were in Eden's garden freely placed
Each thing that's pleasant to the sight or taste,
'Twas filled with beasts and birds, trees hung with fruit,
That might with man's celestial nature suit:
The world being made thus spacious and complete,
Then man was formed, who seemed nobly great.
When heaven surveyed the works that it had done,
Saw male and female, but found man alone,
A barren sex, and insignificant,
Then heaven made woman to supply the want,
And to make perfect what before was scant:
Surely then she a noble creature is,
Whom heaven thus made to consummate all bliss.
Though man had being first, yet methinks she
In nature should have the supremacy;
For man was formed out of dull senseless earth,
But woman had a much more noble birth:
For when the dust was purified by heaven,
Made into man, and life unto it given,
Then the Almighty and all-wise God said,
That woman of that species should be made;
Which was no sooner said, but it was done,
'Cause 'twas not fit for man to be alone.

Thus have I proved woman's creation good,
And not inferiour, when right understood,
To that of man's; for both one maker had,
Which made all good; then how could Eve be bad:
But then you'll say, though she at first was pure,
Yet in that state she did not long endure.
'Tis true; but yet her fall examine right;
We find most men have banished truth for spite:
Nor is she quite so guilty as some make,
For Adam most did of the guilt partake;
While he from God's own mouth had the command,
But woman had it at the second hand:

The Devil's strength weak woman might deceive,
But Adam only tempted was by Eve:
She had the strongest tempter, and least charge;
Man's knowing most, doth make his sin more large.
But though that woman man to sin did lead,
Yet since her seed hath bruised the serpent's head:
Why should she thus be made a public scorn,
Of whom the great almighty God was born?
Surely to speak one slighting word, must be
A kind of murmuring impiety:
But yet their greatest haters still prove such
Who formerly have loved them too much;
And from the proverb they are not exempt,
Too much familiarity has bred contempt.
And as in Adam all mankind did die,
They make all base for one's immodesty;
Nay, make the name a kind of magic spell,
As if 'twould conjure married men to hell.

Woman! By heaven, the very name's a charm,
And will my verse against all critics arm.
The Muses or Apollo doth inspire
Heroic poets; but yours is a fire
Pluto from hell did send by incubus,
Because we make their hell less populous,
Or else you ne'er had damned the females thus:
But if so universally they are
Disposed to mischief, what need you declare
Peculiar faults, when all the world might see
With each approaching morn a prodigy.
Man curse bad woman! I could [hear] as well
The black infernal devils curse their hell;
When there had been no such damned place we know,
If they themselves had not first made it so.
In lust perhaps you others have excelled,
And made all whores that possibly would yield;
And courted all the females in your way,
Then did design at last to make a prey

Of some pure virgins; or what's almost worse,
Make some chaste wives to merit a divorce:
But 'cause they hated your insatiate mind,
Therefore you call what's virtuous, unkind;
And disappointments did your soul perplex,
So in mere spite you curse the female sex.
I would not judge you thus, only I find
You would adulterate all womankind,
Not only with your pen; you higher soar,
You'd exclude marriage, make the world a whore.

But if all men should of your humour be,
And should rob Hymen of his deity,
They soon would find the inconveniency.
Then hostile spirits would be forced to peace,
Because the world so slowly would increase.
They would be glad to keep their men at home,
And every King want more t'attend his throne:
Nay, should an English Prince resolve that he
Would keep the number of's nobility;
And this dull custom some few years maintained,
There would be none less than a peer in the land;
And I do fancy 'twould be pretty sport,
To see a kingdom crammed into a court.
Sure a strange world, when one shall nothing see,
Unless a bawdy-house or nunnery.
For should this act e'er pass, woman would fly
Unto dark caves to save her chastity.
She only in a marriage-bed delights,
The very name of whore her soul affrights:
And when that sacred ceremony's gone,
Woman I'm sure will choose to live alone.

There's none can number all those virtuous dames
Which chose cold death before their lovers' flames.
The chaste Lucretia, whom proud Tarquin loved,
Her self she flew; her chastity she proved.
But I've gone further than I need have done,
Since we have got examples nearer home:

Witness those Saxon ladies who did fear
The loss of honour when the Danes were here;
And cut their lips and noses, that they might
Not pleasing seem, or give the Danes delight:
Thus having done what they could justly do,
At last they fell their sacrifices too.
I could say more, but history will tell
Many examples that do these excel.

In constancy they often men excel,
That steady virtue in their souls do dwell;
She's not so fickle and frail as men pretend,
But can keep constant to a faithful friend;
And though man's always altering of his mind,
He says, inconstancy's in womankind;
And would persuade us that we engross all
That's either fickle, vain or whimsical.
Man's fancied truth small virtue doth express;
Ours is constancy, theirs is stubbornness.
In faithful love our sex do them out-shine,
And is more constant than the masculine:
For where is there that husband that e'er died,
Or ever suffered with his loving bride?
But numerous trains of chaste wives oft' expire
With their dear husbands, wrapt in flaming fire.
We'd to the same if custom did require.
But this is done by Indian women, who
Do make their constancy immortal too,
As is their fame; while happy India yields
More glorious phoenix [sic] than the Arabian fields.
The German women constancy did show
When Wensberg was besieged, begged they might go
Out of the city, with no bigger packs
Than each of them could carry on their backs.
The wondering world expected they'd have gone
Laded with treasures from their native home;
But crossing expectation, each did take
Her husband, as her burden, on her back;

So saved him from intended death, and she
At once gave him both life and liberty.
How many loving wives have often died
Through extreme grief by their cold husbands' side?
If this be not constancy, why then the sun
Or earth do not a constant progress run.

There's thousands of examples that will prove
Woman is true and constant in chaste love:
But when to us pretended love is made,
We yielding, find it lust in masquerade:
Then we disown it, virtue says we must,
We well may change, I think the reason just.
Change did I say, that word I must forbear,
No, she bright star won't wander from her sphere
Of virtue (in which female souls do move)
Nor will she join with an insatiate love;
For she that's first espoused to virtue, must
Be most inconstant when she yields to lust.

The anonymous female author of *Triumphs of Female Wit* (1683) took up the defense of her sex in less pious terms than *The Female Advocate: or, An Answer to a Late Satyr Against the Pride, Lust and Inconstancy of Woman.*

Triumphs of Female Wit in Some Pindaric Odes: or, The Emulation. Together with an Answer to an Objector Against Female Ingenuity, and Capacity of Learning. London, 1683.

The Preface to the Masculine Sex.

Well Gentlemen, your censures I know are ready, and you as willing to bestow them too on a young lady, when ill nature (as you call it) hinders her compliance with the foppish importunities of your desires, or grows cross-grained and won't submit to the usual slavery of her sex. Indeed I expect to find my appearance in the behalf of injured females condemned not only as immodest and unfashionable, but as unnatural and unreasonable also; it being the common experienced policy of usurpers in wit or government, to overthrow the justness of a claimer's title with aspersions of incapacity or weakness. But as for our fate, so far as it can be influenced either by your brains or tongues, I think we need not much value it, be the severity thereof never so great or so keenly urged: for, ingenuity of revenge, and the witty management of a passion, was always looked on as a talent peculiar to our sex alone; a female-province, in which we were ever allowed to be absolute. And I am of [the] opinion, that there are very few of you sparks, who have been so happy as to be engaged in innocent intrigues with us ladies, but must confess that we have briskness of parts sufficient to baffle the ablest of you; nay, and to your own sorrow too, many times have experimented the acuteness of our senses in resenting, and our wit and resolution in revenging injuries. I fancy, had mother Eve but foreseen this unjust oppression of her daughters, she would scarce have been so prodigal of the happiness and ease of her sex, or so free in complaisance to her husband, to engage in so mean and difficult a duty; but would rather have condemned him to the drudgeries of life, whilst her easy task should be the delightful study of natural curiosity, with its variety of productions, to make remarks on the labour of toiling men, and to be judge of their performances. Thus far did woman's complaisancy become her crime and her disadvantage; who instead of an easy pleasurable life, is now confined to labour all the day in the kitchen mines of a family, and at night to the ungratifying divertisement of an unperforming husband. Well, after all, I see if ever we hope to have these grievances redressed, we must e'en appeal to Dame Nature, to know what she at first designed us for, and whether the excellency of a female soul could possibly be raised no higher than the management of a needle or the ingenuity of a pudding. Why we should not be thought capable of all the endowments of human nature, I cannot apprehend: I am sure we seem framed with as much skill and exactness, with the same materials too, both of body and mind, as best composed of you all, with this only difference, that the yielding female lump was with more ease wrought into perfection, and the curious line of natural beauty and ingenuity, when man's more rugged knotty matter could not be carved into excellency without flaws and imperfections: and do not your addresses and amours daily confess us to be the chiefest instruments of conveying your blessings; nature having made us the stewards of all those delights and pleasures which men enjoy or wish for, and entrusted our discretion with their disposal. Why then should not ladies set up for wits, in whom it is so natural to please; for wit is nothing else but an agreeable relish of an object on the apprehension: besides, the faculties of our souls are always brisk and sprightful, our senses quick and intelligent, and then for the organs of our senses, the instruments of action, they are always in tune, ever ready for exercise and engagement. Nay, so far are we from the unpardonable crime of dullness, (a virtue proper only to you men) that at pleasure we (when the occasion proves inviting) can raise our obliged senses into the pleasing extravagancy of rapture or diverting wit or passion: and then again, with as much facility and ease, can command them back unto the sober rules of solid wisdom. We scorn to flag, like you sparks, in the midst of a half-enjoyed pleasure, for want of life to relish, and vigour to finish the innocent enjoyment. Thus far nature furnishes us with ability. And were but the liberty of an artificial improvement, and the great advantages of a suitable education added to the strength of our parts and our natural capacity, on my conscience we should outdo you in the trade of ingenuity, and soon get a stock of acquired excellency wherewith to set up for accomplished professors of arts and sciences: and I dare say that there are none of all you sparks but would be glad to be dealing with us for wit and pleasure. Don't you see, whenever generosity and bravery of mind (disdaining to be fettered to the mean employments of her sex) drives the noble female's soul from the slavery of an entailed ignorance unto the freedom and more agreeable pursuit of learning and wisdom, how soon and with what ease she becomes the deserved envy of mankind, the emulation of the ingenious, and the glory of her sex for a rare ingenuity. And let me tell you, gentlemen, since we are thus happily become acquainted with our strength, we shall often make bold to let our wit sally out upon you the enemies of our growing reputation, and the unjust invaders of our native rights; not doubting but to return with the grateful spoils of a just applause, and to signalize the prevailing power of our charms in the triumphs of our wit, as well as beauty: the last of which was ever allowed to be irresistible, and by the first you shall see that our methods of conquering are not always the same, but that we can captivate defenceless men which way we please.

The Emulation. A Pindaric Ode.

Ah! tell me why, deluded sex, thus we
Into the secret beauty must not pry
Of our great Athenian deity.
Why do we Minerva's blessings slight,
And all her tuneful gifts despise?
Shall none but the insulting sex be wise?
Shall they be blessed with intellectual light,
Whilst we drudge on in ignorance's night?
We've souls as noble, and as fine as clay,
And parts as well composed to please as they.
Men think perhaps we best obey,
And best their servile business do,
When nothing else we know
But what concerns a kitchen or a field,
With all the meaner things they yield.
As if a rational unbounded mind
Were only for the sordidest task of life designed.

II.

They let us learn to work, to dance, or sing,
Or any such like trivial thing,
Which to their profit may increase or pleasure bring.

But they refuse to let us know
What sacred sciences doth [sic] impart
Or the mysteriousness of art.
In learning's pleasing paths denied to go,
From knowledge banished, and their schools;
We seem designed alone for useful fools,
And foils for their ill-shapen sense, condemned to prize
And think them truly wise,
Being not allowed their follies to despise.
Thus we from ignorance to wonder run.
(For admiration ceases when the secret's known.)
Seem witty only in their praise
And kind, congratulating lays.
Thus to the repute of sense they rise,
And thus through the applauder's ignorance are wise,
For should we understand as much as they,
They fear their empire might decay.
For they know women heretofore
Gained victories, and envied laurels wore:
And now they fear we'll once again
Ambitious be to reign
And to invade the dominions of the brain.
And as we did in those renowned days,
Rob them of laurels, so we now will take their bays.

III.

But we are peaceful and will not repine,
They still may keep their bays as well as wine.
We've now no Amazonian hearts,
They need not therefore guard their magazine of arts.
We will not on their treasure seize,
A part of it sufficently will please.
We'll only so much knowledge have
As may assist us to enslave
Those passions which we find
Too potent for the mind.
'Tis o're them only we desire to reign,
And we no nobler, braver, conquest wish to gain.

IV.

We only so much will desire
As may instruct us how to live above
Those childish things which most admire,
And may instruct us what is fit to love.
We covet learning for this only end,
That we our time may to the best advantage spend:
Supposing 'tis below us to converse
Always about our business or our dress;
As if to serve our senses were our happiness.
We'll read the stories of the ancient times,
To see, and then with horror hate their crimes:
But all their virtues with delight we'll view,
Admired by us, and imitated too.
But for rewarding sciences and arts,
And all the curious products which arise
From the contrivance of the wise,
We'll tune and cultivate our fruitful hearts.
And should man's envy still declare,
Our business only to be fair;
Without their leave we will be wise,
And beauty, which they value, we'll despise.
Our minds, and not our faces, we'll adorn,
For that's the employ to which we are born.
The Muses gladly will their aid bestow,
And to their sex their charming secrets show.
Whilst man's brisk notions owe their rise
To an inspiring bottle, wench, or vice,
Must be debauched and damned to get
The reputation of a wit.
To nature only, and our softer Muses, we
Will owe our charms of wit, of parts, and poetry.

The Answer to the Emulation.

What daring female is't who thus complains,
In masculine Pindaric strains,
Of great Apollo's Salic law;
Both breaks it, and pretends that she
Pleads only for her native liberty.
Whilst in a rapid over-flowing tide
Of wit and fancy, which no banks are able to abide,
She strikes the guards of Helicon
With a surprising awe,
And Amazonian-like, compells 'em to withdraw.

II.

Stand, valiant she, a parley I desire;
Whence had you this poetic fire?
I fear, Prometheus-like, y'have stole
A spark designed to form a manly soul.
Forbear, bold Nymph, thus to aspire,
You needs must know, ingenious dame,
'Twas from Jove's brain alone Minerva came.
Nature indeed hath made your sex of use
Unknowing infants to produce.
But sure she ne're designed it
To make your brains prolific, or your wit.

III.

Which of the arts,
Except that one of captivating hearts,
Doth the world owe to womankind?
And 'tis not to monopolise
The law allows it to the wise,
That he who proves so happy as to find
Some undiscovered useful skill
Should use it at his will.
And the sole profit be to him confined.

At least until
Some tolerable gains
Have recompensed his cost and pains.
But when, alas! will arts repay
The time, health, cost, and pains upon them thrown away.

IV.

'Tis not that men insult or would enslave
Your sex, that they engross Apollo's mines;
Methinks you should more pity have
For those whom you have robbed of all their store,
Than thus to envy them their toil and pains
To gain some part of what they had before.
No, let 'em dig and delve, what need you care,
'Tis too hard labour for the fair.
And when the dross is purged and gone,
'Tis not for ourselves alone
That we such tedious labour take,
Next to our selves, 'tis for your sake.
To your fair sex we willingly commit
Our golden wisdom and our silver wit.

V.

Nature hath made your sex with curious art,
Your souls too are ingenious and bright,
Both full of beauty as the sons of light.
And woman is the rib that lies most near the heart.
Therefore I must advise the witty she
Not to indulge this longing still,
Lest you miscarry when you see
Your power not equal to your will.
Alas! forbidden fruit you know
Did on the tree of knowledge grow.
And when hardy thick-skulled man
Spends and cracks his studious brain,
And instead of gaining more
Loses what he had before,
So those whom emulation sets at strife
To gain the Tree of Knowledge often lose the Tree of Life.

VI.

That muddy stream of time
In which your sex, that prison of your souls,
Your rational unbounded mind controuls,
Swiftly into the eternal ocean rolls;
And then
You'll find no cause to envy men.
It will not be who studied most,
No one his attainments then shall boast.
'Tis not a studious life that brings
The necessary knowledge of revealed things.
And all will then receive,
Not as they knew, but as they did believe.
Then trouble not your quiet so,
Hard and unnecessary things to know:
Knowledge divine you may attain
Without the labour of the brain.
Histories and moral precepts too
Are not denied to you;
But for the learning of the schools,
That can't make women wise, that makes men fools.
Philosophy's uncertain light
Is but a wild fire in the night.
And all the rest we wisdom call,
Is either little so, or not at all.
Each limb of learning hath the gout
Of an incurable and painful doubt.
And by the acute disease
The richest men are always least at ease.

VII.

But you have passions to subdue;
More you would know, because you more would do;
You're sensible of ignorance's night,
And fain would glut your sight
With a full view of intellectual light.
And may your wish successful prove,
For ladies should enjoy whate're they love.

May you walk safe in learning's milky way,
Know all that men and angels say,
Expand your souls to truth as wide as day.
But when you're grown wise as well as fair,
Then, Lady, have a care.
Ambitious thoughts will rise,
And you will know that you are wise.
A woman fair, wise, learned, and humble too,
Will be a species alone,
A Phoenix true,
Talked of by all but seen by none.

Written by Mr. H.

The anonymous author of *An Essay in Defence of the Female Sex* was clearly moved to publish her argument in answer to the continuous stream of "wits" who have "so strongly attacked our sex." But she was, interestingly enough, also angered by an "apology" for women, *A Dialogue Concerning Women, Being a Defence of the Sex*, written by William Walsh, with a preface by John Dryden. The anonymous female "defender" accuses Walsh of bad faith: "he has taken more care to give an edge to his satire, than force to his apology," she observes. Walsh's "defense" takes the form of a dialogue between Misogynes and Philogynes, who pleads the case for women. The ravings of Misogynes are energetic and amusing, while the lukewarm defense that follows laboriously lists "illustrious women" from history to prove that the sex is capable of achievement. This argument infuriated the female defender, who notes: "He levels his scandal at the whole sex, and thinks us sufficiently fortified, if out of the story of two thousand years he has been able to pick up a few examples of women illustrious for their wit, learning or virtue. . . ."

Walsh ends his catalogue of women wonders of the ages by remarking that "there might be as advantageous characters perhaps given of ladies of our own country now living did not their modesty, that inseparable quality of wit and woman, deter me from it." He goes on to praise the modesty in women that keeps them from joining "those eternal [male] scribblers who are continually plagueing the world with their works," and points out the extraordinary circumstances that produced "famous" women. "Had not Anna Maria van Schurman's works been published by a friend without her consent," Walsh confides, "we had lost the benefit of them."

An Essay in Defence of the Female Sex. London, 1696.

Preface:

. . . I suppose, I shall not be thought vain, if, as I pretend not to the applause, so I fear not the contempt of the world: yet I presume not so far upon the merits of what I have written, as to make my name public with it. I have elsewhere held, that vanity was almost the universal mover of all our actions, and consequently of mine, as well as of others; yet it is not strong enough in me, to induce me to bring my name upon the public stage of the world.

There are many reasons that oblige me to this cautious, reserved way of procedure; tho' I might otherwise be very ambitious of appearing in the defence of my sex, could I persuade my self, that I was able to write any thing suitable to the dignity of the subject, which I am not vain enough to think. This indeed is one reason; because I am sensible it might have been much better defended by abler pens, such as many among our own sex are; though I believe scarce thus much would have been expected from me, by those that know me . . . the consideration of the tenderness of reputation in our sex, (which as our delicatest fruits and finest flowers are most obnoxious to the injuries of weather, is submitted to every infectious blast of malicious breath) made me very cautious, how I exposed mine to such poisonous vapours. I was not ignorant, how liberal some men are of their scandal, whenever provoked, especially by a woman; and how ready the same men are to be so, tho' upon never so mistaken grounds. This made me resolve to keep 'em in ignorance of my name, and if they have a mind to find me out, let 'em catch me (if they can) as children at blindman's bluff do one another, hoodwinked; and I am of opinion I have room enough to put 'em out of breath before they come near me. . . .

There are some men (I hear), who will not allow this piece to be written by a woman; did I know what estimate to make of their judgements, I might perhaps have a higher opinion of this trifle, than I ever yet had. For I little thought while I was writing this, that any man (especially an ingenious man) should have the scandal of being the reputed author. For he must think it scandalous to be made to father a woman's productions unlawfully. But these gentlemen, I suppose, believe there is more wit, than they'll find in this piece, upon the credit of the bookseller, whose interest it is to flatter it. But were it as well written as I could wish it, or as the subject would bear, and deserves, I see no reason why our sex should be robbed of the honour of it; since there have been women of all ages, whose writings might vie with those of the greatest men, as the present age as well as past can testify. I shall not trouble the reader with their names, because I would not be thought so vain, as to rank myself among 'em; and their names are already too well known, and celebrated to receive any additional luster from so weak encomiums as mine. I pretend not to imitate, much less to rival those illustrious ladies, who have done so much honour to their sex, and are unanswerable proofs of, what I contend for. I only wish that some ladies now living among us (whose names I forbear to mention in regard to their modesty) would now exert themselves, and give us more recent instances, who are both by nature and education sufficiently qualified to do it, which I pretend not to. I freely own to the reader, that I know no other tongue besides my native, except French, in which I am but very moderately skilled. I plead not this to excuse the meanness of my performance; because I know I may reasonably be asked why I was so forward to write. For that I have already given my reasons above, if they will not satisfy the reader, he must endeavour to please himself with better, for I am very little solicitous about the matter. I shall only add, that for my good will I hope the favour of my own sex, which will satisfy my ambition. . . .

The defence of our sex against so many and so great wits as have so strongly attacked it, may justly seem a task too difficult for a woman to attempt. Not that I can, or ought to yield, that we are by nature less enabled for such an enterprise than men are, which I hope at least to show plausible reasons for, before I have done: but because through the usurpation of men, and the tyranny of custom (here in England especially) there are at most but few, who are by education, and acquired wit, or letters sufficiently qualified for such an undertaking. For my own part, I shall readily own that, as few as there are, there may be and are abundance, who in their daily conversations approve themselves much more able, and sufficient assertors of our cause, than my self; and I am sorry that either their business, their other diversions, or too great indulgence of their ease, hinder them from doing public justice to their sex. The men by interest or inclination are so generally engaged against us, that it is not to be expected, that any one man of wit should arise so generous as to engage in our quarrel, and be the champion of our sex against the injuries and oppressions of his own. Those romantic days are over, and there is not so much as a Don Quixote of the quill left to succour the distressed damsels. 'Tis true, a feint of something of this nature was made three or four years since by one;* but how much soever his Eugenia may be obliged to him, I am of the opinion the rest of her sex are but little beholding to him. For as you rightly observed, Madam, he has taken more care to give an edge to his satire, than force to his apology; he has played a sham prize, and receives more thrusts than he makes; and like a false renegade fights under

* This is a reference to William Walsh's *A Dialogue Concerning Women, Being a Defence of the Sex* (London, 1691). The text of Walsh's dialogue is addressed to a "Eugenia."

our colours only for a fairer opportunity of betraying us. But what could be expected else from a beau? An animal that can no more commend in earnest a woman's wit, than a man's person, and that compliments ours, only to show his own good breeding and parts. He levels his scandal at the whole sex, and thinks us sufficiently fortified, if out of the story of two thousand years he has been able to pick up a few examples of women illustrious for their wit, learning or virtue, and men infamous for the contrary; though I think the most inveterate of our enemies would have spared him that labour, by granting that all ages have produced persons famous or infamous of both sexes; or they must throw up all pretense to modesty, or reason.

I have neither learning, nor inclination to make a precedent, or indeed any use of Mr. W's laboured common place book; and shall leave pedants and school-boys to rake and tumble the rubbish of antiquity, and muster all the heros and heroines they can find to furnish matter for some wretched harangue, or stuff a miserable declamation with instead of sense or argument.

I shall not enter into any dispute, whether men, or women be generally more ingenious, or learned; that point must be given up to the advantages men have over us by their education, freedom of converse, and variety of business and company. But when any comparison is made between 'em, great allowances must be made for the disparity of those circumstances. Neither shall I contest about the pre-eminence of our virtues; I know there are too many vicious, and I hope there are a great many virtuous of both sexes. Yet this I may say, that whatever vices are found amongst us, have in general both their source, and encouragement from them.

The question I shall at present handle is, whether the time an ingenious gentleman spends in the company of women may justly be said to be misemployed, or not? . . .

It remains then for us to inquire whether the bounty of nature be wholly neglected, or stifled by us, or so far as to make us unworthy [of] the company of men? Or whether our education (as bad as it is) be not sufficient to make us a useful, nay a necessary part of society for the greatest part of mankind. This cause is seldom indeed urged against us by the men, though it be the only one, that gives 'em any advantage over us in understanding. But it does not serve their pride; there is no honour to be gained by it: for a man ought no more to value himself upon being wiser than a woman, if he owe his advantage to a better education, and greater means of information, than he ought to boast of his courage, for beating a man, when his hands were bound. Nay it would be so far from honourable to contend for preference upon this score, that they would thereby at once argue themselves guilty both of tyranny, and of fear: I think I need not have mentioned the latter; for none can be tyrants but cowards. For nothing makes one party slavishly depress another, but their fear that they may at one time or other become strong or couragious enough to make themselves equal to, if not superiour to their masters. This is our case; for men being sensible as well of the abilities of mind in our sex, as of the strength of body in their own, began to grow jealous, that we, who in the infancy of the world were their equals and partners in dominion, might in process of time, by subtlety and stratagem, become their superiours; and therefore began in good time to make use of force (the origin of power) to compel us to a subjection nature never meant; and made use of nature's liberality to them to take the benefit of her kindness from us. From that time they have endeavoured to train us up altogether to ease and ignorance; as conquerors use to do those, they reduce by force, that so they may disarm 'em, both of courage and wit; and consequently make them tamely give up their liberty, and abjectly submit their necks to a slavish yoke. As the world grew more populous, and men's necessities whetted their inventions, so it increased their jealousy, and sharpened their tyranny over us, till by degrees, it came to that height of severity, I may say cruelty, it is now at in all the eastern parts of the world, where the women, like our negroes in our western plantations, are born slaves, and live prisoners all their lives. Nay, so far has this barbarous humour prevailed, and spread itself, that in some parts of Europe, which pretend to be most refined and civilized, in spite of Christianity, and the zeal for religion which they so much affect, our condition is not very much better. And even in France, a country that treats our sex with more respect than most do, we are by the Salic Law excluded from sovereign power. The French are an ingenious people, and the contrivers of that law knew well enough, that we were no less capable of reigning, and governing well, than themselves; but they were suspicious that if the regal power should fall into the hands of women, they would favour their own sex, and might in time restore 'em to their primitive liberty and equality with the men, and so break the neck of that unreasonable authority they so much affect over us; and therefore made this law to prevent it. The historians indeed tell us other reasons, but they can't agree among themselves, and as men are parties against us, and therefore their evidence may justly be rejected. To say the truth, Madam, I can't tell how to prove all this from ancient records; for if any histories were anciently written by women, time, and the malice of men have effectually conspired to suppress 'em; and it is not reasonable to think that men should transmit, or suffer to be transmitted to posterity, any thing that might show the weakness and illegality of their title to a power they still exercise so arbitrarily, and are so fond of. But since daily experience shows, and their own histories tell us, how earnestly they endeavour, and what they act, and suffer to put the same trick upon one another, 'tis natural to suppose they took the same measures with us at first, which now they have effected, like the rebels in our last civil wars, when they had brought the Royal Party under, they fall together by the ears about the dividend.

In a sermon preached at a wedding in Dorsetshire on May 11, 1699, the Reverend John Sprint took it upon himself to instruct the bride in her proper duties, deportment, and attitude. His remarks on the subject sparked a great deal of resentment on the part of his female listeners, and the sermon became an issue of public debate. Two women published replies to Sprint's sermon, one an anonymous "Female Advocate," and the other a (then) unpublished poet who was also an unhappy wife, Lady Mary Chudleigh. A few years later, Mary Astell addressed the question of marriage in a long essay entitled *Some Reflections upon Marriage.*

John Sprint, *The Bride-Woman's Counseller: Being a Sermon Preached at a Wedding, May the 11th, 1699, at Sherbourne in Dorsetshire.* London, 1700.

The Epistle to the Reader.

Courteous Reader,

When thou hast perused this discourse, thou wilt see cause enough to believe me, if I tell thee it was designed only for the pulpit, not for the press; but it hath so often fallen out, that the doctrine therein contained is so unhappily represented to the world, by some ill-natured females, that I am necessitated to offer it to public view; by means of which, yet I hope I shall get the advantage of convincing of the world that I am not such an impudent villain as my waspish accusers have reported me to be. Be it known unto thee, reader, whosoever thou art, that I have not met with one woman amongst all my accusers whose husband is able to give her the character of a dutiful and obedient wife. I observe also, that good wives are no more offended with my discourse, than modest matrons are when vile strumpets are painted in their proper colours; the most that such have to say is, that I might have done well to have said as much to the men, which for their satisfaction I will promise to do, when I see this discourse hath had that happy success as to reform those imperious wives, who never think their husbands love them well, unless they obey them too.

Upon the whole, I find 'tis women's guilt which makes them so uneasy, and puts them to that pain which they feel in their consciences, for which

I know no better an anodyne than a speedy repentance and reformation; which if they neglect, in despite of all their loud noise and clamours, the truths which I here publish will pursue them to judgement, and there witness against them, not only as traitors to their husbands, whose authority they usurp, but as rebels to the great monarch of the world, whose sacred laws they impiously violate.

I. Cor. Chap.7. Ver.34.

But she that is married careth for the things of the world, how she may please her husband.

The word *careth*, in the original, signifieth more than ordinary care, and implies a dividing of the mind into divers thoughts, casting this way, and that way, and every way, how to give best content. Finding no other verbal difficulties, I shall leave words and pass to things, and shall lay the foundation of my discourse in this proposition.

It is a duty incumbent on all married women, to be extraordinary careful to content and please their husbands.

From which doctrine I shall take occasion faithfully to represent the duty of married women to their husbands.

Obj. And why so? May the women say, why could you not have pitched upon v.33. and have taken occasion from thence to have told married men their duty to their wives? Or if we must be told our duty, why could you not have come to a composition with us, and have brought our husbands in to have shared with us?

Answ. Truly I foresaw not only these, but a whole *Iliad* of female objections, would be started against my design; but if reason may take place, I hope I am able to silence them all: and here, amongst the many reasons which might be produced to justify my attempt, I shall only offer to your consideration these few.

1st. Because the woman's duty is harder and more difficult than that of the man. Precepts for ruling and governing are more taking, and have a more pleasing relish, than those which enjoin subjection and obedience. You women will acknowledge that men can learn to command and rule fast enough, which as husbands they ought to do; but 'tis very rare to find that women learn so fast to submit and obey, which as wives they ought to do: women have need of *line, upon line, precept upon precept, here a little and there a little,* and all little enough to make them perfect in their lesson.

2nd. Because women are so weaker capacities to learn than men, and therefore when they have a hard and difficult lesson, and but weak abilities to learn it, they had need of more help and assistance afforded them; and so it behoves us not only to tell them their duty in conjunction with their husbands', but also to teach them singly and by themselves.

3rd. Because that (according to the observation which I have made) most of those distractions and disturbances which have attended a married life, and that have brought so much reproach and disgrace on that honourable state, are owing to the indiscretion and folly, if not to the obstinacy and stubbornness of disobedient wives; and I shall not scruple to affirm, that the number of those bad husbands, which their wives have made so, is greater by far than the number of those whom their wives have found so when they were first married.

4th. Because the love of a husband does very much depend upon the obedience of a wife: stubbornness and obstinacy in a wife may check and quench the affections of a husband, but are no proper methods to kindle and enflame them. When the wife becomes pliant and yielding to her husband's will and desire, she then leads him captive at her pleasure, and leaves him so fast bound in the golden fetters of love, that she may even do with him what she pleases. "An obedient wife, (says one) is the likeliest woman in the world to command her husband": so that in plain terms, you are more afraid than hurt, and instead of being so scrupulous of having your duty told you, you should use your utmost diligence to learn and practise it, if ever you mean to have your husbands loving and kind to you.

5th. Because that all that I pretend to, is to lay your duty before you; and shall I therefore become your enemy, because I am come to tell you the truth? As for good wives, the knowledge and practice of their duty is so comfortable and pleasant to them, that I am sure they are not listed in the number of these objectors, and I wish, that where there is one of these, there were a thousand: as for bad ones, I am sure they have need of being told their duty more than a little, and of this sort I wish there were none at all; and if by my poor endeavours in this discourse, I can but be instrumental either of lessening their number, or of preventing their increase, I shall obtain my end. Under the shelter of these reasons I shall adventure in the face of all objections to pursue my design, which is to prosecute this doctrine, *viz.*

That 'tis a duty incumbent on all married women to be extraordinary careful to content and please their husbands. . . .

The Female Advocate, or A Plea for the Just Liberty of the Tender Sex, and Particularly of Married Women, Being Reflections on a Late Rude and Disingenuous Discourse Delivered by Mr. John Sprint, in a Sermon at a Wedding, May 11, at Sherbourne in Dorsetshire, 1699. By a Lady of Quality. London, 1700.

Preface to the Female Sex:

Ladies, If you enquire who I am, I shall only tell you in general, that I am one that never yet came within the clutches of a husband, and therefore what I write may be the more favourably interpreted as not coming from a party concerned. Nor really do I hope to make any condition the easier if ever I resign myself into the arms of one of the other sex. No, I am very well satisfied that there are a great many brave men whose generous principles make them scorn the methods that very reason condemns. Not that I can boast of any great beauty, or a vast fortune—two things (especially the latter) which are able to make us conquerors through the world. But I have endeavoured to furnish myself with something more valuable: I shall not brag that I understand a little Greek and Latin (languages being only the effect of confusion), having made some attempt to look into the more solid parts of learning, and having adventured a little abroad into the world, and endeavoured to understand men and manners. And having seen something of the Italian and Spanish humours, I solemnly profess I never observed in Italy, nor Spain itself, a slavery so abject as this author would fain persuade us to.

As for those of you that are already in the house of bondage, and have found all the charms of innocence and good humour, and the most exact prudence ineffectual long to recommend you to the smiles of your new lords and masters. I think indeed 'twill be very well if you can, as he advises you, bring down the very desires of your hearts to their will and pleasure, and fancy yourselves happy in the midst of all.

And for those of you that are happily married, your life and actions are a sufficient contradiction to this gentleman. While you let the world see that you can please your husbands without that extraordinary way which he recommends in his sermon, that was thought so unmanly and scandalous, that (as I am informed) Mr. L——, the minister who is resident at Sherbourne, looked on himself as obliged to tell the world in the public news that he was not the author of that discourse, lest, it being preached where he lives, they who knew not his name might impute it to him.

In a word, Ladies, I would recommend to your thoughts something that is great and noble, that is to say, to furnish your minds with true knowledge, that (as an ingenious lady tells us) you may know something more than a well-chosen petticoat, or a fashionable commode. Several of the French ladies, and with us the late incomparable Mrs. Baynard, and that lady that is Mr. Norris's correspondent, and many more, are witnesses of this. Hereby we shall be far enough from being charmed with a great estate, or moved with the flowing nonsense and romantic bombast of every foppish beau, and shall learn (if we choose companions for our lives) to select the great, the generous, the brave and deserving souls, men who will as much hate to see us uneasy, as this gentleman is afraid of coming under the discipline of the apron.

Yours,
Eugenia

The Ladies' Defence; or, "The Bride-Woman's Counseller" Answer'd: A Poem. In a Dialogue Between Sir John Brute, Sir William Loveall, Melissa, and a Parson. London, 1701.

To All Ingenious Ladies:

The love of truth, the tender regard I have for your honour, joined with a just indignation to see you so unworthily used, makes me assume the confidence of employing my pen in your service. The knowledge I had of my inability for so great a task made me for a while stifle my resentments, as thinking it much better privately to lament the injuries that were done you, than expose you by a weak defence to the fresh insults of a person who has not yet learned to distinguish between railing and instruction, and who is so vain as to fancy, that the dignity of his function will render everything he thinks fit to say becoming: but when I found that some men were so far from finding fault with his sermon, that they rather defended it, and expressed an ill-natured sort of joy to see you ridiculed, and that those few among 'em who were pretenders to more generosity and good humour, were yet too proud, too much devoted to their interest, and too indulgent to their pleasures to give themselves the trouble of saying anything in your vindication, I had not the patience to be silent any longer. Besides, it vexed me to think he should have the satisfaction of believing, that what by the malice of some, the neutrality of others, and the sacredness of his character, he was secured from all opposition, and might triumph over you at his pleasure. It also troubled me to find that but one of our own sex had the courage to enter the lists with him:* I know there are several other ladies, who, if they would be so kind themselves, and you, as to undertake the quarrel, would manage it with more learning, eloquence and address, than I dare pretend to, as being infinitely my superiors in all the endowments of the mind; but since they think fit to decline it, I hope they will permit me to enter the field, and try my fortune with our mighty antagonist. I assure 'em I do not do it out of an ambitious desire of being talked of, or with hopes of having it said [that] I can write well; no, if I know my own heart, I am far from any such vanity, as being too well acquainted with my own insufficiency to entertain any such unbecoming thoughts of my mean performance. . . . I solemnly declare that what I

* The anonymous author of *The Female Advocate.*

Being forced to parade through town wearing a metal cage over the head was standard punishment for gossips and scolds. The woman's tongue was depressed by a bar extending from the frame of the cage.

There was a woman known to be so bold,
That she was noted for a common scold . . .
She should be ducked over head and ears,
In a deep pond, before her overseers.
The Anatomy of a Woman's Tongue, 1638.

Tittle-Tattle; Or, the sev

AT THE CHILDBED

AT THE CONDIT

AT THE BAKEHOVSE

AT Child-bed when the Goſſips meet, | Together they will crack a Pot, | At Alehouſe you ſee how jovial they
  Fine Stories we are told; | Before they can get Home. | With every one her Noggin :
And if they get a Cup too much, | The Bake-houſe is a Place you know, | For till the Skull and Belly be ful',
  Their Tongues they cannot hold. | Where Maids a Story hold, | None of them will be jogging.

At Market when good Houſewives meet, | And if their Miſtreſſes will prate, | To Church fine Ladies do reſort,
    | They muſt not be control'd. | New Faſhions for to ſay :

"As is usual at such gossiping meetings . . . the ladies fell into a discourse of husbands, complaining of ill husbands, and so from husbands in general, to their own particular husbands." Margaret Cavendish, Duchess of Newcastle, *Sociable Letters*, 1664.

al Branches of Gossipping.

THE GOVERNMENT OF THE TONGUE

"[Women's] tongues are held their defensive
armour, but in no particular detract they more
from their honour, than by giving too free scope
to that glibbery member." Richard Brathwaite,
The English Gentlewoman, 1631.

Illustration from Robert Codrington's
*The Second Part of Youth's Behaviour;
or, Decency in Conversation Amongst
Women*, 1664.

VERTVE

VICE

T. Cross sculp

Education. | Vocation. | Decency. | Complement

Spes in cælis, Pes in terris. | Grace my guide, Glory my goale.

THE ENGLISH GENTLEMAN AND ENGLISH GENTLEWOMAN,

Both

In one Volume couched,
The 3d. Edition, revised,
corrected & enlarged;

with

A LADIES Love Lecture,
And a Supplement
Lately annexed,
and
Entitled

The TURTLES
TRIVMPH.

By Rich. Brathwait Esq;

Qui genus jactat suum, aliena laudat. | Casta fides sponsam me fecerit.

Creation. | Acquaintance. | Estimation. | Fancy.

Generoso Germine. Germino.

Moderation. | Perfection. | Gentility. | Honour

THE
ARRAIGNMENT
of Lewd, Idle, Froward, and
Vnconſtant Women :

O R,

The vanitie of them; chuſe you whether.

W I T H

A Commendation of the Wiſe, Vertuous, and
Honeſt Women.

*Pleaſant for married-Men, profitable for Young-
Men, and hurtfull to none.*

Printed at London by *T. C.* and are to be ſold by *F. Grove,* at his Shop, at
upper-end of Snowzhill, neere the Sarazens head without Newzgate, 1634.

Frontispiece, *Swetnam,
the Woman-Hater,
Arraigned by Women,*
1620.

Ester hath hang'd Haman:

OR

AN ANSVVERE TO

a lewd Pamphlet, entituled,
The Arraignment of Women.

With the arraignment of lewd, idle,
froward, and vnconstant men, and
HVSBANDS.

Diuided into two Parts.

The first proueth the dignity and worthinesse
of Women, out of diuine Testimonies.

The second shewing the estimation of the Fœ-
minine Sexe, in ancient and Pagan times ; all which
is acknowledged by men themselues in their
daily actions.

VVritten by *Ester Sowernam*, neither Maide,
Wife nor Widdowe, yet really all, and therefore experienced to defend all.

IOHN 8.7.
He that is without sinne among you, let him first cast a stone at her.

Neque enim lex iusticior vlla
—— *Quam necis Artificem arte perire sua.*

LONDON,
Printed for *Nicholas Bourne*, and are to be sold at his shop
at the entrance of the Royall Exchange. 1617.

The Man-Woman:

Being a Medicine to cure the Coltiſh Diſeaſe of
the Staggers in the Maſculine-Feminines
of our Times.

Expreſt in a briefe Declamation.

Non omnes poſſumus omnes.

Miſtris, will you be trim'd or truſſ'd?

London printed for I. T. and are to be ſold at Chriſt Church gate. 1620.

write is wholly intended for such as are on the same level with my self, and have not been blessed with a learned and ingenious education, and cannot boast of such a strength of resolution, such a constancy of mind, such a depth of reason and solidity of judgement. . . .

So well, so entirely well, I love my sex, that if 'twere in my power they should be all wholly faultless, and as much admired for the comprehensiveness of their knowledge as they are now despised for their ignorance, and have souls as beauteous as their faces, thoughts as bright and sparkling as their eyes. . . . And if it is their hard fortune to be married to men of brutish unsociable tempers, to monsters in human shape, to persons who are at open defiance with their reason, and fond of nothing but their folly, and under no government but their irregular passions, I would persuade them to struggle with their afflictions, and never leave contending, 'till they have gained an absolute victory over every repining thought, every uneasy reflection. And though 'tis extremely difficult, yet I would advise them to pay [their husbands] as much respect, and to obey their commands with as much readiness, as if they were the best and most endearing husbands in the world; this, will not only put a stop to the invidious censures of their spiteful enemies, but give 'em [the ladies] the possession of that inward joy, that unspeakable satisfaction, which naturally arises from the apprehension of having done good and laudable actions. In order to the gaining such a happy disposition of mind, I would desire 'em seriously to consider what those things are which they can properly call their own, and of which fortune cannot deprive 'em. . . . This, if often and heedfully reflected on, will make them moderate their desires, and teach them never with earnestness to wish for any thing that has no dependence on [themselves], nor to entertain an aversion for things that 'tis not in their power to avoid.

Mary Astell, *Some Reflections upon Marriage*. London, 1706.

They only who have felt it, know the misery of being forced to marry where they do not love; of being yoked for life to a disagreeable person and imperious temper, where ignorance and folly (the ingredients of a coxcomb, who is the most unsufferable fool) tyrannizes over wit and sense: to be perpetually contradicted for contradiction-sake, and bore down by authority, not by argument; to be denied one's most innocent desires, for no other reason but the absolute will and pleasure of a Lord and Master, whose follies a wife, with all her prudence, cannot hide, and whose commands she cannot but despise at the same time that she obeys them.

Or, suppose on the other hand, she has married the man she loves, heaped upon him the highest obligations, by putting into his power the fortune he coveted, the beauty he professed to adore; how soon are the tables turned? It is her part now to court and fawn; his real or pretended passion soon cools into indifference, neglect, or perhaps aversion. 'Tis well if he preserves a decent civility, takes a little care of appearances, and is willing to conceal his breach of faith.

But shall a wife retaliate? God forbid! No provocation, though ever so great, can excuse the sin, or lessen the folly: it were indeed a revenging the injury upon herself in the most terrible manner. The Italian proverb shows a much better way, "If you would be revenged of your enemies, live well."

Devotion is the proper remedy, and the only infallible relief in all distresses; when this is neglected or turned into ridicule, we run, as from one wickedness, so from one misfortune, to another. Unhappy is that grandeur which is too great to be good, and that which sets us at a distance from true wisdom. Even bigotry, as contemptible as it is, is perferable to profane wit; for *that* requires our pity, but *this* deserves our abhorrence.

A woman who seeks consolation under domestic troubles from the gaieties of a court, from gallantry, gaming, rambling in search of odd adventures, childish, ridiculous and ill-natured amusements, such as we find in the most unhappy Madam M——'s *Memoirs*, the common methods of getting rid of time, that is, of our very being, and keeping as much as we can at a distance from ourselves, will find these are very insignificant applications; they hardly skin the wound, and can never heal it, they even hurt; they make it fester, and render it almost incurable.

What an ill figure does a woman make, with all the charms of her beauty, and sprightliness of her wit, with all her good humour and insinuating address, though she be the best oeconomist in the world, the most entertaining company, if she remit her guard, abate in the severity of her caution, and strictness of her virtue? If she neglects those methods which are necessary to keep her, not only from a crime, but from the very suspicion of one? She justifies the injury her husband has done her, by publishing to the world, that whatever good qualities she may possess, discretion, the mistress of all the rest, is wanting: though she be really guiltless, she cannot prove her innocence, the suspicions in her prejudice are so strong. When she is censured, charity, that thinks no evil, can only be silent; though it believes and hopes the best, it cannot engage in her defence, nor apologize for irregular actions.

An ill husband may deprive a wife of the comfort and quiet of her life, give occasion of exercising her virtue, try her patience and fortitude to the utmost, which is all he can do; it is herself only that can accomplish her ruin. . . .

These destroyers [seducers] avoided, and better care taken than usual in women's education, marriage might recover the dignity and felicity of its original institution; and men be very happy in a married state, if it be not their own fault. The great author of our being, who does nothing in vain, ordained it as the only honourable way of continuing our race; as a distinction between reasonable creatures and mere animals, into which we degrade our selves, by forsaking the divine institution. God ordained it for a blessing, not a curse: we are foolish as well as wicked, when that which was appointed for mutual comfort and assistance, has quite contrary effect through our folly and perverseness. Marriage therefore, notwithstanding all the loose talk of the town, the satires of ancient, or modern pretenders to wit, will never lose its just esteem from the wise and good. . . .

If therefore it be a woman's hard fate to meet with a disagreeable temper, and of all others, the haughty, imperious, and self-conceited are the most so, she is as unhappy as any thing in this world can make her. For when a wife's temper does not please, if she makes her husband uneasy, he can find entertainments abroad; he has a hundred ways of relieving himself; but neither prudence nor duty will allow a woman to fly out: her business and entertainment are at home; and tho' he makes it every [sic] so uneasy to her, she must be content, and make her best on't. She who elects a monarch for life, who gives him an authority, she cannot recall, however he misapply it, who puts her fortune and person entirely in his power, nay, even the very desires of her heart, according to some learned casuists, so as that it is not lawful to will or desire any thing but what he approves and allows, had need be very sure that she does not make a fool her head, nor a vicious man her guide and pattern; she had best stay till she can meet with one who has the government of his own passions, and has duly regulated his own desires, since he is to have such an absolute power over hers. But he who dotes on a face, he who makes money his idol, he who is charmed with vain and empty wit, gives no such evidence, either of wisdom or goodness, that a woman of any tolerable sense should care to venture her self to his conduct. . . .

She then who marries, ought to lay it down for an indisputable maxim, that her husband must govern absolutely and entirely, and that she has nothing else to do but to please and obey. She must not attempt to divide his authority, or so much as dispute it; to struggle with her yoke will only make it gall the more, but must believe him wise and good, and in all respects the best, at least he must be so to her. She who can't do this is no way fit to be a wife, she may set up for that peculiar coronet the ancient fathers talked of, but is not qualified to receive that great reward which attends the eminent exercise of humility and self-denial, patience and resignation, the duties that a wife is called to.

But some refractory woman perhaps will say, how can this be? Is it possible for her to believe him wise and good, who by a thousand demonstrations convinces her, and all the world, of the contrary? Did the bare name of husband confer sense on a man, and the mere being in authority infallibly qualify him for government, much might be done. But since a wise man and a husband are not terms convertible, and how loath soever one is to own it, matter of fact won't allow us to deny, that the head many times stands in need of the inferiour's brains to manage it, she must beg leave to be excused from such high thoughts of her sovereign, and if she submits to her power, it is not so much reason as necessity that compels her.

Now of how little force soever this objection may be in other respects, methinks it is strong enough to prove the necessity of a good education, and that men never mistake their true interest more than when they endeavour to keep women in ignorance. Could they indeed deprive them of their natural good sense at the same time they deny them the true improvement of it, they might compass their end; otherwise natural sense unassisted may run into a false track, and serve only to punish him justly, who would not allow it to be useful to himself or others. If man's authority be justly established, the more sense a woman has, the more reason she will find to submit to it; if according to the tradition of our fathers, (who having had possession of the pen, thought they had also the best right to it) women's understanding is but small, and man's partiality adds no weight to the observation, ought not the more care to be taken to improve them?

III
The Female Pen

Anna Maria van Schurman (1607–78)

Though Anna Maria van Schurman was Dutch, and therefore does not properly belong to a discussion of English women writers, I have included her nevertheless because she had an important influence. She was, perhaps, the most celebrated "learned lady" of the seventeenth century, not only in her native country, where she was treated with great respect, but throughout all of Europe. She was expert in all the classical languages, as well as more exotic ones like Syriac and Chaldee, and even published her own *Ethopian Grammar*. She was so respected as a Latinist that when the University of Utrecht was founded, it was Schurman who was asked to write the commemorative ode. She corresponded with many of the famous scholars of her day, including Descartes, whose friendship she enjoyed as well.

In 1641 Anna Maria van Schurman published a treatise arguing that women ought to be allowed a classical education. It was originally written in Latin, but in 1659 an English translation was published under the title *The Learned Maid; or, Whether a Maid May Be a Scholar. A Logic Exercise Written in Latin by That Incomparable Virgin Anna Maria van Schurman of Utrecht.* Apparently, another translation had appeared earlier, but it has since dropped from sight. Schurman's work was well known in England, however, as she was frequently cited as proof that women *might* be learned. "That incomparable Virgin" also had a more direct influence on English women through her friendship and correspondence with Bathsua Makin, who founded a highly respected school for girls in London. Acknowledging Schurman's precedent, Makin herself later wrote a tract pleading for the improvement of feminine education in her time.

Anna Maria van Schurman's *The Learned Maid* begins by setting forth what reads like an early version of Woolf's *A Room of One's Own:* she stipulates that the potential scholar must be "provided of necessaries and not oppressed with want," but also must be to some degree free from household duties, which might apply either to "virgins" or "celibates" or those who could rely on "the ministry of handmaids, which are wont to free the richer sort of matrons also from domestic troubles." As records of "household oeconomy" from the period tell us, even a woman with a number of servants was seldom entirely free from "domestic troubles." The women who might possibly become scholars, then, were for the most part those who, like Schurman, remained "virgins."

Schurman's text is written in the awkwardly stiff form of a "logic exercise," an expedient, one can't help feeling, to which the author resorted in order to provide a protective shield against attack. Though the ultimate purpose of *The Learned Maid* is to defend the rights of women, the arguments Schurman uses are often derived from some of the most traditionally restrictive attitudes or negative "received opinions" about woman's nature. She argues, for example, that because of their "imbecility and inconstancy of disposition or temper," women are more in need of the "solid and continual employment" that learning can supply. Furthermore, she does not question the assumption that women's "proper sphere" is in the home—"forsooth the vocation of a maid, or woman is included in very narrow limits"—but uses it as an argument to demonstrate that "the study of letters is more convenient for them [women]." Schurman also supports the standard view of "modesty," using this as an argument as well: "What teaches prudence without any detriment to fame or modesty, is convenient for a Christian woman. . . ."

Anna Maria van Schurman is an interesting example of the way in which a woman could challenge certain social restrictions that applied to her sex, and yet defend equally restrictive assumptions at the same time—either explicitly or implicitly.

The Learned Maid; or, Whether a Maid May Be a Scholar. A Logic Exercise Written in Latin by That Incomparable Virgin Anna Maria van Schurman of Utrecht. London, 1659.

We hold the affirmative, and will endeavour to make it good. . . .

Wherefore we make use of these limitations:

First, of the subject; and first, that our maid be endued at least with an indifferent good wit, and not unapt for learning.

Secondly, that she be provided of necessaries and not oppressed with want: which exception I therefore put in, because few are so happy to have parents to [breed] them up in studies, and teachers are chargeable.

Thirdly, that the condition of the times, and her quality be such, that she may have spare hours from her general and special calling, that is, from the exercises of piety and household affairs. To which end will conduce, partly her immunity from cares and employments in her younger years, partly in her elder age either celibate, or the ministry of handmaids, which are wont to free the richer sort of matrons also from domestic troubles.

Fourthly, let her end be, not vainglory and ostentation, or unprofitable curiosity: but beside the general end, God's glory and the salvation of her own soul; that both her self may be the more virtuous and the more happy, and that she may (if that charge lie upon her) instruct and direct her family, and also be useful, as much as may be to her whole sex.

Next, limitations of the predicate, scholarship, or the study of letters I so limit, that I clearly affirm all honest discipline, or the whole . . . circle and crown of liberal arts and sciences (as the proper and universal good and ornament of mankind) to be convenient for the head of our Christian maid: yet so, that according to the dignity and nature of every art or science, and according to the capacity and condition of the maid herself, all in their order, place and time succeed each other in the learning of them, or be commodiously conjoined. But especially let regard be had unto those arts which have nearest alliance to theology and the moral virtues, and are principally subservient to them. In which number we reckon grammar, logic, rhetoric; especially logic, fitly called the key of all sciences: and then, physics, metaphysics, history, &c. and also the knowledge of languages, chiefly of the Hebrew and Greek. All which may advance to the more facile and full understanding of Holy Scripture: to say nothing now of other books. The rest, i.e. mathematics (to which is also referred music) poetry, picture, and the like, not illiberal arts, may obtain the place of pretty ornaments and ingenious recreations.

Lastly, those studies which pertain to the practice of the law, military discipline, oratory in the Church, Court, University, as less proper and less necessary, we do not very much urge. And yet we in no wise yield that our maid should be excluded from the scholastic knowledge or theory of those; especially not from understanding the most noble doctrine of the politics or civil government. . . .

Therefore let our thesis or proposition be:
a Maid may be a scholar.

For the confirmation whereof we bring these arguments: . . .

IV. *Argument:*

Whosoever is in most need of solid and continual employment may conveniently give himself to learning:

But woman is in most need of solid and continual employment: therefore, &c.

The major [premise] is good, because nothing doth more exercise and intend all the nerves and powers of the mind (and as the great Erasmus saith), nothing takes so full possession of the fair temple of a virgin's breast, as learning and study, whither, on all occasions she may fly for refuge.

The minor [premise]* is proved by these two reasons.

1. Whosoever through imbecility and inconstancy of disposition or temper, and the innumerable snares of the world, is in most danger of vanity, is in most need of solid and perpetual employment.

But woman, through the imbecility and inconstancy, &c. Therefore, &c. The major in this syllogism is true; because contraries are best cured by contraries: and nothing doth more effectually oppose vanity than serious and constant employment. . . .

V. *Argument:*

They that have the happiness of a more quiet and free course of life, may with most convenience follow their studies:

But maids, for the most part have the happiness of a more quiet and free course of life: Therefore. . . .

The reason of the major is evident: for nothing is so great a friend to studies as tranquility and liberty.

The minor is proved thus:

They which for the most part have their time to bestow upon themselves, and are exempt from public cares and employments, have the happiness of a more quiet and free course of life:

But maids (especially during their celibate, or single life) [for the] most part have their time to bestow on themselves, &c. Therefore. . . .

* The minor premise contains the minor term, the subject of the conclusion of a categorical syllogism.

VII. *Argument:*

The study of letters is convenient for them, for whom it is more decent to find themselves both business and recreation at home and in private than abroad among others.

But it is more decent for a Christian maid to find herself both work and recreation at home and in private than abroad: therefore &c.

The major is most true: because studies have this prerogative, to give us a delightful exercise, and to recreate us when we have no other company. . . .

The minor is no less: because the Apostle requireth women to be keepers at home. And moreover, experience testifies; whose tongues, ears, eyes often travail abroad, hunting after pleasures; their faith, diligence, and modesty too, is generally called into question. . . .

XII. *Argument:*

What teacheth prudence without any detriment of fame or modesty, is convenient for a Christian woman:

But the studies of good learning teach prudence, &c.

Therefore:

The major is confessed: for no man is ignorant, that the honour of the female sex is most tender, and needeth nothing more than prudence: and how hard a thing it is and full of hazard, to draw prudence from use and experience.

The minor is proved, because the writings of learned men do offer us not only excellent precepts, but notable examples, and lead us as it were by the hand to virtue. . . .

The Thesis of the Adversaries.

A Christian maid (or woman) except she be perhaps divinely excited to it by some peculiar motion or instinct, may not conveniently give herself to the study of letters.

I. *Argument on the part of the subject:*

Whosoever has a weak wit may not give her self to the study of letters:
But women are of weak wits.
Therefore:

They will prove the major; because, to the study of letters is required a wit firm and strong: unless we will labour in vain, or fall into the danger of a disease of the intellect.

The minor, they think, needeth no proof.

We answer to the major: that by our limitation such are exempted, which by imbecility of their wit are altogether unapt for studies, when we state it, that at least indifferent good wits are here required. Then, we say, not always heroical wits are precisely necessary to studies: for the number even of learned men, we see, is made up in good part of those that are of the middle sort.

To the minor, we answer: it is not absolutely true, but comparatively only, in respect of the male sex. For, though women cannot be equaled for their wit with those more excellent men . . . yet, the matter itself speaks thus much; not a few are found of so good wit, that they may be admitted to studies, not without fruit.

But on the contrary we infer:

They are less able by dexterity of wit, may most conveniently addict themselves to studies:

But women are less able by dexterity of wit. Therefore.

We prove the major, because studies do supply us with aids and helps for our weakness:

Therefore:

II. *Objection:*

Whose mind is not inclined to studies, they are not fit to study;

But the minds of women are not inclined to studies.

They prove the major, because nothing is to be done *invita Minerva*, as we say, against the hair.

The minor they will prove from use and custom; because very seldom do women apply their mind to study.

We answer to the major. It should be thus: Whose mind, after all means duly tried, is not inclined to studies: otherwise it [the major] is denied.

To the minor we say, no man can rightly judge of our inclination to studies, before he has encouraged us by the best reasons and means to set upon them: and withall hath given us some taste of their sweetness, although in the meantime we do not want examples to evince the contrary to be true.

III. *Objection:*

The studies of learning are not convenient for those that are destitute of means necessary to their studies.

But women are destitute of means, &c.

Therefore:

The major is without controversy.

They endeavour to prove the minor, because there be no academies and colleges, wherein they may exercise themselves.

But we deny this consequence; for it sufficeth, that under the conduct of their parents, or of some private teacher, they may exercise themselves at home.

IV. *Objection:*

Studies are not fit for them whose labour misseth of its proper end.

But the labour of women misseth of its proper end.

Therefore:

The major may be proved, because the end is that for which all things are done.

They prove the minor by this, that women are seldom or never preferred to public offices, political, ecclesiastical, or academical. We answer to the major: women, in speculative sciences are never frustrated of their end: and in the practical (now spoken of) though they attain not the primary, or that public end; yet do they attain a secondary end, as I may say, and more private.

V. *Objection:*

To whom, for their vocation, it is sufficient to know a little, to them is not convenient the encyclopaedia, or a more sublime degree of knowledge.

But it is sufficient to women, &c.

Therefore:

They prove the major, because it is not convenient for anyone to study things superfluous and impertinent to his calling.

The minor they will prove, because forsooth the vocation of a maid, or woman is included in very narrow limits, the terms of a private or oeconomical† life.

† I.e., household management was referred to as "oeconomy."

Let the major pass, we answer to the minor. There is an ambiguity in the words; first, vocation: for if here they understand the vocation of a private life, opposed to public offices, we say, by the same reason the encyclopaedia or a more sublime degree of knowledge is denied all men too, that lead a private life. When yet, that most grave sentence of Plutarch is pronounced of all men of what rank soever, without exception: "It becomes a perfect man to know what is to be known, and to do what is to be done." But if they understand a special vocation, in order to a family and oeconomical cares, we say, that the universal calling which pertains chiefly to us all, either as Christians, or at least as men, is in no way excluded by it. Yea, I may be bold to affirm, that a virgin both may and ought especially to attend upon this universal calling, as being usually more free from the impediments of the former. *She that is unmarried careth for the things of the Lord.* [1 Cor. 7:34] Again, there is ambiguity in the words "it is sufficient," which is sufficiently taken away by what is above said in the limitation of the convenience and necessity of studies.

Wherefore our thesis stands firm:

A Christian maid, or woman, may conveniently give her self to learning, whence we draw this consectary.

That maids may and ought to be excited and encouraged by the best and strongest reasons, by the testimonies of wise men: and lastly, by the examples of illustrious women, to the embracing of this kind of life, especially those who are above others provided of leisure, and other means and aids for their studies; and, because it is best, that the mind be seasoned with learning from the very infancy: therefore the parents themselves are chiefly to be stirred up, as we suppose, and to be admonished of their duty.

Margaret Cavendish, Duchess of Newcastle (1624–74)

The Duchess of Newcastle was the first Englishwoman to publish a
large body of literary work (as opposed to religious tracts) under her
own name. She began writing at an early age, and claimed that by
the time she was twelve her first work of philosophy had already
been written. Her first book was published before she was thirty, and
in the space of fifteen years, from 1653 to 1668, the Duchess published more than thirteen additional volumes: plays, poems, scien-
tific and natural observations, philosophical discourses, and social
commentaries are among the forms her prolific "wit" took. Her
published oeuvre includes *Poems and Fancies* (1653), *Philosophical
Fancies* (1653), *The Worlds Olio* (1655), *The Philosophical and
Physical Opinions* (1655), *Natures Pictures Drawn by Fancies Pencil*
(1656), *Orations of Divers Sorts Accomodated to Divers Places*
(1662), *Sociable Letters* (1664), *Philosophical Letters* (1664), *Observations upon Experimental Philosophy. To Which Is Added, the
Description of a Blazing New World* (1666), *The Life of the Thrice
Noble, High and Puisant Prince William Cavendish, Duke, Mar-
quess, and Earl of Newcastle; Earl of Ogle; Viscount Mansfield; and
Baron of Bolsover, or Ogle, Bothal and Hepple; Gentleman of His
Majesties Bedchamber; one of his Majesties most Honourable Privy-
Council; Knight of the Most Noble Order of the Garter; His Majesties Lieutenant of the County and Town of Nottingham; and Justice
in Ayre Trent-North; Who Had the Honour to be Governor to Our
Most Glorious King* (1667), *Playes* (1668). The author of this biography of the noble duke and of the other aforementioned works was
always described on the title page as the "thrice Noble, Illustrious,
and Excellent Princess, Margaret, Duchess of Newcastle."

The Duchess of Newcastle began life more prosaically, as Margaret Lucas, the daughter of one Thomas Lucas, of Colchester, in
Essex—as she tells us in the autobiography she appended to the
narrative of her husband's life. Margaret's father seems to have been
quite well-off, but died when she was still a baby, leaving his wife to
manage the complicated business of their estates, which she appears

to have done most competently. Margaret, the youngest of the daughters, was given the typical "polite education" of the time, and later recalled that she and her sisters had tutors "for all sorts of virtues, as singing, dancing, playing on music, reading, writing, working [needlework] and the like." She seems to have had no instruction at all in any of the classics or indeed in any serious subject. The Duchess added to the account of her education the observation that her mother hired tutors "more for formality than for benefit," and was much less concerned about what they could teach, than that "we should be bred virtuously, modestly, civilly, honourably and on honest principles."

At twenty, Margaret Lucas met and married the Duke of Newcastle, a man more than thirty years her senior. The marriage seems to have been a very happy one: the Duke encouraged his young wife "in my harmless pastime of writing," and paid printers huge sums to publish lavish editions of her work. When rumors began to circulate that he was the *true* author of the books that appeared under her name, the Duke began to write introductions that were printed at the beginning of all her works, commending the wit and learning of his wife and defending her from attack. His commendation was usually followed by a letter from her thanking him for permission to publish—a favor, she noted, few men allowed their wives. She was always careful to signal her proper position of inferiority and wrote of her husband: "He creates himself with his pen, writing what his wit dictates to him, but I pass my time rather with scribbling than with writing, with words than with wit. . . . I am so far from thinking myself able, to teach, as I am afraid I have not capacity to learn, yet I must tell the world, that I think that not any hath a more abler master to learn from, than I have, for if I had never married the person I have, I do believe I should never have writ so, as to have adventured to divulge my works."

The Duke of Newcastle's wealth and high position provided the Duchess with a large degree of freedom to do as she liked, but ultimately her evident desire for recognition and eagerness for literary fame made her a figure of ridicule in the eyes of the public. She was thought bold even to the point of madness. When the Duchess's first book of poems was published in 1653, Dorothy Osborne wrote to her fiancé, William Temple, to ask him to send her the rarity, commenting: "Sure the poor woman is a little distracted, she could never be so ridiculous else as to venture at writing books and in verse too. If I could not sleep this fortnight I should not come to that." A few weeks later, she added: "You need not send me my Lady Newcastle's book, for I have seen it, and am satisfied there are many soberer people in Bedlam, I'll swear her friends are much to blame to let her go abroad. . . ." The Duchess, known popularly as "Mad Madge," did in fact retreat more and more into the isolation of her country estate, where she and the Duke surrounded themselves with hangers-on. The cushion of flattery they provided only partially obscured the Duchess's awareness that the outside world generally regarded her with either disapproval or scorn.

The number of prefaces, introductions, and words "To the Reader" printed at the beginning of the Duchess of Newcastle's works multiplied to as many as nine or ten (appended to a single work) as she increasingly felt the need to justify herself. The issues addressed in these defenses ultimately all refer to the difficulties (both internal and external) introduced by the author's sex. Interestingly enough, the Duchess is not overly worried about the "immodesty" of her undertaking: the fact that her husband gave such unusual support to her literary endeavors may have freed her from the excessive guilt and conflict over "modesty" that a great many other women writers expressed. It is not that the Duchess doubted the importance of "feminine modesty," but simply that she assumes her innate "chastity" as understood—certainly not a subject open to question. Occasionally one finds her making a remark like "I am chaste, both by nature, and education, in as much as I do abhor an unchaste thought," but the remark is much more an expression of self-satisfaction than a gesture of defense.

The Duchess's insecurities about the fact of her sex in the matter of publication had much more to do with her sense of transgression into a sphere not "properly" her own: knowledge. The attitudes expressed by the Duchess on this subject are strikingly contradictory: in one preface she protests against the inadequate education she received as a girl, and in another she emphatically states that women are "by nature" less educable than men. She apologizes constantly for her lack of learning, but then rails against the "artificial" knowledge of scholars, whose natural understanding is crowded out by reading the opinions of others. Her own understanding, the

Duchess tells us, is entirely innocent of the blemish of "knowledge"; yet she assiduously sought the approval of the scholars at Cambridge, and even tried to persuade them to insert her works into the curriculum there.

I have tried to give some idea of the extent to which the Duchess was torn by the apparent contradictions between her "feminine education" and her desire to become a famous writer in the following texts excerpted from her work.

Sociable Letters. London, 1664.

Madam,

In your last letter you advised me to write a book of orations, but how should I write orations, who know no rules in rhetoric, nor never went to school, but only learned to read and write at home, taught by an ancient decayed gentlewoman whom my mother kept for that purpose; which my ill hand (as the phrase is) may sufficiently witness; yet howsoever, to follow your advice, I did try to write orations, but I find I want wit, eloquence, and learning for such a work, and though I had wit, eloquence, and learning, I should not find so many subjects, to write so many orations as will fill a book, for orations for the most part, are concerning war, peace, and matters of state, and business in the commonwealth, all which I am not capable of, as being a woman, who hath neither knowledge, ability, nor capacity in state affairs, and to speak in writing of that I understand not, will not be acceptable to my reading auditors. . . .

The World's Olio. London, 1655.

Preface to the Reader.

It cannot be expected that I should write so wisely or wittily as men, being of the effeminate sex, whose brains nature hath mixed with the coldest and softest elements; and to give my reason why we cannot be so wise as men, I take leave and ask pardon of my own sex, and present my reasons to the judgement of truth; but I believe all of my own sex will be against me out of partiality to themselves, and all men will seem to be against me, out of compliment to women, or at least for quiet and ease's sake, who know women's tongues are like stings of bees; and what man would endure our effeminate monarchy to swarm about their ears? For certainly he would be stung to death; so I shall be condemned of all sides, but truth, who helps to defend me. True it is, our sex make great complaints, that men from their first creation usurped a supremacy to themselves, although we were made equal by nature, which tyrannical government they have kept ever since, so that we could never come to be free, but rather more and more enslaved, using us either like children, fools, or subjects, that is, to flatter or threaten us, to allure or force us to obey, and will not let us divide the world equally with them, as to govern and command, to direct and dispose as they do; which slavery has so dejected our spirits, as we are become so stupid, that beasts are but a degree below us, and men use us but a degree above beasts; whereas in nature we have as clear an understanding as men, if we were bred in schools to mature our brains, and to manure our understandings, that we might bring forth the fruits of knowledge. But to speak truth, men have great reason not to let us in to their government, for there is great difference betwixt the masculine brain and the feminine, the masculine strength and the feminine; for could we choose out of the world two of the ablest brain and strongest body of each sex, there would be great difference in the understanding and strength; for nature has made man's body more able to endure labour, and man's brain more clear to understand and contrive than women's; and as great a difference there is between them, as there is between the longest and strongest willow, compared to the strongest and largest oak; though they are both trees, yet the willow is but a yielding vegetable, not fit nor proper to build houses and ships, as the oak, whose strength can grapple with the greatest winds, and plough the furrows in the deep. It is true, the willows may make fine arbours and bowers, winding and twisting its wreathy stalks about, to make a shadow to eclipse the light; or as a light shield to keep off the sharp arrows of the sun, which cannot wound deep, because they fly far before they touch the earth; or men and women may be compared to the blackbirds, where the hen can never sing with so strong and loud a voice, nor so clear and perfect notes as the cock; her breast is not made with that strength to strain so high. Even so, women can never have so strong judgement nor clear understanding nor so perfect rhetoric, to speak orations with that eloquence, as to persuade so forcibly, to command so powerfully, to entice so subtly, and to insinuate so gently and softly into the souls of men; or they may be compared to the sun and moon, according to the description in the Holy Writ, which saith, *God made two great lights, the one to rule the day, the other the night:* so man is made to govern commonwealths, and women their private families. And we find by experience, that the sun is more dry, hot, active, and powerful every way than the moon; besides, the sun is of a more strong and ruddier complexion than the moon; for we find she is pale and wan, cold, moist, and slow in all her operations; and if it be as philosophers hold, that the moon hath no light but what it borrows from the sun, so women have no strength nor light of understanding but what is given them from men; this is the reason why we are not mathematicians, arithmeticians, logicians, geometricians, cosmographers, and the like; this is the reason we are not witty poets, eloquent orators, subtle schoolmen, subtracting chemists, rare musicians, curious limners; this is the reason we are not navigators, architectures, exact surveyors, inventive artisans; this is the reason we are not skilful soldiers, politic statists, dispatchful secretaries, or conquering Caesars; but our governments would be weak, had we not masculine spirits and councillors to advise us; and for our strength, we should make but feeble mariners to tug and pull up great ropes and weighty sails in blustring storms, if there were no other pilots than the effeminate sex; neither would there be such commerce of nations as there is, nor would there be so much gold and silver and other minerals fetched out of the bowels of the earth if there were none but effeminate hands to use the pick-ax and spade; nor so many cities built, if there were none but women labourers to cut out great quarries of stone, to hew down great timber trees, and to draw up such materials and engines thereunto belonging; neither would there be such bars of iron, if none but women were to melt and hammer them out, whose weak spirits would suffocate and so faint with the heat, and their small arms would sooner break than lift up such a weight, and beat out a life, in striving to beat out a wedge; neither would there be such steeples and pyramids, as there have been in this world, if there were no other than our tender feet to climb, nor could our brains endure the height, we should soon grow dizzy and fall down drunk with too much thin air; neither have women such hard chests and strong lungs to keep in so much breath, to dive to the bottom of the sea, to fetch up the treasures that lie in the watery womb; neither can women bring the furious and wild horse to the bit, quenching his fiery courage, and bridling his strong swift speed. This is the reason we are not so active in exercise, nor able to endure hard labour, nor far travels, nor to bear weighty burdens, to run long journeys, and many the like actions which we by nature are not made fit for. It is true, education and custom may add something to harden us, yet never make us so strong as the strongest of men, whose sinews are tougher, and bones stronger, and joints closer, and flesh firmer, than ours are, as all ages have shown, and times have produced. What woman was ever so strong as Samson, or so swift as Hazael? Neither have women such tempered brains as men, such high imaginations, such subtle conceptions, such fine inventions, such solid reasons, and such sound judgement, such prudent forecast, such constant resolutions, such quick, sharp, and ready flowing wits. What women ever made such laws as Moses, Lycurgus, or Solon did? What woman was ever so wise as Solomon, or Aristotle? So politic as Achitophel? So eloquent as Tully? So demonstrative as Euclid? So inventive as Seth, or Archimedes? It was not a woman that found out the card, and needle, and the use of the loadstone; it was not a woman that invented perspective-glasses to pierce into the moon; it was not a woman that found out the invention of writing letters, and the arts of printing; it was not a woman that found out the invention of gunpowder, and the arts of guns. What women were such soldiers as Hannibal, Caesar, Tamberlain *[sic]*, Alexander, and Scanderbeg? What woman was such a chemist as Paracelsus? Such a physician as Hippocrates or Galen? Such a poet as Homer? Such a painter as Apelles? Such a carver as Pigmalion *[sic]*? Such an architect as Vitruvious *[sic]*? Such a musician as Orpheus? What women ever found out the Antipodes in imagination, before they were found out by navigation, as a Bishop did? Or what ever did we do but like apes, by imitation? Wherefore women can have no excuse, or complaints of being subjects, as a hindrance from thinking; for thoughts are free, those can never be enslaved, for we are not hindered from studying, since we are allowed so much idle time that we know not how to pass it away, but may as well read in our closets, as men in their colleges; and contemplation is as free to us as to men to beget clear speculation. Besides, most scholars marry, and their heads are so full of their school lectures, that they preach them over to their wives when they come home, so that they know as well what was spoke, as if they had been there; and though most of our sex are bred up to the needle and spindle, yet some are bred in the public theatres of the world; wherefore, if nature had made our brains of the same temper as men's, we should have had as clear speculation, and had been as ingenious and inventive as men: but we find she hath not, by the effects.

And thus we may see by the weakness of our actions, the constitution of our bodies; and by our knowledge, the temper of our brains; by our unsettled resolutions, inconstant to our promises, the perverseness of our wills;

by our facile natures, violent in our passions, superstitious in our devotions, you may know our humours; we have more wit than judgement; more active than industrious, we have more courage than conduct, more will than strength, more curiosity than secrecy, more vanity than good housewifery, more complaints than pains, more jealousy than love, more tears than sorrow, more stupidity than patience, more pride than affability, more beauty than constancy, more ill nature than good. Besides, the education and liberty of conversation which men have, is both unfit and dangerous to our sex, knowing that we may bear and bring forth branches from a wrong stock, by which every man would come to lose the property of their own children; but nature, out of love to the generation of men, hath made women to be governed by men, giving them strength to rule, and power to use their authority.

And though it seem to be natural, that generally all women are weaker than men, both in body and understanding, and that the wisest woman is not so wise as the wisest of men, wherefore not so fit to rule; yet some are far wiser than some men; like earth; for some ground, though it be barren by nature, yet, being well mucked and well manured, may bear plentiful crops, and sprout forth divers sorts of flowers, when the fertiler and richer ground shall grow rank and corrupt, bringing nothing but gross and stinking weeds, for want of tillage; so women by education may come to be far more knowing and learned than some rustic and rude-bred men. Besides, it is to be observed that nature hath degrees in all her mixtures and temperaments, not only to her servile works, but in one and the same matter and form of creatures, throughout all her creations. Again, it is to be observed that, although nature has not made women so strong of body, and so clear of understanding as the ablest of men, yet she has made them fairer, softer, slenderer, and more delicate than they, separating as it were the finer parts from the grosser, which seems as if nature had made women as purer white manchet, for her own table and palate, where men are like coarse household bread which the servants feed on; and if she hath not tempered women's brains to that height of understanding, nor has put in such strong species of imaginations, yet she hath mixed them with sugar of sweet conceits; and if she hath not planted in their dispositions such firm resolutions, yet she hath sowed gentle and willing obedience; and though she hath not filled the mind with such heroic gallantry, yet she hath laid in tender affections, [such] as love, piety, charity, clemency, patience, humility, and the like, which makes them nearest to resemble angels, which are the perfectest of all her works; whereas men by their

Effigies of a Maid all Hairy, and an
infant that was black by the Imagination
of their Parents.

...n illustration of the dangers which await
...ward women; this one has grown hair
... over her body from thinking masculine
...oughts.

Frontispiece, John Taylor, A *Juniper
Lecture*, 1639. *The Women's Sharpe
Revenge*, 1640, was written in answer.

Rise you drunken Slave.

A QVAKER

Weake as you say we are, yett wee command,
all flesh to fall, that doth against us stand.
The light within us, of such force is found,
showld satan come, twill lay him on the grund.

The Light they talke of keepes a heavy rout,
ile search all corners, but ile find it out.
By yea and nay, she is a dareing Gule,
ile try a fall, or els I am a Chirle.

With face of brass, this woman that you see
most Impudently doth afirm, that shee.
The mind of God, in all poynts, more doth know,
then from the Sacred Scriptures, ere could flow.
Presumptious wretch; it were more fitt that shee.
at home showld keepe, and mind hir howsewifery.
And if noe meanes to live on, woorke for bread,
then idlye gossop with hir maget head.

Their light within doth so prevayle.
it makes them hot about the tayle.
Exsept afreind that poynt doth cleare.
they could them selves in pecces teare.

A woman preacher.

Response to a "woman's speaking."

Husband and wife fighting over who will wear the breeches. From a popular ballad.

A New yeares guift for Shrews

Who marieth a Wife vppon a Moneday. ff she will not be good vppon a Tewesday. Lett him go to y wod vppon a Wen
And cutt him a cudgell vppon the Thursday. And pay her soundly vppon a Fryday. And she mend not y Diuil take her a Sa
Then may he eate his meate in peace on the Sonday.

Trevill Sculp

Edward lee Ex

Instructions on how to govern an unruly wife.

Anna Maria van Schurman.

ANNA MARIA A SCHVRMAN.
AN. ÆTAT .LII. CIƆ IƆC LIX
Cernitis hic picta nostros in imagine vultus:
Si negat ars formâ, gratia vestra dabit.

THE

LEARNED MA

OR,

Whether a MAID may
Scholar?

A LOGICK EXERC

Written
In Latine by that incomparable V
Anna Maria à Schurman
of Vtrecht.

With some Epistles to the famous Gasse
and others.

Ignat:

LONDON,
Printed by JOHN REDMAYNE. 16
Thom. Banner

Dorothy Osborne [Temple]

Bathsua Makin.

Margaret Cavendish, Duchess of Newcastle.

Aphra Behn.

Katherine Philips, "the Matchless Orinda."

Anne Finch, Countess of Winchilsea.

Catherine Trotter Cockburn

Eliza Haywood and the
editorial committee of
The Female Spectator.

ambitions, extortion, fury, and cruelty, resemble the Devil. But some women are like devils too, when they are possessed with those evils; and the best of men by their heroic, magnanimous minds, by their ingenious and inventive wits, by their strong judgements, by their prudent forecast and wise managements, are like to gods.

Epistle

Some say, as I hear, that my book of poems, and my book of *Philosophical Fancies*, was not my own; and that I had gathered my opinions from several philosophers. To answer the first, I do protest, upon the grounds of honour, honesty and religion, they are my own, that is, my head was the forge, my thoughts the anvil to beat them out, and my industry shaped them and sent them forth to the use of the world; if any use may be made thereof, but my Lord was the master and I the prentice, for gathering them from philosophers, I never conversed in discourse with any an hour, at one time in my life. And I may swear on my conscience, I never had a familiar acquaintance, or constant conversation with any professed scholar, in my life, or a familiar acquaintance with any man, so as to learn by them, but those that I have near relation to, as my husband, and brothers; it is true, I have had the honour sometime to receive visits of civility from my noble and honourable acquaintance, wherein we talk of the general news of the times, and the like discourse, for my company is too dull to entertain, and too barren of wit to afford variety of discourse, wherefore I bend myself to study nature; and though nature is too specious to be known, yet she is so free as to teach, for every straw, or grain of dust, is a natural tutor, to instruct my sense and reason, and every particular rational creature, is a sufficient school to study in; and our own passions and affections, appetites and desires, are moral doctors to learn us; and the evil that follows excess, teaches us what is bad, and by moderation we find, and do so learn what is good, and how we ought to live, and moderate them by reason, and discourse them in the mind, and there is few that have not so much natural capacity, and understanding, but may know, if not find out what is needful for life, without artificial education; for nature is the chief master; art and education but the under-ushers, in the school of life; for natural objections may be applied without the help of arts, and natural rules of life, may lead us safe, and easy ways to our journey's end; and questionless nature was the first guide, before art came to the knowledge, and if it were not for nature, art many times would lose her followers; yet let nature do what she can, art oft-times will go out of the right way; but many will say it is the nature of man that invents, and the nature of man to err; that is, 'tis the nature of man to be so ambitious, as to strive to be wiser than nature her self, but if nature hath given men ambition, yet nature hath given men humility to allay that fiery appetite; and though nature hath given men ignorance, yet nature hath given men understanding, to bring them out of that darkness into the light of knowledge; and though nature hath obscured the secrets of the natural cause, yet he [sic] hath given men nature to observe her effects, and imaginations, to conjecture of her ways, and reason to discourse of her works, and understanding to find some out, and these gifts are general to mankind: wherefore I find no reason, but my readers may allow me to have natural imagination, understanding and inquiries, as well as other philosophers, and to divulge them as they have done, if that they believe that I am produced by nature, and not by artifice's hand, cut out like a stone-statue; but if my readers will not allow my opinions, and fancies to be my own, yet truth will; but there is a natural education to all, which comes without pains-taking, not tormenting the body with hard labour, nor the mind with perturbed study, but comes easy and free through the senses; and grows familiar and sociable with the understanding, pleasant and delightful to the contemplation, for there is no subject that the sense can bring into the mind, but is a natural instructor to produce the breeding of rational opinions, and understanding truths; besides, imaginary fancies, if they will give their mind time as to think, but most spend their time in talk rather than in thought; but there is a wise saying, think first, and speak after; and an old saying that many speak first, and think after; and doubtless many, if not most do so, for we do not always think of our words we speak, for most commonly words flow out of the mouth, rather customarily than premeditatedly, just like actions of our walking, for we go by custom, force and strength, without a constant notice or observation; for though we design our ways, yet we do not ordinarily think of our pace, nor take notice of every several step; just so, most commonly we talk, for we seldom think of our words we speak, nor many times the sense they tend to; unless it be some affected person that would speak in fine phrases; and though speech is very necessary to the course of man's life, yet it is very obstructive to the rational part of man's mind; for it employs the mind with such busy, and unprofitable matters, as all method is run out of breath, and gives not contemplation leave to search, and inquire after truth, nor understanding leave to examine what is truth, nor judgement how to distinguish truth from false-

1ood, nor imagination leave to be ingenious, nor ingenuity leave to find
nvention, nor wit leave to spin out the fine and curious thread of fancy,
put only to play with words on the tongue, as balls with rackets. Besides a
multiplicity of words confounds the solid sense, and rational understand-
ng, the subject in the discourse; yet to think very much and speak very
seldom, make speech uneasy, and the tongue apt to falter, when it is to
deliver sense of the matter they have, and want of uncustomary speaking
makes the orator to seek for words to declare the sense of his meaning, or
the meaning of his sense; because, want of eloquence many times, loseth
not only rational opinions, but conceals truth itself, for want of persuading
rhetoric, to raise up belief, or to get understanding; so that a contem-
platory person hath the disadvantage of words; although most commonly
they have the advantage of thoughts, which brings knowledge; but life
being short, those that speak much, have not time to think much, that is,
not time to study and contemplate; wherefore it is a great loss of time to
speak idle word[s], that is, words that are to no purpose, and to think idle
thoughts, that bring no honest profit to the life of man, nor delight for
life's pastime, nor news to the knowledge and understanding; but most
men speak of common matters, and think of vulgar things, beat upon
what is known, and understood, not upon what ought to be known, and
understood; but upon known improbabilities, or vain ambitions, or upon
that which nothing concerns them, or upon evil designs to work distractions, or upon that which cannot advantage them, nor anybody else; but it
is very probable, my readers will at this discourse condemn me, saying, I
take upon me to instruct, as if I thought myself a master, when I am but a
novice, and fitter to learn. I answer, it is easier to instruct what ought to
be done, than to practise what is best to be done; but I am so far from
thinking myself able, to teach, as I am afraid I have not capacity to learn,
yet I must tell the world, that I think not any hath a more abler master to
learn from, than I have, for if I had never married the person I have, I do
believe I should never have writ so, as to have adventured to divulge my
works, for I have learned more of the world from my Lord's discourse,
since I have been his wife, than I am confident I should have done all my
life, should I have lived to an old age; and though I am not so apt a scholar
as to improve much in wit, yet I am so industrious a scholar to remember
whatsoever he hath said, and discoursed to me, and though my memory is
dull, and slow, and my capacity weak to all other discourses, yet when I am
in company, I had rather show my simplicity than be thought rude; wherefore I choose rather to speak, though foolishly, than say nothing, as if I

were dumb, when I am to entertain my acquaintance, and though I do not speak so well as I wish I could, yet it is civility to speak. But it is my Lord's discourse that gets me understanding, and makes such impressions in my memory, as nothing but death can rub it out: and my greatest fear is, that I the scholar should disgrace him the master, by the vulgar phrases and the illiterate expressions in my works: but the truth is, I am neither eloquent by nature, nor art; neither have I took the accustomary way of often speaking, to make my words, or letters fluent, not but my tongue runs fast and foolish when I do speak, but I do not often speak, for my life is more contemplary [sic], than discoursing, and more solitary than sociable, for my nature being dull and heavy, and my disposition not merry, makes me think myself not fit for company.

The Philosophical and Physical Opinions. London, 1655.

To the Two Most Famous Universities of England:

Most Famously Learned,

I here present to you this philosophical work, not that I can hope wise school-men and industrious laborious students would value it for any worth, but to receive it without scorn, for the good encouragement of our sex, lest in time we should grow irrational as idiots, by the dejectedness of our spirits, through the careless neglects and despisements of the masculine sex to the female, thinking it impossible we should have either learning or understanding, wit or judgement, as if we had not rational souls as well as men, and we out of a custom of dejectness think so too, which makes us quit all industry towards profitable knowledge, being employed only in low and petty employments, which take away not only our abilities towards arts, but higher capacities in speculations, so as we are become like worms, that only live in the dull earth of ignorance, winding ourselves sometimes out by the help of some refreshing rain of good education, which seldom is given us, for we are kept like birds in cages, to hop up and down in our houses, not suffered to fly abroad, to see the several changes of fortune, and the various humours, ordained and created by nature, and wanting the experience of nature, we must needs want the understanding and knowledge, and so consequently prudence, and invention of men. Thus by an opinion, which I hope is but an erroneous one in men, we are shut out of all power and authority, by reason we are never employed either in civil or martial affairs, our counsels are despised, and laughed at, the best of our actions are trodden down with scorn, by the overweaning conceit men have of themselves, and through a despisement of us.

But I, considering with myself, that if a right judgement, and a true understanding, and a respectful civility live any where, it must be in learned universities, where nature is best known, where truth is oftenest found, where civility is most practised, and if I find not a resentment here, I am very confident I shall find it nowhere, neither shall I think I deserve it, if you approve not of me; but if I deserve not praise, I am sure to receive so much courtship from your sage society, as to bury me in silence, that thus I may have a quiet grave, since not worthy a famous memory, for to lie entombed under the dust of a university will be honour enough for me, and more than if I were worshipped by the vulgar as a deity. Wherefore, if your wisdoms cannot give me the Bays*, let your charity strew me with cypress; and who knows, but, after my honourable burial, I may have a glorious resurrection in following ages, since time brings strange and unusual things to pass: I mean unusual to men, though not in nature; and I hope this action of mine is not unnatural, though unusual for a woman to present a book to the university, nor impudent, for it is honest, although it seem vainglorious; but if it be, I am to be pardoned, since there is little difference between man and beast, but what ambition and glory makes.

Orations of Divers Sorts. London, 1662.

To His Excellency the Lord Marquis of Newcastle:

My Lord,

I have mentioned in my other books, that I think it not fit I should dedicate unto your Lordship the single parts of my works, before I dedicate all the parts in the whole; yet I cannot choose but declare to the world how happy I and my works are in your approvement, which makes the pastime of my writing very delightful; besides, it makes me confident and resolute to put them to the press, and so to the public view, in despite of these critical times and censorious age, which is apt to find fault with every action, let it be never so innocent or harmless, or with any work

* Laurels.

although good and profitable, yet they will sling spiteful aspersions on them . . . but your Lordship, who is full of truth and generosity, reason and knowledge, will give your opinion clearly and uprightly, and my works having your approbation, I regard not the dislike of other men, for I have dedicated myself and all my actions to your Lordship, as becomes

Your Lordship's honest wife and humble servant,
M. Newcastle.

Philosophical Letters: or, Modest Reflections upon Some Opinions in Natural Philosophy, Maintained by Several Famous and Learned Authors of This Age, Expressed by Way of Letters. London, 1664.

To His Excellency the Lord Marquis of Newcastle

My Noble Lord,

Although you have always encouraged me in my harmless pastime of writing, yet was I afraid that your Lordship would be angry with me for writing and publishing this book, by reason it is a book of controversies. . . . But your Lordship will be pleased to consider in my behalf, that it is impossible for one person to be of everyone's opinion, if their opinions be different, and that my opinions in philosophy, being new, and never thought of, at least not divulged by any, but my self, are quite different from others: for the ground of my opinions is, that there is not only a sensitive, but also a rational life and knowledge, and so a double perception in all creatures: and thus my opinions being new, are not so easily understood as those, that take up several pieces of old opinions, of which they patch up a new philosophy, (if new may be made of old things), like a suit made up of old stuff bought at the brokers: wherefore to find out a truth, at least a probability in natural philosophy by a new and different way from other writers, and to make this way more known, easy and intelligible, I was in a manner forced to write this book; for I have not contradicted those authors in any thing, but what concerns and is opposite to my opinions; neither do I any thing, but what they have done themselves, as being common amongst them to contradict each other. . . .

All which considered, was the cause of publishing this book; wherein although I dissent from their opinions, yet doth not this take off the least of the respect and esteem I have of their merits and works. But if your

Lordship do but pardon me, I care not if I be condemned by others; for your favour is more than the world to me, for which all the actions of my life shall be devoted and ready to serve you, as becomes,

My Lord,
Your Lordship's
honest Wife, and humble Servant,
M.N.

The Philosophical and Physical Opinions. London, 1655.

An Epistle to the Reader:

Noble Readers,

To treat of every particular motion in every particular part of every particular creature, is beyond my capacity, and to treat of some particular motions in some particular parts of some particular creatures, is very difficult for me to do, having a weak body, and a weak mind, so that I fear my readers would think my mind a busy fool, and my body an idle animal, if I should offer or endeavour to do it. But, howsoever, I am resolved to venture on their censure, rather than bury my opinions in oblivion. . . . I do not know how they will seem to your understanding, for they being new opinions, never broached before but by me, are like new extracts, essences or spirits, whose substance is not easily discerned or found out, and therefore not generally known of what matter they were made, and I being a woman cannot, or if I could, it were not fit for me publicly to preach, teach, declare or explain them by words of mouth, as most of the most famous philosophers have done, who thereby have made their philosophical opinions more famous, than I fear mine will ever be; for, though writing and printing explains the text, yet it doth not so clearly expound it as speech would do. But I am in hope, this my work will meet with understanding readers, to whom I leave it.

Sociable Letters. London, 1664.

. . . As for the matter of governments, we women understand them not; yet if we did, we are excluded from intermeddling therewith, and almost from being subject thereto; we are not tied, nor bound to State or Crown; we are free, not sworn to allegiance, nor do we take the oath of supremacy; we are not made citizens of the Commonwealth, we hold no offices, nor bear we any authority therein; we are accounted neither useful in peace, nor serviceable in war; and if we be not citizens in the Commonwealth, I known no reason we should be subjects to the Commonwealth: and the truth is, we are no subjects, unless it be to our husbands, and not always to them, for sometimes we usurp their authority, or else by flattery we get their good wills to govern; but if nature had not befriended us with beauty, and other good graces, to help us to insinuate ourselves into men's affections, we should have been more enslaved than any other of nature's creatures she hath made; but nature be thanked, she hath been so bountiful to us, as we oftener enslave men, than men enslave us; they seem to govern the world, but we really govern the world, in that we govern men: for what man is he, that is not governed by woman more or less? None, unless some dull stoic, or an old miserable usurer, or a cold, old, withered bachelor, or a half-starved hermit, and such like persons, which are but here and there one. And not only wives and mistresses have prevalent power with men, but mothers, daughters, sisters, aunts, cousins, nay, maid-servants have many times a persuasive power with their masters, and a land-lady with her lodger, or a she-hostess with her he-guest; yet men will not believe this, and 'tis the better for us, for by that we govern as it were by an insensible power, so as men perceive not how they are led, guided, and ruled by the feminine sex.

Orations of Divers Sorts. London, 1662.

An Oration Against the Liberty of Women

Although I am sure to be hated of all the women in this city, and perchance elsewhere, yet by reason I think it fit to reprove their liberties, vanities, and expences, I shall not be silent, although I were sure to be tortured with their railing tongues, and to be exclaimed in all their female societies, which societies ought to be dissolved, allowing no public meetings to that sex, no not child-bed gossipings, for women corrupt and spoil each other, striving to out-brave, out-beauty, and out-talk each other, with their vanities, paintings, and gossipings; wherefore it were fit, that women should be restrained not only from the company of men, but their own

sex, unless it be those they have near relations to, and not to suffer them
to make acquaintance with strangers; this would cause moderation, sobriety, and silence amongst them; also it would cause them to be housewifely
in their families, obedient to their husbands, and careful of their children,
but liberty is an enemy to women, nay it is an enemy to men, not only to
fathers, husbands, and sons, but even to wanton lovers, or rather courtiers,
making them as vain and expensive as women, to gain their mistresses'
favours, knowing women, especially amorous women, are soonest won
with gays, toys, and shows; but women are so far from being restrained in
this age, and in these nations round about, that they have liberty to spend
what they will, to keep what company they will, and to use their husbands
and natural friends as they please; the truth is, liberty makes all women
wild and wanton, both maids, wives, and widows, which defames themselves and their families. Thus in short, women are the chief ruiners of
men in their estates, fortunes, and honours, and so I leave them.

An Oration for the Liberty of Women

It is not only uncivil and ignoble, but unnatural, for men to speak
against women and their liberties, for women were made by nature for
men, to be loved, accompanied, assisted, and protected; and if men are
bound to love them by nature, should they restrain them by force? Should
they make them slaves, which nature made to be their dearest associates,
their beautifulest objects, and sweetest delights? And shall man restrain
them of their harmless pleasures, chaste societies, and gentle conversations? And as it is natural for men to love women, so it is natural for love
to please what they love, and not to cross, oppose, or restrain them, but to
grant them all their lawful requests and desires, as far as lies in their
powers; for can men dispose of their estates more generously than to
women? Or think any fortune better, than when they can serve them? Or
is there a greater happiness than to be beloved of them? Whereas they are
the chiefest good, that nature hath made for men, and the greatest delight, she hath given to men; for can there be any sound sweeter than their
voices? Any object brighter than their beauties, or any society more divine
than theirs? Yet these celestial creatures, a terrestrial man in the former
Oration did plead against them, persuading you, o horrid persuasions! to
use them as your slaves, which ought to be your goddesses on earth, for
nature made them to be beloved, admired, desired, adored, and worshipped, sued and praised by our sex.

Sociable Letters. London, 1664.

. . . It be the part of every good wife to desire children to keep alive the memory of their husband's name and family by posterity, yet a woman hath no such reason to desire children for her own sake, for first her name is lost as to her particular, in her marrying, for she quits her own, and is named as her husband; also her family, for neither name nor estate goes to her family according to the laws and customs of this country; also she hazards her life by bringing them into the world, and hath the greatest share of trouble in bringing them up; neither can women assure themselves of comfort of happiness by them, when they are grown to be men, for their name only lives in sons, who continue the line of succession, whereas daughters are but branches which by marriage are broken off from the root from whence they sprang, and engrafted into the stock of another family, so that daughters are to be accounted but as moveable goods or furnitures that wear out; and though sometimes they carry the lands with them, for want of heir-males, yet the name is not kept nor the line continued with them, for these are buried in the grave of the males, for the line, name and life of a family ends with the male issue; but many times married women desire children, as maids do husbands, more for honour than for comfort or happiness, thinking it a disgrace to live old maids, and so likewise to be barren, so that for the most part maids and wives desire husbands and children upon any condition, rather than to live maids or barren. But I am not of their minds, for I think a bad husband is far worse than no husband, and to have unnatural children is more unhappy than to have no children, and where one husband proves good, as loving and prudent, a thousand prove bad, as cross and spendthrifts, and where one child proves good, as dutiful and wise, a thousand prove disobedient and fools, as to do actions both to the dishonour and ruin of their families. Besides, I have observed, that breeding women, especially those that have been married some time, and have had no children, are in their behaviour like new-married wives, whose actions of behaviour and speech are so formal and constrained, and so different from their natural way, as it is ridiculous; for new-married wives will so bridle their behaviour with constraint, or hang down their heads so simply, not so much out of true modesty, as a forced shamefulness; and to their husbands they are so coyly amorous, or so amorously fond and so troublesome kind, as it would make the spectators sick, like fulsome meat to the stomach; and if new-married men were not wise men, it might make them ill husbands, at least to dislike a married life, because they cannot leave their fond or amorous wives so readily or easily as a mistress; but in truth that humour doth not last long, for after a month or two they are like surfeited bodies, that like any meat better than what they were so fond of, so that in time they think their husbands worse company than any other men.

. . .

Madam,

You writ in your last letter, that I had given your sex courage and confidence to write, and to divulge what they writ in print; but give me leave humbly to tell you, that it is no commendation to give them courage and confidence, if I cannot give them wit. But, Madam, I observe, our sex is more apt to read than to write, and most commonly when any of our sex doth write, they write some devotions, or romances, or [recipes] of medicines, for cookery or confectioners, or complimental letters, or a copy or two of verses, all which seem rather as briefs than volumes, which express our brief wit in our short works, and to express myself according to the wit of our sex, I will end this letter, only give me leave to subscribe myself, as truly I am,

Madam,

your ladyship's faithful servant.

The Philosophical and Physical Opinions. London, 1655.

To His Excellence the Lord Marquis of Newcastle:

My Noble Lord,

Since your return from a long banishment into your native country, retiring to a shepherd's life, I, your shepherdess, was resolved, to employ all my thoughts and industry in good housewifery, knowing your Lordship had great debts after your great losses; and though I am as industrious and careful to serve your Lordship in such employments, which belong to a wife, as household affairs, as ever I can, and not to be sordidly base, which is a vice, your Lordship hates, yet I cannot for my life be so good a housewife, as to quit writing, to follow my sheep so carefully, but that they will go astray sometimes; the truth is, I have somewhat erred from good housewifery, to write *Nature's Philosophy*, where, had I been prudent, I should have translated natural philosophy into good housewifery; for your Lordship, who hath as deep conceptions and subtle observation in natural philosophy, and as curious fancies and clear distinguishing in poetry, and as much ingenuity to arts as speculation into sciences, yet you are in a manner forced, to lay them by, since your return into your native country, employing your thoughts and actions in helping to repair your ruined estate, that was caused by cross and malicious fortune, which, I have heard your Lordship say, was never your friend.

Sarah Jinner (fl. 1658)

There is no known record of Sarah Jinner's life and opinions except
the brief note to the reader prefacing her *An Almanack or Prognostication for Women* of 1658.

An Almanack or Prognostication for Women. 1658.

To the Reader:
   You may wonder to see one of our sex in print, especially in the celestial
sciences: I might urge much in my defence, yea, more than the volume of
this book can contain: in which I am confined, not to exceed ordinary
bulk. But, why not women write, I pray? Have they not souls as well as
men, though some witty coxcombs strive to put us out of conceit of
ourselves, as if we were but imperfect pieces, and that nature intending a
man, when the seminal conception proves weak, there issues a woman:
many other rare benefits the world reapeth by women, although it is the
policy of men, to keep us from education and schooling, wherein we might
give testimony of our parts by improvement: we have as good judgement
and memory, and I am sure as good fancy as men, if not better. We will
not boast of strength of body, let horses or mules do that. What rare
things have women done? What cures in physick, which great doctors
have left? How many commonwealths have been ruled by women, [such]
as the Amazons. . . . When, or what Commonwealth was ever better
governed than this by the virtuous Queen Elizabeth? I fear I shall never
see the like again; your Princes now a days are like dunces in comparison
to her: either they have not the wit, or the honesty that she had: somewhat is the matter that things do not forge so well! Well, no more of that.
To our business again: what rare poets of our sex were of old, and now of
late the Countess of Newcastle. And, I pray you, what a rare poem hath
one Mistris Katherine Philips near Cardigan writ. It is printed before
Cartwright's *Poems,* who, if her modesty would permit, her wit would put
down many men's in a masculine strain. I could tell you of many more,
that have been famous in philosophy and physick, [such] as the Countess

of Kent, and others. And lastly, of Cunetia, a German lady, that lately did set out tables of the planets' motion: therefore, why should we suffer our parts to rust? Let us scour the rust off, by ingenious endeavouring the attaining higher accomplishments. This I say, not to animate our sex, to assume or usurp the breeches: no, but perhaps if we should shine in the splendour of virtue, it would animate our husbands to excell us: so that by this means we should have an excellent world.

Katherine Philips, "the Matchless Orinda" (1631–64)

The woman who became the most renowned "model" poetess of the seventeenth century, known as "the matchless Orinda," was born Katherine Fowler, daughter of John Fowler, an eminent merchant of Bucklersbury, and Katherine Oxenbridge, whose father was a Fellow of the Royal College of Physicians in London. According to John Aubrey, who had his account from Katherine Fowler's "cousen Blacket," Orinda was remarkably precocious: "When a child, she was mighty apt to learn . . . she had read the Bible through before she was full four years old; she could have sayed *[sic]* I know not how many places of Scripture and chapters. She was a frequent hearer of sermons, had an excellent memory and could have brought away a sermon in her memory."[1]

After this auspicious start, Katherine was sent to a school for girls at Hackney, where she began to write verse. In this, cousin Blacket pointed out to Aubrey, she took after her grandmother Oxenbridge, who was "much inclined to poetrie herself." Katherine's other great passion was religion: she was an ardent Presbyterian, and as a child, prayed out loud at great length, and could be overheard declaring against the bishops.

At sixteen, she married James Philips, a man she had come to know because her mother had married his father. Katherine's husband shared her love of poetry, and together they gathered a literary "Society of Friendship," whose members took on "poetic" names to suit their pastoral verse. The principal parties were "Atenor" (James Philips), "Lucasia" (Anne Owen), "Rosania" (Mary Aubrey), "Regina" (John Collier), "Palaemon" (Jeremy Taylor), "Silvander" (Sir Edward Dering), and "Policrite" (Lady Margaret Cavendish). There were at least twenty-eight others in the circle addressed (under their pastoral "disguises") by Katherine Philips in her poems. The poems were widely circulated in manuscript, and Orinda enjoyed a high literary vogue.

In 1662 Orinda was persuaded to undertake the translation of Corneille's *La Mort de Pompée* by Lord Orrery, a recent acquaintance whose attention was most flattering, given his high social standing. The play was performed with great success, and Sir Charles Cotterell, another friend, took charge of its publication. Orinda most emphatically did not wish to sign her name to the text, but found herself in an uncomfortable position, since the original manuscript had been dedicated to the Duchess of York, and it would have been insulting to leave out the dedication in the published version, but equally rude to affix a dedication to an unsigned play. Orinda wrote to "Poliarchus" (Sir Charles Cotterell) to explain her dilemma: "I would beg leave publicly to address it to the Dutchess, but that I must then put my name to it, which I can never resolve to do; for I shall scarce ever pardon myself the confidence of having permitted it to see the light at all, tho' it was partly in my own defence that I did; for had I not furnished a true copy, it had been printed from one that was very false and imperfect. But should I once own it publicly, I think I should never be able to show my face again; and thus her Highness will be freed from the trouble of protecting a trifle, which indeed had never been exposed at all, but for her approbation, which was my sole encouragement to let it first be seen by those, who even compelled me to suffer it to be acted and then printed."[2]

Not long after this, an edition of Orinda's poems appeared. The events that followed have already been discussed in the Introduction, pp. 15–16. Orinda's response is described in her own words in the text that follows.

1. John Aubrey, *Brief Lives* (Oxford, 1898) 2:153–54.
2. *Letters from Orinda to Poliarchus* (London, 1705), pp. 127–28.

Letters from Orinda to Poliarchus. London, 1705.

Letter XLIV.

I am so obliged to you for the generous and friendly concern you take in the unfortunate accident of the unworthy publishing of my foolish rhymes, that I know not which way to express, much less to deserve the least part of so noble an obligation. Philaster gave me a hint of this misfortune last post, and I immediately took an opportunity of expressing

to him the great but just affliction it was to me, and begged him to join
with you in doing what I see your friendship had urged you both to do
without that request; for which I now thank you, it being all that could be
done to give me ease, but the smart of that wound still remains, and hurts
my mind. You may be assured I had obeyed you by writing after my old ill
rate on the occasion you mention, had you not in your next letter seemed
to have changed your opinion, advising me rather to hasten to London
and vindicate myself by publishing a true copy. Besides, I considered it
would have been too airy a way of resenting such an injury, and I could
not be so soon reconciled to verse, which had been so instrumental to
afflict me, as to fall to it again already; however, if you still think it proper
I will resign my judgement and humour to yours, and try what I can do
that way. Meanwhile I have sent you enclosed [the following letter, which
was sent enclosed in this]* my true thoughts on that occasion in prose,
and have mixed nothing else with it, to the end that you may, if you
please, show it to anybody that suspects my ignorance and innocence of
that false edition of my verses; and I believe it will make a greater impression on them, than if it were written in rhyme: besides, I am yet in too
great a passion to solicit the Muses, and think I have at this time more
reason to rail at them than court them; only that they are very innocent of
all that I write, and I can blame nothing but my own folly and idleness for
having exposed me to this unhappiness; but of this no more till I hear
from you again.

Letter XLV.

'Tis well you chid me so much for endeavouring to express a part of the
sense I have of your obligations; for while you go on conferring them past
all possibility of acknowledgement, 'tis very convenient for me to be forbidden to attempt it. Your last generosity in vindicating me for the unworthy usage I have received from the press at London, as much transcends
all your former favours, as the injury done me by that printer and publisher surpasses all the troubles that to my remembrance I ever had. All I
can say to you for it is only this, that you assert the cause of an innocent,
tho' a very unhappy person, and that 'tis impossible for malice itself to
have printed those rhymes, which you tell me are got abroad so impudently, with so much wrong and abuse to them, as the very publication of

* Poliarchus's note.

them at all, tho' never so correct, had been to me, who never writ a line in
my life with intention to have it printed; and am truly of my Lord Falkland's mind, when he says,

> —He danger feared than cen-
> sure less,
> Nor could he dread a breach like
> to the press.

You know me, Sir, to have been all along sufficiently distrustful of whatever my own want of company and better employment, or the commands
of others have seduced me to write, and that I have rather endeavoured
never to have those trifles seen at all, than that they should be exposed to
all the world in this impudent manner in which they now most unhappily
are. But is there no retreat can shield me from the malice of this world? I
thought that rocks and mountains might have hidden me, that 'twas free
for all to beguile their solitude with what harmless thoughts they pleased,
and that our rivers, tho' they are babbling, would not have betrayed the
follies of impertinent thoughts that were produced on their banks. But I
am the only unfortunate person who cannot so much as think in private,
who must have all my imaginations and idle notions rifled and exposed to
play the mountebanks and dance upon the ropes to entertain the rabble,
to undergo all the raillery of the wits, and all the severity of the wise, to be
the sport of some that can, and derision of others that cannot read a verse.
This is the most cruel accident that could ever have befallen me, and has
already made a proportionate impression on me; for it has cost me a sharp
fit of sickness since I heard it; and I believe would have been more fatal,
but that I considered what a champion I have in you, whose credit in the
world will gain me a belief with all the better sort of persons, that I am so
innocent of that wretched artifice of a secret consent, of which I fear I am
suspected, that whoever would have brought me those copies corrected
and amended, and a thousand pounds to have bought my permission to
print them, should not have obtained it. You know too besides, that tho'
there are many things in this villanous impression, which the ignorance of
what occasioned them, and the falseness of the copies may represent very
ridiculous and extravagant, yet I could give some account of them even to
the severest Cato; and sure they must be more abused than I can believe it
possible for them to be, (for I have not yet seen the book, nor can imagine
what is in it) before they can be disguised in such a manner, as not to

deserve the character of these lines of Sir Edward Dering in his epilogue
to *Pompey,*

> —No bolder thoughts can
>   tax
> Those rhymes of blemish to the
>   blushing sex:
> As chaste the lines, as harmless
>   is the sense,
> As the first smiles of infant in-
>   nocence.

So that I hope there will be no need of justifying them to virtue and
honour: and I am so little concerned for the reputation of writing sense,
that provided the world will believe me wholly innocent of the least
knowledge, much more of any connivance at this publication, I will willingly compound never to trouble them with the true copies, which nevertheless you advise me to do; though if you still judge it absolutely necessary
to the reparation of this misfortune, and to the general satisfaction, and if,
as you tell me, all the rest of my friends will press me to it, I shall resolve
upon it with the same reluctancy that I would cut off a limb to save my
life. However, I hope you will satisfy all your acquaintance of my aversion
to it, and did they know me as well as you do, that apology were very
unnecessary, for I am so far from expecting applause on account of any
thing I write, that I can scarce expect a pardon: and sometimes I think
that to make verses is so much above my reach, and a diversion so unfit for
the sex to which I belong, that I am about to resolve against it forever; and
could I have recovered those fugitive papers that have escaped my hands,
I had long since, I believe, made a sacrifice of them all to the flames. The
truth is, I have always had an incorrigible inclination to the vanity of
rhyming, but intended the effects of that humour only for my own amusement in a retired life, and therefore did not so much resist it as a wiser
woman would have done: but some of my dearest and best friends having
found my ballads (for they deserve no better a name) they made me so
much believe they did not dislike them, that I was betrayed to permit
some copies to be taken for their diversion, but this with so little concern
for them, that I have lost most of the originals, which I suppose to be the
cause of my present misfortune; for some infernal spirits or other have
catched those rags of paper, and what the careless blotted writing kept

them from understanding, they have supplied by conjecture, till they have at length put them into the shape wherein you saw them, or else I know not which way 'tis possible for them to have been collected, and so abominably printed as I hear they are. I believe too there are some among them that are not mine, and thus I am not only injured in my own particular, but on the account likewise of those worthy persons, who had then the ill luck to be of my conversation, whose names are without their leave exposed in this impression, so that there are but few things in the power of fortune that could have afflicted me more than this treacherous accident. To conclude, I know you so much my friend, that I need not ask your pardon for making you this tedious complaint, but I own 'tis a great injustice to revenge my self thus on you for the wrongs [that] have been done me by others; and therefore will only tell you, that the sole advantage I gain by this cruel news is, that it has convinced me by dear experience, that no adversity can shake the constancy of your friendship, and that in the worst humour that ever I was in, I still am, &c.

Jan. 29, 1663.   Orinda

Interestingly enough, the encomium that prefaced the posthumous edition of Katherine Philips's verse was a strongly argued defense of women's right to the pen.

Poems. London, 1669 (posthumous edition).

To the Excellent Orinda

Let the male poets their male Phoebus choose,
Thee I invoke, Orinda, for my Muse;
He could but force a branch, Daphne her tree
Most freely offers to her sex and thee,
And says to verse, so unconstrained as yours,
Her laurel freely comes, your fame secures:
And men no longer shall with ravished Bays
Crown their forced poems by as forced a praise.
    Thou glory of our sex, envy of men,
Who are both pleased and vexed with thy bright pen:
Its luster doth entice their eyes to gaze,
But men's sore eyes cannot endure its rays;

It dazzles and surprises so with light,
To find a noon where they expected night:
A woman translate *Pompey!* which the famed
Corneille with such art and labour framed!
To whose close version the wits club their sense,
And a new lay-poetic S M E C sprigs thence!
Yes, that bold work a woman dares translate,
Not to provoke, nor yet to fear men's hate.
Nature doth find that she hath erred too long,
And now resolves to recompense that wrong:
Phoebus to Cynthia must his beams resign,
The rule of day and wit's now feminine.

    That sex, which heretofore was not allowed
To understand more than a beast, or crowd;
Of which problems were made, whether or no
Women had souls; but to be damned, if so;
Whose highest contemplation could not pass,
In men's esteem, no higher than the glass;
And all the painful labours of their brain,
Was only how to dress and entertain:
Or, if they ventured to speak sense, the wise
Made that, and speaking ox, like prodigies.
From these thy more than masculine pen hath reared
Our sex; first to be praised, next to be feared.
And by the same pen forced, men now confess,
To keep their greatness, was to make us less.

    Men know of how refined and rich a mould
Our sex is framed, what sun is in our gold:
They know in lead no diamonds are set,
And jewels only fill the cabinet.
Our spirits purer far than theirs, they see;
By which even men from men distinguished be:
By which the soul is judged, and does appear
Fit or unfit for action, as they are.

    When in an organ various sounds do stroke,
Or grate the ear, as birds sing, or toads croak;
The breath, that voices every pipe's the same,
But the bad metal doth the sound defame.
So, if our souls by sweeter organs speak,
And theirs with harsh false notes the air do break;

The soul's the same, alike in both doth dwell,
'Tis from her instruments that we excell.
Ask me not then, why jealous men debar
Our sex from books in peace, from arms in war;
It is because our parts will soon demand
Tribunals for our persons, and command.
    Shall it be our reproach, that we are weak,
And cannot fight, nor as the schoolmen speak?
Even men themselves are neither strong nor wise,
If limbs and parts they do not exercise.
    Trained up to arms, we Amazons have been,
And Spartan virgins strong as Spartan men:
Breed women but as men, and they are these;
Whilst Sybarite men are women by their ease.
Why should not brave Semiramis break a lance,
And why should not soft Ninyas curl and dance?
Ovid in vain bodies with change did vex,
Changing her form of life, Iphis changed sex.
Nature to females freely doth impart
That, which the males usurp, a stout, bold heart.
Thus hunters female beasts fear to assail:
And female hawks more mettaled* than the male:
Men ought not then courage and wit engross,
Whilst the fox lives, the lion, or the horse.
Much less ought men both to themselves confine,
Whilst women, such as you, Orinda, shine.
    That noble friendship brought thee to our coast,
We thank Lucasia, and thy courage boast.
Death in each wave could not Orinda fright,
Fearless she acts that friendship she did write:
Which manly virtue to their sex confined,
Thou rescuest to confirm our softer mind;
For there's required (to do that virtue right)
Courage, as much in friendship as in fight.
The dangers we despise, doth this truth prove,
Though boldly we not fight, we boldly love.
    Engage us unto books, Sappho comes forth,
Though not of Hesiod's age, of Hesiod's worth.

* mettled.

If souls no sexes have, as 'tis confessed,
'Tis not the He or She makes poems best:
Nor can men call these verses feminine,
Be the sense vigorous and masculine.
'Tis true, Apollo sits as judge of wit,
But the nine female learned troop are it:
Those laws, for which Numa did wise appear,
Wiser Aegeria [sic] whispered in his ear.
The Gracchi's mother taught them eloquence;
From her breasts courage flowed, from her brain sense;
And the grave beards, who heard her speak in Rome,
Blushed not to be instructed, but o'ercome.
Your speech, as hers, commands respect from all,
Your very looks, as hers, rhetorical:
Something of grandeur in your verse men see,
That they rise up to it as Majesty.
The wise and noble Orrery's regard,
Was much observed, when he your poem heard:
All said, a fitter match was never seen,
Had Pompey's widow been Arsamnes' Queen.

One of the most important themes of Katherine Philips's poetry was
that of "friendship." Philips and the society of friends she gathered
around her attached a special meaning to the word: "friendship"
was a Platonic ideal, a sacred connection between persons (male or
female), far removed from the sphere of the merely sexual. Katherine Philips defined it as "love refin'd and purg'd from all its dross."
This rejection of the possibility of sex frees Philips to express her
feelings far more passionately than she might otherwise have done.

A Friend

1.

Love, nature's plot, this great creation's soul,
    The being and the harmony of things,
Doth still preserve and propagate the whole,
    From whence man's happiness and safety springs:

The earliest, whitest, blessedest times did draw
From her alone their universal law.

2.

Friendship's an abstract of this noble flame,
   'Tis love refin'd and purg'd from all its dross,
The next to angels' love, if not the same,
   As strong as passion is, though not so gross:
It antedates a glad eternity,
And is an Heaven in epitome.

3.

Nobler than kindred or than marriage-band,
   Because more free; wedlock-felicity
Itself doth only by this union stand,
   And turns to friendship or to misery.
Force or design matches to pass may bring,
But friendship doth from love and honour spring.

4.

If souls no sexes have, for men t'exclude
   Women from friendship's vast capacity,
Is a design injurious or rude,
   Only maintain'd by partial tyranny.
Love is allowed to us and innocence,
And noblest friendships do proceed from thence.

5.

The chiefest thing in friends is sympathy:
   There is a secret that doth friendship guide,
Which makes two souls before they know agree,
   Who by a thousand mixtures are allied,
And changed and lost, so that it is not known,
Within which breast doth no reside their own.

6.

Essential honour must be in a friend,
   Not such as every breath fans to and fro;
But born within, is its own judge and end,
   And dares not sin though sure that none should know

Where friendship's spoke, honesty's understood;
For none can be a friend that is not good.

7.

Friendship doth carry more than common trust,
  And treachery is here the greatest sin.
Secrets deposed then none ever just
  Presume to open, but who put them in.
They that in one chest lay up all their stock,
Had need be sure that none can pick the lock.

8.

A breast too open friendship does not love,
  For that the other's trust will not conceal;
Nor one too much reserved can it approve,
  Its own condition this will not reveal.
We empty passions for a double end,
To be refreshed and guarded by a friend.

9.

Wisdom and knowledge friendship does require,
  The first for counsel, this for company;
And though not mainly, yet we may desire
  Both complaisance and ingenuity.
Though ev'ry thing may love, yet 'tis a rule,
He cannot be a friend that is a fool.

10.

Discretion uses parts, and best knows how;
  And patience will all qualities commend:
That serves a need best, but this doth allow
  The weakness and passions of a friend.
We are not yet come to the quire above:
Who cannot pardon here, can never love.

11.

Thick waters show no images of things;
  Friends are each other's mirrours, and should be

Clearer than crystal or the mountain springs,
　　And free from clouds, design or flattery.
For vulgar souls no part of friendship share:
Poets and friends are born to what they are. . . .

To Mrs. M.A. at Parting.

1.

I have examin'd and do find,
　　Of all that favour me
There's none I grieve to leave behind
　　But only, only thee.
To part with thee I needs must die,
Could parting sep'rate thee and I.

2.

But neither chance nor compliment
　　Did element our love;
'Twas sacred sympathy was lent
　　Us from the quire above.
That friendship fortune did create,
Still fears a wound from time or fate.

3.

Our chang'd and mingled souls are grown
　　To such acquaintance now,
That if each would resume their own,
　　Alas! we know not how.
We have each other so engrossed,
That each is in the union lost.

4.

And thus we can no absence know,
　　Nor shall we be confin'd;
Our active souls will daily go
　　To learn each other's mind.
Nay, should we never meet to sense,
Our souls would hold intelligence.

5.

Inspired with a flame divine
    I scorn to court a stay;
For from that noble soul of thine
    I ne're can be away.
But I shall weep when thou dost grieve;
Nor can I die whil'st thou dost live.

6.

By my own temper I shall guess
    At thy felicity,
And only like my happiness
    Because it pleaseth thee.
Our hearts at any time will tell
If thou, or I, be sick, or well.

7.

All honour sure I must pretend,
    All that is good or great;
She that would be Rosania's friend,
    Must be at least complete.
If I have any bravery,
'Tis cause I have so much of thee.

8.

Thy leiger [sic] soul in me shall lie,
    And all thy thoughts reveal;
Then back again with mine shall fly,
    And thence to me shall steal.
Thus still to one another tend;
Such is the sacred name of friend. . . .

Katherine Philips's ideal of "friendship" was much discussed in certain circles. The idea that women and men can only find a happy
equilibrium outside sex is suggested in a private letter to another
woman, written not long after Katherine Philips's death. The writer
was Mary Beale (1632–97), the first Englishwoman to make a living
as a painter. She painted portraits of Charles II, Nell Gwyn, Abraham Cowley, Aphra Behn, and countless other notables of her time.

Letter Written March 9, 1666*

Friendship is the nearest union which distinct souls are capable of (and is as rare to be found in sincerity, as it is excellent in its qualities). . . . For when God had at first created him, it is not fit, said he, that Man should be alone, as then he gave him Eve to be a great help, and what can that imply but that God gave her for a friend, as well as for a wife? A wife and friend, but not a slave, for we find her not in the beginning made subject to Adam, but always of equal dignity of honour with him, 'till by her own great credulity, sinning herself and then seducing her husband, she lost her share in that rule which before they had in common, and as a just reward of her transgression had both her desires and person subjected to him. A curse which she not only procured to herself, but entailed upon all her female posterity; except a small number who by friendship's inter-position, have restored the marriage-bond to its first institution. . . . The name of friend has certainly in it more charms than that of any other in the world . . . for how oft has the dividing of an estate separated breth-ren, and the selling of a jointure alienated the love of a husband or wife?

* B.L., Harl. Ms. 6828, fols. 510–23.

Aphra Behn (c. 1640–89)

Aphra Behn was the first Englishwoman to make a living by her pen. In a London that boasted only two theaters, she had seventeen plays produced in seventeen years. In addition, she wrote thirteen "novels" (thirty years before Daniel Defoe wrote *Robinson Crusoe)* and published several collections of poems and translations. Her novel *Oroonoko* contained the first literary portrayal of the horrors of slavery, and her bawdy poems were probably the first instance in which a woman dared to write openly about sex. Despite the scandalous reputation she acquired during her lifetime, she was the first woman writer to be buried in Westminster Abbey. Aphra Behn's career undoubtedly represents a watershed in the history of feminine writing. Her influence on women who came after is acknowledged constantly in prefaces "To the reader," where she is cited as a precedent.

Aphra Behn's birth and parentage are a matter of much dispute among scholars. Contemporary accounts are contradictory and incomplete. I have argued in my biography of Aphra Behn that she may have been the illegitimate daughter of an aristocrat (possibly belonging to the Willoughby family). This theory, while speculative, explains the contradiction between the obscurity of Aphra Behn's origins and the court connections that she was later able to take advantage of.*

When she was in her early twenties, Aphra Behn went to Surinam with her family. Her father, she claimed, had been appointed Lieutenant-General of the British colony, but died on the voyage there. Aphra, her mother, sisters, and brother remained in South America for a short time before returning home. More than twenty years later, Aphra gave an impressively realistic account in her novel *Oroonoko* of the flora and fauna, geography, climate, and scurrilous customs she had observed. The focus of the narrative, however, was

---

* See my biography of her *(Reconstructing Aphra: A Social Biography of Aphra Behn* [New York: Dial Press, 1980]) for a full account of Behn's origins.

her friendship with the slave Oroonoko and the dramatic slave rebellion Aphra claimed to have been involved in.

Aphra's next adventure was marriage to a Mr. Behn, a shadowy figure who seems to have left her a widow in short order. His death apparently left her without financial resources, a difficulty she hoped to meet by signing on as a spy in the service of Charles II. In July of 1666, she was sent to Antwerp with instructions to gather what information she could about English dissidents in exile there. She performed her task admirably, but fell victim to Charles's notorious dilatoriness in reimbursing those who worked for him. Aphra borrowed the money to return to England and a short time later was imprisoned for debt.

It is not known to what expedient Aphra resorted to extricate herself from prison, but in September of 1670 her first play, *The Forced Marriage*, was produced at Lincoln's Inn Fields. *The Amorous Prince* followed in February, and two years later *The Dutch Lover* was staged at the Dorset Garden Theatre. As the texts reproduced here demonstrate, Aphra Behn suffered violent attacks from critics. She continued to write steadily, however, until her death in 1689.

The Forced Marriage. London, 1671.

Prologue

Gallants, our poets have of late so us'd ye,
In play and prologue too so much abus'd ye,
That should we beg your aids, I justly fear,
Ye're so incensed you'd hardly lend it here.
But when against a common foe we arm,
Women those charming victors, in whose eyes
Lie all their arts, and their artilleries,
Not being contented with the wounds they made,
Would by new stratagems our lives invade.
Beauty alone goes now at too cheap rates;
And therefore they, like wise and politic states,
Court a new power that may the old supply,
To keep as well as gain the victory.

The'll join the force of wit to beauty now,
And so maintain the right they have in you.
If the vain sex this privilege should boast,
Past cure of a declining face we're lost.
You'll never know the bliss of change; this art
Retrieves (when beauty fades) the wandring heart;
And though the airy spirits move no more,
Wit still invites, as beauty did before.
Today one of their party ventures out,
Not with design to conquer, but to scout.
Discourage but this first attempt, and then,
They'll hardly dare to sally out again. . . .

Epilogue

By a Woman.

We charged you boldly in our first advance,
And gave the onset *à la mode de France,*
As each had been a Joan of Orleance.

Like them our heat as soon abated too;
Alas we could not vanquish with a show,
Much more than that goes to the conquering you.

The trial though will recompense the pain,
It having wisely taught us how to reign;
'Tis beauty only can our power maintain.

But yet, as tributary Kings, we own
It is by you that we possess that throne,
Where had we victors been, we'ad reign'd alone.

And we have promised what we could not do;
A fault, methinks, might be forgiven too,
Since 'tis but what we learnt of some of you.

But we are upon equal treatment yet,
For neither conquer, since we both submit;
You to our beauty bow, we to your wit.

The Dutch Lover. London, 1673.

Epistle to the Reader

Good, Sweet, Honey, Sugar-Candied Reader,

Which I think is more than anyone has called you yet, I must have a word or two with you before you do advance into the treatise; but 'tis not to beg your pardon for diverting you from your affairs, by such an idle pamphlet as this is, for I presume you have not much to do and therefore are to be obliged to me for keeping you from worse employment, and if you have a better you may get you gone about your business: but if you will misspend your time, pray lay the fault upon yourself; for I have dealt pretty fairly in the matter, told you in the title page what you are to expect within. Indeed, had I hung a sign of the Immortality of the Soul, of the Mystery of Godliness, or of Ecclesiastical Policy, and then had treated you with Indiscerptibility and Essential Spissitude (words, which though I am no competent judge of, for want of languages, yet I fancy strongly ought to mean just nothing) with a company of Apocryphal midnight Tales culled out of the choicest insignificant authors; if I had only proved in folio that Apollonius was a naughty knave, or had presented you with two or three of the worst principles transcribed out of the peremptory and ill-natured (though prettily ingenious) Doctor of Malmesbury* undigested and ill-managed by a silly, saucy, ignorant, impertinent, ill-educated chaplain, I were then indeed sufficiently in fault; but having inscribed Comedy on the beginning of my book, you may guess pretty near what pennyworths you are like to have, and ware your money and your time accordingly. I would not yet be understood to lessen the dignity of plays, for surely they deserve a place among the middle if not the better sort of books; for I have heard the most of that which bears the name of learning, and which has abused such quantities of ink and paper, and continually employs so many ignorant, unhappy souls for ten, twelve, twenty years in the university (who yet poor wretches think they are doing something all the while) as logic, etc. and several other things (that shall be nameless lest I misspell them) are much more absolutely nothing than the errantest play that e'er was writ. Take notice, reader, I do not assert this purely upon my own knowledge, but I think I have known it very fully proved, both sides

* Hobbes.

being fairly heard, and even some ingenious opposers of it most abominably baffled in the argument: some of which I have got so perfectly by rote, that if this were a proper place for it, I am apt to think myself could almost make it clear; and as I would not undervalue poetry, so neither am I altogether of their judgement who believe no wisdom in the world beyond it. I have often heard indeed (and read) how much the world was anciently obliged to it for most of that which they called science, which my want of letters makes me less assured of than others happily may be: but I have heard some wise men say that no considerable part of useful knowledge was this way communicated, and on the other way, that it hath served to propagate so many idle superstitions, as all the benefits it hath or can be guilty of, can never make sufficient amends for; which unaided by the unlucky charms of poetry, could never have possessed a thinking creature such as man. However true this is, I am myself well able to affirm that none of all our English poets, and least the dramatic (so I think you call them) can be justly charged with too great reformation of men's minds or manners, and for that I may appeal to general experiment, if those who are the most assiduous disciples of the stage, do not make the fondest and lewdest crew about this town; for if you should unhappily converse them through the year, you will not find one dram of sense amongst a club of them, unless you will allow for such a little link-boy's ribaldry thick-larded with unseasonable oaths and impudent defiance of God, and all things serious; and that at such a senseless damned unthinking rate, as, if 'twere well distributed, would spoil near half the apothecaries' trade, and save the sober people of the town the charge of vomits; and it was smartly said (how prudently I cannot tell) by a late learned Doctor, who, though himself no great asserter of a deity, (as you'll believe by that which follows) yet was observed to be continually persuading of this sort of men (if I for once may call them so) of the necessity and truth of our religion; and being asked how he came to bestir himself so much this way, made answer that it was because their ignorance and indiscreet debauch make them a scandal to the profession of atheism. And for their wisdom and design I never knew it reach beyond the invention of some notable expedient, for the speedier ridding them of their estate, (a devilish clog to wit and parts), than other growling mortals know, or battering half-a-dozen fair new windows in a morning after their debauch, whilst the dull unjantee rascal they belong to is fast asleep. But I'll proceed no farther in their character, because that miracle of wit (in spite of academic frippery) the mighty Eachard hath already done it to my satisfaction; and whoever undertakes a supplement to anything he hath discoursed, had better for their reputation be doing nothing.

Besides this theme is worn too threadbare by the whiffling would-be wits of the town, and of both the stone-blind-eyes of the kingdom. And therefore to return to that which I before was speaking of, I will have leave to say that in my judgement the increasing number of our latter plays have not done much more towards the amending of men's morals, or their wit, than hath the frequent preaching, which this last age hath been pestered with, (indeed without all controversy they have done less harm), nor can I once imagine what temptation anyone can have to expect it from them; for sure I am no play was ever writ with that design. If you consider tragedy, you'll find their best of characters unlikely patterns for a wise man to pursue: for he that is the Knight of the play, no sublunary feats must serve his Dulcinea; for if he can't bestride the moon, he'll ne'er make good his business to the end, and if he chance to be offended, he must without considering right or wrong confound all things he meets, and put you half-a-score likely tall fellows into each pocket; and truly if he come not something near this pitch I think the tragedy's not worth a farthing; for plays were certainly intended for the exercising of men's passions, not their understandings, and he is infinitely far from wise that will bestow one moment's meditation on such things: and as for comedy, the finest folks you meet with there are still unfitter for your imitation, for though within a leaf or two of the prologue, you are told that they are people of wit, good humour, good manners, and all that: yet if the authors did not kindly add their proper names, you'd never know them by their characters; for whatsoe'er's the matter, it hath happened so spitefully in several plays, which have been pretty well received of late, that even those persons that were meant to be the ingenious censors of the play, have either proved the most debauched, or most unwitty people in the company: nor is this error very lamentable, since as I take it comedy was never meant, either for a converting or a conforming ordinance. In short, I think a play the best divertisement that wise men have: but I do also think them nothing so who do discourse as formally about the rules of it, as if 'twere the grand affair of human life. This being my opinion of plays, I studied only to make this as entertaining as I could, which whether I have been successful in, my gentle reader, you may for your shilling judge. To tell you my thoughts of it, were to little purpose, for were they very ill, you may be sure I would not have exposed it; nor did I so till I had first consulted most of those who have a reputation for judgement of this kind; who were at least so civil (if not kind) to it as did encourage me to venture it upon the stage, and in the press: nor did I take their single word for it, but used their reasons as a confirmation of my own.

Indeed that day 'twas acted first, there comes me into the pit, a long, lither, phlegmatic, white, ill-favoured, wretched fop, an officer in masquerade newly transported with a scarf and feather out of France, a sorry animal that has nought else to shield it from the uttermost contempt of all mankind, but that respect which we afford to rats and toads, which though we do not well allow to live, yet when considered as a part of God's creation, we make honourable mention of them. A thing, reader—but no more of such a smelt: this thing, I tell ye, opening that which serves it for a mouth, out issued such a noise as this to those that sat about it, that they were to expect a woeful play, God damn him, for it was a woman's. Now how this came about I am not sure, but I suppose he brought it piping hot from some who had with him the reputation of a villanous wit: for creatures of his size of sense talk without all imagination, such scraps as they pick up from other folks. I would not for a world be taken arguing with such a property as this; but if I thought there were a man of any tolerable parts, who could upon mature deliberation distinguish well his right hand from his left, and justly state the difference between the number of sixteen and two, yet had this prejudice upon him; I would take a little pains to make him know how much he errs. For waiving the examination why women having equal education with men, were not as capable of knowledge, of whatsoever sort as well as they: I'll only say as I have touched before, that plays have no great room for that which is men's great advantage over women, that is learning. We all well know that the immortal Shakespeare's plays (who was not guilty of much more of this than often falls to women's share) have better pleased the world than Jonson's works, though by the way 'tis said that Benjamin was no such Rabbi neither, for I am informed that his learning was but grammar high; (sufficient indeed to rob poor Salust [sic] of his best orations) and it hath been observed that they are apt to admire him most confoundedly, who have just such a scantling of it as he had; and I have seen a man the most severe of Jonson's sect, sit with his hat removed less than a hair's breadth from one sullen posture for almost three hours at *The Alchemist;* who at that excellent play of *Harry the Fourth* (which yet I hope is far enough from farce) hath very hardly kept his doublet whole; but affectation hath always had a greater share both in the actions and discourse of men than truth and judgement have; and for our modern ones, except our most unimitable Laureat, I dare to say I know of none that write at such a formidable rate, but that a woman may well hope to reach their greatest heights. Then for their musty rules of unity, and God knows what besides, if they meant anything, they are enough intelligible and as practicable by a woman; but really methinks they that disturb their heads with any other rule of plays besides the making them pleasant, and avoiding of scurrility, might much better be employed in studying how to improve men's too imperfect knowledge of that ancient English game which hight long Laurence:† and if comedy should be the picture of ridiculous mankind I wonder anyone should think it such a sturdy task, whilst we are furnished with such precious originals as him I lately told you of; if at least that character do not dwindle into farce, and so become too mean an entertainment for those persons who are used to think. Reader, I have a complaint or two to make to you and I have done. Know then that this play was hugely injured in the acting, for 'twas done so imperfectly as never any was before, which did more harm to this than it could have done to any of another sort; the plot being busy (though I think not intricate) and so requiring a continual attention, which being interrupted by the intolerable negligence of some that acted in it, must needs much spoil the beauty on't. My Dutch Lover spoke but little of what I intended for him, but supplied it with a great deal of idle stuff, which I was wholly unacquainted with until I had heard it first from him; so that Jack-pudding ever used to do: which though I knew before, I have him yet the part, because I knew him so acceptable to most o' th' lighter periwigs about the town, and he indeed did vex me so, I could almost be angry. Yet, but reader, you remember, I suppose a fusty piece of Latin that has passed from hand to hand this thousand years they say (and how much longer I can't tell) in favour of the dead. I intended him a habit much more notably ridiculous, which if ever it be important was so here, for many of the scenes in the three last acts depended upon the mistakes of the Colonel for Haunce, which the ill-favoured likeness of their habits is supposed to cause. Lastly my epilogue was promised me by a person who had surely made it good, if any, but he failing of his word, deputed one, who has made it as you see, and to make out your penny-worth you have it here. The prologue is by misfortune lost. Now, reader, I have eased my mind of all I had to say, and so *sans* farther compliment, Adieu.

† "To play at Laurence": "to laze." Laurence is the personification of indolence.

Sir Patient Fancy. London, 1686.

To the Reader

I printed this play with all the impatient haste one ought to do, who would be vindicated from the most unjust and silly aspersion, woman could invent to cast on woman, and which only my being a woman has procured me: *That it was bawdy*—the least and most excusable fault in the men writers, to whose plays they all crowd, as if they came to no other end than to hear what they condemn in this: *but from a woman it was unnatural:* but how so cruel an unkindness came into their imaginations I can by no means guess; unless by those whose lovers by long absence, or those whom age or ugliness have rendered a little distant from those things they would fain imagine here—But if such as these durst profane their chaste ears with hearing it over again, or taking it into their serious consideration in their cabinets; they would find nothing that the most innocent virgins can have cause to blush at: but confess with me that no play either ancient or modern has less of that bug-bear bawdry in it. Others to show their breeding (as Bays* says) cried it was made out of at least four French plays, when I had but a very bare hint from one, the *Malad Imagenere[sic]*, which was given me translated by a gentleman infinitely to advantage; but how much of the French is in this, I leave to those who do indeed understand it and have seen it at the Court. The play had no other misfortune but that of coming out for a woman's: had it been owned by a man, though the most dull, unthinking rascally scribbler in town, it had been a most admirable play. Nor does its loss of fame with the ladies do it much hurt, though they ought to have had good nature and justice enough to have attributed all its faults to the author's unhappiness, who is forced to write for bread and not ashamed to own it, and consequently ought to write to please (if she can) an age which has given several proofs it was by this way of writing to be obliged, though it is a way too cheap for men of wit to pursue who write for Glory, and a way which even I despise as much below me.

* The poet laureate, John Dryden.

Epilogue, Spoken by Mrs. [Nell] Gwyn.

I here an there o'erheard a coxcomb cry,   [Looking about.]
Ah, rot it—'tis a woman's comedy,
One, who because she lately chanced to please us,
With her damned stuff, will never cease to tease us.
What has poor woman done, that she must be
Debarred from sense, and sacred poetry.
Why in this age has Heaven allowed you more,
And women less of wit than heretofore?
We once were famed in story, and could write
Equal to men; could govern, nay, could fight.
We still have passive valour, and can show,
Would custom give us leave, the active too,
Since we no provocations want from you.
For who but we could your dull fopperies bear,
Your saucy love, and your brisk nonsense hear;
Endure your worse than womanish affectation,
Which renders you the nuisance of the nation;
Scorned even by all the Misses of the town,
A jest to vizard mask, the pit-buffoon;
A glass by which the admiring country fool
May learn to dress himself *en ridicule:*
Both striving who shall most ingenious grow
In lewdness, foppery, nonsense, noise and show.
And yet to those fine things we must submit
Our reason, arms, our laurels, and our wit.
Because we do not laugh at you, when lewd,
And scorn and cudgel ye when you are rude.
That we have nobler souls than you, we prove,
By how much more we're sensible of love;
Quickest in finding all the subtlest ways
To make your joys, who not to make you plays?
We best can find your foibles, know our own,
And jilts and cuckolds now best please the town;
Your way of writing's out of fashion grown.
Method, and rule—you only understand;
Pursue that way of fooling, and be damned.

Your learned cant of action, time and place,*
Must all give way to the unlaboured farce.
To all the men of wit we will subscribe:
But for your half wits, you unthinking tribe,
We'll let you see, whate'er besides we do,
How artfully we copy some of you:
And if you're drawn to th' life, pray tell me then,
Why women should not write as well as men.

The Lucky Chance. London, 1686.

Preface.

   The little obligation I have to some of the witty sparks and poets of the
town, has put me on a vindication of this comedy from those censures that
malice, and ill nature have thrown upon it, though in vain: the poets I
heartily excuse, since there is a sort of self-interest in their malice, which I
should rather call a witty way they have in this age, of railing at everything
they find with pain successful, and never to show good nature and speak
well of any thing; but when they are sure 'tis damned, then they afford it
that worse scandal, their pity. And nothing makes them so thorough-
stitched an enemy as a full third day.† That's crime enough to load it with
all manner of infamy; and when they can no other way prevail with the
town, they charge it with that old never failing scandal—that 'tis not fit
for the ladies: as if (if it were as they falsely give it out) the ladies were
obliged to hear indecencies only from their pens and plays; and some of
them have ventured to treat 'em [the ladies] as coarsely as 'twas possible,
without the least reproach from them; and in their most celebrated plays
have entertained 'em with things, that if I should here strip from their wit
and occasion that conducts 'em in and makes them proper, their fair
cheeks would perhaps wear a natural colour at the reading [of] them: yet
are never taken notice of because a man writ them, and they may hear
that from them [which] they blush at from a woman—But I make a
challenge to any person of common sense and reason—that is not willfully
bent on ill nature, and will in spite of sense wrest a double *entendre* from
every thing, lying upon the catch for a jest or a quibble, like a rook for a

---

* A reference to the dramatists and critics who insisted that the three unities be respected.
† The author's royalties were the receipts of the box office at the third day's performance.

cully; but any unprejudiced person that knows not the author, to read any of my comedys and compare 'em with others of this age, and if they find one word that can offend the chastest ear, I will submit to all their peevish cavils; but right or wrong they must be criminal because a woman's; condemning them without having the Christian charity to examine whether it be guilty or not, with reading, comparing, or thinking; the Ladies taking up any scandal on trust from some conceited sparks, who will in spite of nature be wits and beaus; then scatter it for authentic all over the town and court, poisoning of others' judgements with their false notions, condemning it to worse than death, the loss of fame. And to fortify their detraction, charge me with all the plays that have ever been offensive; though I wish with all their faults I had been the author of some of those they have honoured me with.

For the farther justification of this play; it being a comedy of intrigue, Dr. Davenant out of respect to the commands he had from Court, to take great care that no indecency should be in plays, sent for it and nicely looked it over, putting out anything he but imagined the critics would play with. After that, Sir Roger L'Estrange read it and licensed it, and found no such faults as 'tis charged with. Then Mr. Killigrew, who more severe than any, from the strict order he had, perused it with great circumspection; and lastly the Master players, who you will I hope in some measure esteem judges of decency and their own interest, having been so many years prentice to the trade of judging.

I say, after all these supervisors the ladies may be convinced, they left nothing that could offend, and the men, of their unjust reflections on so many judges of wit and decencies. When it happens that I challenge anyone, to point me out the least expression of what some have made their discourse, they cry, that Mr. Leigh opens his nightgown, when he comes into the bride-chamber; if he do, which is a jest of his own making, and which I never saw, I hope he has his clothes on underneath? And if so, where is the indecency? I have seen in that admirable play of *Oedipus,* the gown opened wide, and the man shown in his drawers and waistcoat, and never thought it an offence before. Another cries, "Why we know not what they mean, when the man takes a woman off the stage, and another is thereby cuckolded"; is that any more than you see in the most celebrated of your plays, as the *City Politics,* the *Lady Mayoress,* and the *Old Lawyer's Wife,* who goes with a man she never saw before, and comes out again the joyfullest woman alive, for having made her husband a cuckold with such dexterity, and yet I see nothing unnatural nor obscene: 'tis proper for the characters. So in that lucky play of the *London Cuckolds*, not to recite particulars. And in that good comedy of *Sir Courtly Nice*, the tailor to the young lady—in the famed Sir Fopling Dorimont and Bellinda, see the very words—in *Valentinian*, see the scene between the court bawds. And Valentinian all loose and ruffled after the rape, and all this you see without scandal, and a thousand others, the *Moor of Venice*, in many places. The *Maid's Tragedy*—see the scene of undressing the bride, and between the King and Amintor, and after between the King and Evadne —All these I name as some of the best plays I know. If I should repeat the words expressed in these scenes I mention, I might justly be charged with coarse ill manners, and very little modesty, and yet they so naturally fall into the places they are designed for, and so are proper for the business, that there is not the least fault to be found with them; though I say those things in any of mine would damn the whole piece, and alarm the town. Had I a day or two's time, as I have scarce so many hours to write this in (the play, being all printed off and the press waiting) I would sum up all your beloved plays, and all the things in them that are passed with such silence by, because written by men; such masculine strokes in me, must not be allowed. I must conclude those women (if there be any such) greater critics in that sort of conversation than myself, who find any of that sort in mine, or anything that can justly be reproached. But 'tis vain by dint of reason or comparison to convince the obstinate critics, whose business is to find fault, if not by a loose and gross imagination to create them, for they must either find the jest, or make it; and those of this sort fall to my share; they find faults of another kind for the men writers. And this one thing I will venture to say, though against my nature, because it has a vanity in it: that had the plays I have writ come forth under any man's name, and never known to have been mine; I appeal to all unbiased judges of sense, if they had not said that person had made as many good comedies, as any one man that has writ in our age; but a devil on't—the woman damns the poet.

Ladies, for its further justification to you, be pleased to know, that the first copy of this play was read by several ladies of very great quality, and unquestioned fame, and received their most favourable opinion, not one charging it with the crime, that some have been pleased to find in the acting. Other ladies who saw it more than once, whose quality and vertue can sufficiently justify anything they design to favour, were pleased to say, they found an entertainment in it very far from scandalous; and for the generality of the town, I found by my receipts it was not thought so criminal. However, that shall not be an encouragement to me to trouble the critics with new occasion of affronting me, for endeavouring at least to divert; and at this rate, both the few poets that are left, and the players who toil in vain will be weary of their trade.

I cannot omit to tell you, that a wit of the town, a friend of mine at Will's Coffee House, the first night of the play, cried it down as much as in him lay, who before had read it and assured me he never saw a prettier comedy. So complaisant one pestilent wit will be to another, and in the full cry make his noise too; but since 'tis to the witty few I speak, I hope the better judges will take no offence, to whom I am obliged for better judgements; and those I hope will be so kind to me, knowing my conversation not at all addicted to the indecencies alleged, that I would much less practice it in a play, that must stand the test of the censoring world. And I must want common sense, and all the degrees of good manners, renouncing my fame, all modesty and interest for a silly saucy fruitless jest, to make fools laugh, and women blush, and wise men ashamed; my self all the while, if I had been guilty of this crime charged to me, remaining the only stupid, insensible [one]. Is this likely, is this reasonable to be believed by anybody, but the wilfully blind? All I ask, is the privilege for my masculine part, the poet in me, (if any such you will allow me) to tread in those successful paths my predecessors have so long thrived in, to take those measures that both the ancient and modern writers have set me, and by which they have pleased the world so well. If I must not, because of my sex, have this freedom, but that you will usurp all to yourselves; I lay down my quill, and you shall hear no more of me, no not so much as to make comparisons, because I will be kinder to my brothers of the pen, than they have been to a defenceless woman; for I am not content to write for a third day only. I value fame as much as if I had been born a hero; and if you rob me of that, I can retire from the ungrateful world, and scorn its fickle favours.

The following text is an example of the kind of sexually vicious attack the "immodest" Mrs. Behn was often subjected to.

"The Description of a Poetress" (c. 1670–80).*

A famous poetess has lately writ
A bawdy ballad without sense or wit.
She satires them whose virtues all admire
Tried like best metals in the keenest fire.
Fair innocence she basely does asperse
Railing and silly in obscenest verse.
She writes and lives just at the selfsame rate
To lewdness destined by indulgent fate.
Envy and malice are her darling twins
Though she is guilty of all other sins.
The porter's vices all in her combine
Most vicious and most base of all her sins.
Her elder sister fairly stuck to one,
But she kind soul denial gives to none.
The upper galleries she daily plies,
With Whitaker and Boyle she daily lies.
With all the sparkish fops that thither go,
To tease the vizard† from the pit below,
From thence she ravages to the common stews‡
Where she as freely buggers with the Jews.
Even Stratford has denied to take her in
That Lady Abbess of all secret sin.
Swears that she is so lean and ugly grown,
She will not pass with her for half a crown,
Yet Stamford's countess does admire her wit,
But likes it most because 'tis lewdly writ,
For such a beastly friendship only fit,
Thus have you seen the Poetress described,
And so you might have often seen her swived.*

* B.L., Harl. Ms. 6913, Fols. 251–53.
† Prostitute. Prostitutes commonly wore vizard masks in public.
‡ Bawdy houses.
* "To swive": slang for "fornication."

Joan Philips (fl. 1679) "Ephelia"

A few years after Aphra Behn made her debut on the stage, a slim volume of verse, entitled *Female Poems on Several Occasions,* was published under the pseudonym "Ephelia." Research has uncovered the name of the author, but almost no other details of her "identity" are known, other than that she appears to have had some familiarity with the court.

Clearly, Joan Philips was uncomfortable enough about the "immodesty" of publication to choose to remain anonymous, but she also seems to be much reassured by the fact that Katherine Philips and Aphra Behn had gone before her. She praises both of them enthusiastically in her poems, and gives the impression that their success has been an inspiration to her literary ambitions.

Ephelia apparently also wrote a play, entitled *The Pair-Royal of Coxcombs,* which was, according to her, "acted at a dancing school." Though there is no evidence that the play was ever published, Ephelia includes the prologue in her *Female Poems.* One statement she makes in the course of this prologue provides a useful gauge of the important effect Aphra Behn was having on other women writers: Ephelia says of her play, "A woman wrote it; though it be not rare,/It is not common." She then goes on to say that "women seldom dare to reach so high," but nevertheless it is clear that the *precedent* for women's writing for a public was established, even if one might expect adverse reaction from the critics.

Female Poems on Several Occasions, Written by Ephelia. London, 1679.

To Madam Bhen [sic]

Madam! permit a Muse, that has been long
Silent with wonder, now to find a tongue:
Forgive that zeal I can no longer hide,
And pardon a necessitated pride.

When first your strenuous polite lines I read,
At once it wonder and amazement bred,
To see such things flow from a woman's pen,
As might be envied by the wittiest men:
You write so sweetly, that at once you move,
The ladies' jealousies, and gallants' love;
Passions so gentle, and so well expressed,
As needs must be the same fill your own breast;
Then rough again, as your enchanting quill
Commanded love, or anger at your will:
As in your self, so in your verses meet,
A rare connection of strong and sweet;
This I admired at, and my pride to show,
Have took the vanity to tell you so
In humble verse, that has the luck to please
Some rustic swains, or silly shepherdess:
But far unfit to reach your sacred ears,
Or stand your judgement: Oh! my conscious fears
Check my presumption, yet I must go on,
And finish the rash task I have begun.
Condemn it Madam, if you please, to th' fire,
It gladly will your sacrifice expire,
As sent by one, that rather chose to show
Her want of skill, than want of zeal to you.

Prologue to the Pair-Royal of Coxcombs,
Acted at a Dancing School.

Gallants,
If, as you say, you love variety,
We have some hopes, that you so kind will be
To the poor play, to give it your applause,
Though not for wit, nor worth, but yet because
A woman wrote it; though it be not rare,
It is not common. Women seldom dare
To reach so high, to entertain your ears,
Which strikes our poets with a thousand fears
Of your displeasure; yet some little ray
Of hope is left; for women's pardons may

Be gained with ease surely from gentlemen;
Be kind for once then to a female pen.
When you with women in discourse do sit,
Before their faces you'll commend their wit,
Pray flatter now, the poet heareth it:
She hopes too, the great wits, who crowd the age . . .
Won't undervalue so their mighty wit,
To criticize on what a woman writ:
Yet if you'll have it so, it shall be naught,
They that dislike, are welcome to find fault;
For she protests, she had no other ends
In writing this, than to divert her friends. . . .

Jane Barker (1660–?)

Jane Barker was born at the Restoration into a Royalist, Catholic family. At an early age, she was sent to a school for young ladies at Putney but, by her own account, was removed at the age of ten by her mother, who had concluded that such schools were no more than "academies of vanity and expense, no way instructive in the rudiments of a country gentlewoman's life." Presumably, Jane Barker's mother later changed her mind about the sort of instruction a young lady (even one living in the country) might be in need of, because she sent her daughter, at fifteen, to London to learn "town politeness."

Jane Barker's most important exposure to "learning" seems to have come from her brother, who attended both Oxford and Cambridge and cheerfully shared his education and circle of literary friends with this sister. When, at the age of twenty-eight, she published a collection of her poetry, the circle contributed a large number of verses praising her gifts and comparing her to the two famous female poets of the time: Barker's verse was, according to "J.N., Fellow of St. John's," "More than Astrea's soft, more than Orinda's chaste." Barker credits a disappointment in love as the original impetus of her desire to become a "learned lady": "Finding myself abandoned by Bosvil," she recounted, "and thinking it impossible ever to love any mortal more, I resolved to espouse a book, and spend my days in study. . . . I imagined myself the Orinda or Sappho of my time. In order to [do] this, I got my brother, who was not yet returned to Oxford, to set me in the way to learn my grammer. . . ." Barker and her brother also studied medicine together, and she took over management of her father's farm. After her brother's death, she gave up her studies and gradually came to regard learning as an unnatural enterprise for her sex, later writing that a learned woman is "like a forced plant that never has its due or proper relish but is withered by the first blast."

Twenty-five years after the publication of her *Poetical Recreations,* Jane Barker began to publish romantic novels. Her *Love In-*

trigues; or, The History of the Amours of Bosvil and Galisia (1713), proved enormously popular, and was followed by *Exilius* (1715), *A Patch-Work Screen for the Ladies, or Love and Virtue Recommended* (1723), and *The Lining for the Patch-Work Screen* (1726).

Late in life, the special audience for her work that a brother and his friends had represented were replaced by the growing number of women readers who made it possible for a woman writer like Jane Barker to make a living by her pen.

Poetical Recreations. London, 1688.

A Virgin Life

Since, O ye powers, ye have bestowed on me
So great a kindness for virginity,
Suffer me not to fall into the pow'rs
Of men's almost omnipotent amours;
But in this happy life let me remain,
Fearless of twenty-five and all its train,
Of slights or scorns, or being called Old Maid,
Those goblings *[sic]* which so many have betrayed:
Like harmless kids, that are pursued by men,
For safety run into a lion's den.
Ah lovely state how strange it is to see,
What mad conceptions some have made of thee,
As though thy being was all wretchedness,
Or soul deformity i' th' ugliest dress;
Whereas thy beauty's pure, celestial,
Thy thoughts divine, thy words angelical:
And such ought all thy votaries to be,
Or else they're so, but for necessity.
A virgin bears the impress of all good,
In that dread name all virtue's understood:
So equal all her looks, her mien, her dress,
That nought but modesty seems in excess.

And when she any treats or visits make,
'Tis not for tattle, but for friendship's sake;
Her neighb'ring poor she does adopt her heirs,
And less she cares for her own good than theirs;
And by obedience testifies she can
Be's good a subject as the stoutest man.
She to her church such filial duty pays,
That one would think she'd liv'd i' th' pristine days.
Her closet, where she do's much time bestow,
Is both her library and chapel too,
Where she enjoys society alone,
I' th' great three-one———
She drives her whole life's business to these ends,
To serve her God, enjoy her books and friends.

Farther Advice to Young Ladies
By Another Hand.

Be prudent, Ladies; Marry while you may,
Lest, when too late, you do repent and say,
You wish you had, whilst sun had shone, made hay.

If in th' principium of your youthful days,
Your beauty's like to Sol's bright shining rays,
Then you are critical, and hard to please.

When as you do begin to choose your mate,
You choose him first for name and great estate,
And qualified, as I shall here relate.

Good-natured, handsome, eloquent and wise,
Well learned, and skilled in arts, of equal size,
'Tis lady's niceties to be precise.

But when to twenty-one arrived you be,
You do begin to choose reservedly,
Then the young squire who keeps his coach is he.

But when as your meridian is past,
As posting time doth swiftly passing hast,
So will your crystal beauties fade as fast.

Vesper succeeds Aurora in small space,
And time will soon draw wrinkles in that face,
Which was of late adored in every place.

Bathsua Makin (fl. 1673)

Though the exact dates of Bathsua Makin's birth and death are not known, her childhood and "education" belong to the early part of the seventeenth century. Her father was a rector in Sussex and her brother, John Pell (1610–85), became an eminent mathematician. Bathsua acted as tutor to the daughters of Charles I, and instructed them in Greek, Latin, Hebrew, French, Italian, Spanish, and mathematics. After the Princess Elizabeth died in 1650, Makin apparently supported herself as a private governess until she could establish a school of her own in London.

In 1646 Bathsua Makin was introduced to Anna Maria van Schurman by the diarist Sir Simonds D'Ewes and, as earlier noted, engaged in a long-standing friendship and literary correspondence with her. In 1673 Makin put together Schurman's arguments and her own practical experience and ideas about the education of women, producing a polemic entitled *An Essay to Revive the Antient Education of Gentlewomen in Religion, Manners, Arts and Tongues.* The text was published "anonymously": the preface "To the Reader" states that "I am a man myself, that would not suggest anything prejudicial to our sex." The author goes on to assure his [her] reader that he [she] does not mean to incite women to rebellion, or "to equalize women to men," but only to show the benefits that men may derive from the improved education of the other sex. Married persons, for example, would be able to help husbands in their trade. Like Anna Maria van Schurman, the author also emphasizes that the learning advocated need not come into conflict with feminine duties: "I do not deny," he [she] writes, "but women ought to be brought up to a comely and decent carriage, to their needle, to neatness, to understand all those things that do particularly belong to their sex. But when these things are competently cared for . . ." And so on.

Where Bathsua Makin departs significantly from her predecessor Anna Maria van Schurman is in the passionately angry "Dedication to the Ladies" that precedes the note "To the Reader." This dedica-

tion (reprinted on pp. 25–26), when compared to the following tex
gives some indication of the conflicts of feeling Bathsua Makin mu
have experienced.

*An Essay to Revive the Antient Education of Gentlewomen in Reli
gion, Manners, Arts and Tongues.* London, 1673.

To the Reader

I hope I shall not need to beg the patience of ladies to peruse thi
pamphlet: I have bespoken *[sic];* and do not expect your patronage; be
cause it is your cause I plead against an ill custom, prejudicial to you
which men will not willingly suffer to be broken. I would desire men no
to prejudge and cast aside this book upon the sight of the title. If I hav
solidly proved what I do pretend to, and fairly answered the objection
brought against my assertions, and if I have proposed something that ma
be profitable to mankind, let it not be rejected. If this way of educatin
ladies should (as is like, it never will) ever be generally practised, th
greatest hurt, that I foresee, can ensue, is to put your sons upon greate
diligence to advance themselves in arts and languages, that they may b
superior to women in parts as well as in place. This is the great thing
design. I am a man my self, that would not suggest anything prejudicial t
our sex. To propose women rivals with us in learning, will make us cour
Minerva more heartily, lest they should be more in her favour. I do veril
think this to be the best way to dispel the clouds of ignorance, and to stop
the floods of debauchery, that the next generation may be more wise anc
virtuous than any of their predecessors. It is an easy matter to quibble anc
droll upon a subject of this nature, to scoff at women being kept ignorant
on purpose to be made slaves. This savours not at all of a manly spirit, tc
trample upon those that are down. I forbid scoffing and scolding. Let any
think themselves aggrieved, and come forth fairly into the field agains
this feeble sex, with solid arguments to refute what I have asserted, [and]
think I may promise to be their champion. . . .

I do not deny but women ought to be brought up to a comely anc
decent carriage, to their needle, to neatness, to understand all those thing
that do particularly belong to their sex. But when these things are compe
tently cared for, and where there are endowments of nature and leisure
then higher things ought to be endeavoured after. Merely to teach gen

tlewomen to frisk and dance, to paint their faces, to curl their hair, to put on a whisk, to wear gay clothes, is not truly to adorn, but to adulterate their bodies. . . .

My intention is not to equalize women to men, much less to make them superior. They are the weaker sex, yet capable of impressions of great things, something like to the best of men. . . . The inference I make from hence is, that women are not such silly, giddy creatures, as many proud and ignorant men would make them; as if they [women] were incapable of all improvement by learning, and unable to digest arts, that require any solidity of judgement. Many men will tell you [that women] are so unfiable [sic] and unconstant, borne down upon all occasions with such a torrent of fear, love, hatred, lust, pride and all manner of exorbitant passions, that they are uncapable to practise any virtues that require greatness of spirit, or firmness of resolution. Let such but look into history, they will find examples enough of illustrious women to confute them. . . .

Objected: The end of learning is public business, which women are not capable of. They must not speak in the church; and it is more proper for men to act in the commonwealth than they. Answered: They may not speak in the church, but they may inquire of their husbands at home; it is private instruction I plead for, not public employment. Yet there is no such contradiction in the terms . . . sometime women may have occasions for public business, as widows, and wives when their husbands are absent, but especially persons born to government.

Married persons, by virtue of this education, will be very useful to their husbands in their trade, as women are in Holland, and to their children, by timely instructing them. . . . I need not show how any persons thus brought up, if they happen to be widows, will be able to understand and manage their own affairs.

I hope some of these considerations will at least move some of this abused sex to set a right value upon themselves, according to the dignity of their creation, that they might, with an honest pride and magnanimity, scorn to be bowed down and made to stoop to such follies and vanities, trifles and nothings, so far below them, and unproportionable to their noble souls, nothing inferior to those of men and equally precious to God in Christ, in whom there is neither male nor female.

Let a generous resolution possess your minds, seeing men in this age have invaded women's vices, in a noble revenge, reassume those virtues which men sometimes unjustly usurped to themselves, but ought to have left them in common to both sexes.

Hannah Woolley (b. 1623)

Another woman who protested against the parsimonious learning
meted out to women of her time was Hannah Woolley. Like Bathsua Makin, she belonged to the middling class and earned her living
as a teacher, first in a small school, and later as a governess in the
households of two noble families. Later, she began to support herself
by writing extensively on household management, giving practical
advice to women on cooking, cleaning, beautifying themselves, and
concocting medicines and remedies. The works attributed to her
include *The Ladies Directory in Choice Experiments of Preserving
and Candying* (1661, 1662); *The Cooks Guide* (1664); *The Queen-
like Closet, or Rich Cabinet, Stored with All Manner of Rich Receipts* (1672, 1674, 1675, 1681, 1684); *The Ladies Delight . . .
Together with the Exact Cook . . . to Which Is Added the Ladies
Physical Closet, or Excellent Receipts and Rare Waters for Beautifying the Face and Body* (1672). As the number of editions indicate,
these works were much used.

Hannah Woolley's most ambitious work was *The Gentlewoman's
Companion*, which she meant to serve as a "Universal companion
and guide to the female sex, in all places, relations, companies, conditions, and states of life, even from childhood down to old age; And
from the Lady at court, to the cook-maid in the country." There
was, Woolley asserted, no other book that addressed a women's entire experience, though she noted that several other books had been
most useful to her in composing her work, notably Robert Codrington's *The Second Part of Youth's Behaviour; or, Decency in Conversation Amongst Women*. Most of what she had written, however,
was "the product of my thirty years' observation and experience." It
is interesting that she begins the transfer of all this experience and
knowledge by complaining that "the right education of the female
sex . . . is in a manner everywhere neglected. . . ."

Though some of Hannah Woolley's books had been published
anonymously, and though she vigorously insists on the importance
of "feminine modesty" in her text, Woolley seems to feel less ill at

ease with "owning" her work than some of the earlier women writers. This may have something to do with the fact that she earned her living as a teacher and writer; or it may be that she felt the usefulness of her practical advice exempted her from the "ambition of gaining a name publicly in print." In *The Gentlewoman's Companion* she gives an interesting account of her own life:

The Gentlewoman's Companion; or A Guide to the Female Sex: Containing Directions of Behaviour, in All Places, Companies, Relations, and Conditions and States of Life, Even from Childhood down to Old Age. London, 1675.

A Short Account of the Life and Abilities of [the] Authoress of This Book.

I would not presume to trouble you with any passages of my life, or relate my innate qualifications, or acquired, were it not in obedience to a person of honour, who engaged me so to do, if for no other reason than to stop the mouths of such who may be so maliciously censorious as to believe I pretend what I cannot perform.

It is no ambitious design of gaining a name in print (a thing as rare for a woman to endeavour, as obtain) that put me on this bold undertaking; but the mere pity I have entertained for such ladies, gentlewomen, and others, as have not received the benefits of the tithe of the ensuing accomplishments. These ten years and upwards, I have studied how to repair their loss of time, by making public those gifts which God hath bestowed upon me. To be useful in our generation is partly the intent of our creation; I shall then arrive to the top of the pyramid of my contentment, if any shall profit by this following discourse. If any question the truth of what I can perform, their trial of me I doubt not but will convince their infidelity.

The things I pretend greatest skill in, are all works wrought with a needle, all transparent works, shell-work, moss-work, also cutting of prints, and adorning rooms, or cabinets, or stands with them.

All kinds of beugle-works upon wires, or otherwise.

All manner of pretty toys for closets.

Rocks made with shells, or in sweets.

Frames for looking glasses, pictures, or the like.

Feathers of crewel for the corner of beds.

Preserving all kind of sweet-meats wet and dry.

Setting out of banquets.

Making salves, ointments, waters, cordials; healing any wounds not desperately dangerous.

Knowledge in discerning the symptoms of most diseases, and giving such remedies as are fit in such cases.

All manner of cookery.

Writing and arithmetic.

Washing black or white sarsenets.

Making sweet powders for the hair, or to lay among linen.

All these and several things beside, too tedious here to relate, I shall be ready to impart to those who are desirous to learn.

Now to the intent I may increase your wonder, I shall relate how I came to the knowledge of what I profess. When I was fourteen years old, I began to consider how I might improve my time to the best advantage, not knowing at that age any thing but what reason and fancy dictated to me. Before I was fifteen I was entrusted to keep a little school, and was the sole mistress thereof. This course of life I continued till the age of seventeen, when my extraordinary parts appeared more splendid in the eyes of a noble Lady in this kingdom, than really they deserved, who praising my works with the appellation of curious pieces of art, was infinitely pleased therewith. But understanding, withal, that I understood indifferently the smooth Italian, and could sing, dance and play on several sorts of musical instruments, she took me from my school, and greedily entertained me in her house as governess of her only daughter. Unto this honourable person I am indebted for the basis, or ground-work of my preserving and cookery, by my observation of what she ordered to be done. By this Lady's means I came acquainted with the court, with a deportment suitable thereunto.

The death of this Lady gave me a fit opportunity to be entertained by another no way inferiour to the former, with whom I lived seven years. As first I was governess to those of her children, whose forward virtue sufficiently declared the goodness of the stock from whence they came. Time and my Lady's good opinion of me, constituted me afterwards her woman, her stewardess, and her scribe or secretary, by which means I appeared as a person of no mean authority in the family. I kept an exact account of what was spent in the house. And as I profited in externals, so I treasured up things necessary for my understanding, having a happy opportunity so to do, not only by hearing that ingenious and agreeable discourse interfaced between my Lady and persons of honour, but also by inditing all her letters; in the framing and well-fashioning of which (that I might increase my Lady's esteem) I took indefatigable pains. There were not any who both wittily and wisely had published their epistles to view of the world, whom I had not read, and on all occasions did consult: those which I placed in my greatest esteem were the letters of Mr. Ford, Mr. Howel, Mr. Loveday, and Monsieur Voiture.

But that which most of all increased my knowledge was my daily reading to my Lady, poems of all sorts and plays, teaching me as I read, where to place my accents, how to raise and fall my voice, where lay the emphasis of expressions. Romances of the best sort she took great delight in; and being very well versed in the propriety of the French tongue, there was not anything published by the *virtuosi* of France, which carefully and chargeably she procured not; this put me upon the understanding of that language, she was so well experienced therein, which is as great an ornament for young ladies as those learned tongues, of which the academical *studioso* boasts a more than common understanding.

Here as I learned, hourly, courtly phrases and graces, so how to express myself with the attendency of a becoming air. And as I gathered how to manage my tongue gracefully, and discreetly, so I thought it irrequisite to let my hands lie idle. I exercised them daily in carving at table. And when any sad accident required their help in physic and surgery, I was ready to be assisting; in those two excellent arts in this place I acquired a competent knowledge.

In short time I became skilful, and stayed enough to order a house, and all the offices belonging to it; and gained so great an esteem among the nobility and gentry of two counties, that I was necessitated to yield to the importunity of one I dearly loved, that I might free myself from the tedious caresses of a many more.

In the time I was a wife, I had frequent occasion to make use of all, or most of my aforenamed qualities, and what I exercised not within my own roof, I used among my neighbours, friends and acquaintances.

That which qualified me as a governess for children as well as any thing yet I have mentioned, was the great knowledge I had in the humours, inclinations, and dispositions of children, having often had at one time above threescore in number under my tuition.

Besides, as I have been the mistress of many servants, so I have qualified them with my instructions to be mistress to others; the major part of them living very comfortably in a married condition.

As I have taken great pains for an honest livelihood, so the hand of the

Almighty hath exercised me in all manner of afflictions, by death of parents when very young, by loss of husband, children, friends, estate, very much sickness, by which I was disenabled from my employment. Having already given you an account of the duty, and requisite endowments which ought to be in a governess, and how qualified I was myself in that troublesome concern, I shall now proceed in giving young ladies such rules which long experience and observation have taught me, which may be as their perfect guide in all ages and conditions, the practise whereof will assuredly embalm their names here: let their steadfast faith in Jesus Christ only crown them with glory thereafter.

Hannah Woolley's success in dispensing practical instruction to her sex may have inspired other women to do the same. The author of *Advice to the Women and Maidens of London* evidently did not feel, however, that the nature of her advice was sufficient protection against ruination of reputation, and chose not to publish her name with her text. Her setting out of the arguments likely to be brought out in opposition to her project agrees fully with what Bathsua Makin and Hannah Woolley write. The "necessary" separation of spheres (the home, as opposed to the "business of the world") is an impediment she rejects, however.

Advice to the Women and Maidens of London. Showing, that Instead of Their Usual Pastime, and Education in Needlework, Lace, and Pointmaking, It Were Far More Necessary and Profitable to Apply Themselves to the Right Understanding and Practice of the Method of Keeping Books of Account: Whereby, Either Single, or Married, They May Know Their Estates, Carry On Their Trades, and Avoid the Danger of a Helpless and Forlorn Condition, Incident to Widows. By One of That Sex. London, 1678.

Ladies and gentlewomen,

Permit one of your sex to give you, as far as her small knowledge will reach, some hints to the right understanding and use of accounts: an art so useful for all sorts, sexes and degrees of persons, especially for such as ever think to have to do in the world in any sort of trade or commerce, that next to a stock of money, wares, and credit, this is the most necessary thing.

Nor let us be discouraged, or put by the inspection thereof by being bid meddle with our distaff, for I have heard it affirmed by those who have lived in foreign part[s], that merchants and other tradesmen have no other book-keepers than their wives: who by this means (the husband dying) are well acquainted with the nature and manner of their trade, and are so certain how, and where their stock is, that they need not be beholden to servants or friends for guidance.

And for telling us that the government of the house appertains to us, and the trades to our fathers or husbands; (under favour) the one is to be minded, and the other not neglected, for there is not that danger of a family's overthrow by the sauce wanting its right relish, or the table or stools misplaced, as by a widow's ignorance of her concern as to her estate, and I hope husbands will not oppose this when help and ease is intended to them while living, and safety to their name and posterity after death, except they have private trades (too much in mode) whereof they would have their wives wholly ignorant. In such a case indeed, one that knows not that one and two make three suits best. And let us not fear we shall want time and opportunity to manage the decencies of our house; for what is an hour in a day, or half a day in a week, to make inspection into that, that is to keep me and mine from ruin and poverty.

Methinks now the objection may be that this art is too high and mysterious for the weaker sex; it will make them proud: women had better keep to their needlework, point laces, &c. and if they come to poverty, those small crafts may give them some mean relief.

To which I answer, that having in some measure practised both needlework and accounts, I can aver, that I never found this masculine art harder or more difficult than the effeminate achievements of lace-making, gum-work or the like, the attainment whereof need not make us proud: and God forbid that the practice of a useful virtue should prompt us to a contrary vice.

Therefore I might advise you, you should let the poor serve you with these mean things, whilst by gaining or saving an estate you shall never be out of capacity to store your selves more abundantly with those trifles, than your own industry in such matters could have ever blest you.

And now, gentlewomen, I give you those rudiments of accounts which are the subject of this little pamphlet and transmit this learning to you the best I can, in the selfsame manner as it came to me.

Know then that my parents were very careful to cause me to learn writing and arithmetic, and in that I proceeded as far as reduction, the rule of three and practice, with other rules, for without the knowledge of these I was told I should not be capable of trade and book-keeping and in these I found no discouragement, for though arithmetic set my brains at work, yet there was much delight in seeing the end, and how each question produced a fair answer and informed me of things I knew not.

Afterwards I was put to keep an exact account of the expense of housekeeping, and other petty charges. My father made it my office to call all persons to an account every night what they had laid out, and to reimburse it them, and set all down in a book, and this is the way to make one a cashier as they are termed, and one that can keep a fair account of receipts and payments of money or cash-book, is in a good way towards the understanding of book-keeping. She that is so well versed in this as to keep the accounts of her cash right and daily entered in a book, fair without blotting, will soon be fit for greater undertakings.

Lady Damaris Masham (1658–1708)

From her early childhood, Damaris Cudworth had the encouragement, admiration, and conversation of learned men. Her father was Ralph Cudworth, an acclaimed scholar of Hebrew and master of Christ's College at Cambridge. Seeing that his daughter took a lively interest in her studies, Cudworth took great pains to educate her thoroughly; among her tutors was John Locke, who taught her divinity and philosophy. When she married Sir Francis Masham in 1685, Locke became part of an intellectual circle of friends who came to their home, and in 1691 he took up residence there. Locke remained Lady Masham's guest for the next thirteen years, until he died in 1704.

The famous philosopher clearly admired his benefactor and viewed her as a worthy partner in debate, writing in a letter to a friend that "the Lady herself is so well versed in theological and philosophical studies and of such an original mind that you will not find many men to whom she is not superior in wealth of knowledge and ability to profit by it." He was, of course, her teacher.

In 1696 Lady Masham wrote an answer to a theological argument set forth by Mary Astell and John Norris in *Letters Concerning the Love of God* (1694). She published her *A Discourse Concerning the Love of God* anonymously; the general public attributed authorship to Locke. In 1700 Lady Masham published a continuation of her argument, this time at least making the sex of the author fairly clear, though she still chose not to sign her name to the work. In the course of her remarks on Christian life, Lady Masham protests rigorously against the desultory attention given the education of women. She further castigates her contemporaries for their mistrust and ridicule of learned women. A lady with only a smattering of knowledge, she says, "can hardly escape being called learned by the men of our days, and in consequence thereof, becoming a subject of ridicule to one part of them, and of aversion to the other; with but a few exceptions of some virtuous and rational persons. And is not the incurring of general dislike one of the strongest discouragements we can have to anything?"

It seems that, despite the admiration and support of the men closest to her, Lady Masham nevertheless felt the sting of social disapproval. The inscription on her tombstone, written by a friend at her death in 1708, makes it clear that, at least to some extent, the "masculine" understanding she possessed may have "wanted opportunities . . . to shine in the world." Lady Masham's views on education have been included in an earlier section (pp. 29–31); here is an exerpt from her comments on marriage:

Occasional Thoughts in Reference to a Vertuous or Christian Life. London, 1705.

The necessities of a family, very often, and the injustice of parents, sometimes, causes people to sacrifice their inclinations [in marrying] to interest; which must needs make this state uneasy in the beginning . . . yet scarce any virtuous and reasonable man and woman who are husband and wife, can know that it is both their duty and interest (as it is) reciprocally to make each other happy without effectually doing so in a little time. . . . But where there is mutually that predominant disposition to virtuous love, which is the characteristic of the most excellent minds, I think we cannot frame an idea of so great happiness to be formed in anything in this life, as in a married state.

It seems therefore one of the worst marks that can be of the vice and folly of any age when marriage is commonly condemned therein, since nothing can make it so but men's averseness to, or incapacity for those things which most distinguish them from brutes—virtue and friendship.

But it were well if marriage was not become a state almost as much feared by the wise, as despised by fools. Custom and silly opinion, whose consequences yet are (for the most part) not imaginary, but real evils, do usually make it by their best friends thought advisable for those of the female sex once to marry; although the risk which they therein run of being wretched, is yet much greater than that of men; who (not having the same inducement from the hazard of their reputation or any uneasy dependence) are, from the examples of other misfortunes, often deterred from seeking felicity in a condition wherein they so rarely see, or hear of any who find it; it being too true that one can frequent but little company, or know the story of but few families, without hearing of the public divisions, and discords of married people, or learning their private discontents, from their being in that state. But since the cause of such unhappiness lies only in the corruption of manners, were that redressed, there would need nothing more to bring marriage into credit.

Mary Astell (1666–1731)

Born in Newcastle-upon-Tyne, Mary Astell was the daughter of a "hostman," whose duties included welcoming and supervising foreign merchants. Little is known of her childhood or education: tradition has it that her uncle, a clergyman, recognized his niece's potential and took the task of her education on himself. Astell herself lamented the fact that she had no training in the classics: "My ignorance in the Sacred Languages, besides all other disadvantages makes me incapable of expounding Scriptures with the learned," she wrote in 1705.[1]

After her mother's death in 1684, Mary Astell moved to London and settled in Chelsea, where she lived for the rest of her life. She devoted herself to religion, scholarship, and writing, avoiding marriage on principle. A number of intellectual women were drawn to her, and Astell formed close and long-lasting friendships with Lady Mary Wortley Montague, Lady Elizabeth Hastings, Elizabeth Elstob (the Anglo-Saxon scholar), among others.

In 1694 Mary Astell published her first work: *A Serious Proposal to the Ladies for the Advancement of Their True and Greatest Interest.* This polemic argued the case for improving women's education; the proposal was to set up a "seminary" where young ladies, in retreat from the world, could give themselves over to devotion and study. The book excited much interest and controversy, and in 1697 Astell published part two, an elaboration of her argument. Both were printed without the author's name on the title page, but her identity was a matter of public knowledge. It was also well known that a prominent lady (evidence points to Princess Anne) was prepared to furnish ten thousand pounds to further Astell's design for a college, but was dissuaded by Bishop Burnet, who thought the scheme too reminiscent of a Roman Catholic nunnery—unacceptably "popish" for Protestant England. George Ballard, when gathering information for his account of Astell's life, wrote to her friend Elizabeth Elstob in 1738 to inquire whether this story were true and received a confirmation from her.[2]

In 1704 Astell took up religious debate with *A Fair Way with Dissenters and their Patrons,* followed by *An Impartial Enquiry into the Causes of Rebellion and the Civil War* (1704) and then *The Christian Religion as Professed by a Daughter of the Church of England* (1705). In 1706 Mary Astell once again launched into polemic with the publication of *Some Reflections upon Marriage.*

Despite the fact that Mary Astell's most well-known cause, her proposal for a women's college, never was brought to fruition, her book nevertheless exerted a great deal of influence through the wide debate it stirred up. When it finally became clear to Astell that her scheme was not to be realized, she persuaded a number of women friends to give money for a charity school for girls in Chelsea. Two years before she died, the school was established and was to last until the end of the nineteenth century.

1. *The Christian Religion as Professed by a Daughter of the Church of England* (London, 1705), p. 139.
2. Florence Smith, *Mary Astell* (New York, 1916), p. 21.

A Serious Proposal to the Ladies for the Advancement of Their True and Greatest Interest. London, 1694.

Ladies,
Since the profitable adventures that have gone abroad in the world, have met with so great encouragement, tho' the highest advantage they can propose, is an uncertain lot for such matters as opinion, [no] real worth, gives a value to things which if obtained are as flitting and fickle, as that chance which is to dispose of them: I therefore persuade my self, you will not be less kind to a proposition that comes attended with more certain and substantial gain; whose only design is to improve your charms and heighten your value, by suffering you no longer to be cheap and contemptible. Its aim is to fix that beauty, to make it lasting and permanent, which nature with all the helps of art cannot secure, and to place it out of the reach of sickness and old age, by transferring it from a corruptible body to an immortal mind. An obliging design, which would procure them *inward* beauty, to whom nature has unkindly denied the *outward,* and not permit those ladies who have comely bodies to tarnish their glory

with deformed souls; would have you all be wits, or what is better, wise. Raise you above the vulgar by something more truly illustrious, than a sounding title, or a great estate. Would excite in you a generous emulation to excel in the best things, and not in such trifles as every mean person who has but money enough may purchase as well as you. Not suffer you to take up with the low thought of distinguishing your selves by any thing that is not truly valuable; and procure you such ornaments as all the treasures of the Indies are not able to purchase. Would help you to surpass the men as much in virtue and ingenuity, as you do in beauty; that you may not only be as lovely, but as wise as angels. Exalt and establish your fame, more than the best wrought poems and loudest panegyrics, by ennobling your minds with such graces as really deserve it. And instead of the fustian compliments and fulsome flatteries of your admirers, obtain for you the plaudit of good men and angels, and the approbation of him who cannot err. In a word, render you the glory and blessing of the present age, and the admiration and pattern of the next. . . .

Pardon me for the seeming rudeness of this proposal, which goes upon a supposition that there's something amiss in you, which it is intended to amend. My design is not to expose, but to rectify your failures. To be exempt from mistake, is a priviledge few can pretend to; the greatest is to be past conviction, and too obstinate to reform. Even the men, as exact as they would seem, and as much as they divert themselves with our miscar-riages, are very often guilty of greater faults, and such, as considering the advantages they enjoy, are much more inexcusable. But I will not pretend to correct their errors, who either are, or at least *think* themselves too wise to receive instruction from a woman's pen. My earnest desire is, that you ladies, would be as perfect and happy as 'tis possible to be in this imper-fect state; for I love you too well to endure a spot upon your beauties, if I can by any means remove and wipe it off. I would have you live up to the dignity of your nature, and express your thankfulness to God for the benefits you enjoy by a due improvement of them: as I know very many of you do, who countenance that piety which the men decry, and are the brightest patterns of religion that the age affords, 'tis my grief that all the rest of our sex do not imitate such illustrious examples, and therefore I would have them increased and rendered more conspicuous, that vice being put out of countenance (because virtue is the only thing in fashion) may sneak out of the world, and its darkness be dispelled by the conflu-ence of so many shining graces. The men perhaps will cry out that I teach you false doctrine; for because by their seductions some amongst us are

become very mean and contemptible, they would fain persuade the rest to
be as despicable and forlorn as they. We're indeed obliged to them for
their management, in endeavouring to make us so, who use all the artifice
they can to spoil, and deny us the means of improvement. So that instead
of inquiring why all women are not wise and good, we have reason to
wonder that there are any so. Were the men as much neglected, and as
little care taken to cultivate and improve them, perhaps they would be so
far from surpassing those whom they now despise, that they themselves
would sink into the greatest stupidity and brutality. The preposterous
returns that the most of them make, to all the care and pains that is
bestowed on them, renders this no uncharitable, nor improbable conjecture. One would therefore almost think, that the wise disposer of all
things, foreseeing how unjustly women are denied opportunities of improvement from *without*, has therefore by way of compensation endowed
them with greater propensions to virtue and a natural goodness of temper
within, which if duly managed, would raise them to the most eminent
pitch of heroic virtue. Hither, Ladies, I desire you would aspire; 'tis a
noble and becoming ambition, and to remove such obstacles as lie in your
way, is the design of this paper. We will therefore inquire what it is that
stops your flight, that keeps you groveling here below, like Domitian
catching flies, when you should be busied in obtaining empires?

Although it has been said by men of more wit than wisdom, and perhaps of more malice than either, that women are naturally incapable of
acting prudently, or that they are necessarily determined to folly, I must
by no means grant it; that hypothesis would render my endeavours impertinent, for then it would be in vain to advise the one, or endeavour the
reformation of the other. Besides, there are examples in all ages, which
sufficiently confute the ignorance and malice of this assertion.

The incapacity, if there be any, is acquired, not natural, and none of
their follies are so necessary, but that they might avoid them if they
pleased themselves. Some disadvantages indeed they labour under, and
what these are we shall see by and by and endeavour to surmount; but
women need not take up with mean things, since (if they are not wanting
to themselves) they are capable of the best. Neither God nor Nature have
excluded them from being ornaments to their families, and useful in their
generation; there is therefore no reason they should be content to be
ciphers in the world, useless at the best, and in a little time a burden and
nuisance to all about them. And 'tis very great pity that they who are so
apt to over-rate themselves in smaller matters, should, where it most con-

cerns them to know and stand upon their value, be so insensible of their own worth. The cause therefore of the defects we labour under is, if not wholly, yet at least in the first place, to be ascribed to the mistakes of our education; which like an error in the first concoction, spreads its ill influence through all our lives.

The soil is rich, and would, if well cultivated, produce a noble harvest; if then the unskilful managers, not only permit, but encourage noxious weeds, tho' we shall suffer by the neglect, yet they ought not in justice to blame any but themselves, if they reap the fruit of this their foolish conduct. Women are from their very infancy debarred those advantages, with the want of which they are afterwards reproached, and nursed up in those vices which will hereafter be upbraided to them. So partial are men as to expect brick where they afford no straw; and so abundantly civil as to take care we should make good that obliging epithet of ignorant, which out of an excess of good manners, they are pleased to bestow on us!

One would be apt to think indeed, that parents should take all possible care of their children's education, not only for their sakes, but even for their own. And tho' the son convey the name to posterity, yet certainly a great part of the honour of their families depends on their daughters. 'Tis the kindness of education that binds our duty fastest on us: for the being instrumental to the bringing us into the world, is no matter of choice, and therefore the less obliging; but to procure that we may live wisely and happily in it, and be capable of endless joys hereafter, is a benefit we can never sufficiently acknowledge. To introduce poor children into the world, and neglect to fence them against the temptations of it, and so leave them exposed to temporal and eternal miseries, is a wickedness for which I want a name; 'tis beneath brutality; the beasts are better natured, for they take care of their offspring, till they are capable of caring for themselves. And, if mothers had a due regard to their posterity, how great soever they are, they would not think themselves too good to perform what nature requires, nor through pride and delicacy remit the poor little one to the care of a foster parent. Or if necessity enforce them to depute another to perform their duty, they would be as choice at least, in the manners and inclinations, as they are in the complexions of their nurses, lest with their milk they transfuse their vices, and form in the child such evil habits as will not easily be eradicated.

Nature, as bad as it is, and as much as it is complained of, is so far improveable by the grace of God, upon our honest and hearty endeavours, that if we are not wanting to ourselves, we may all in some, tho' not in an equal measure, be instruments of his glory, blessings to this world, and capable of eternal blessedness in that to come. But if our nature is spoiled, instead of being improved at first; if from our infancy we are nursed up in ignorance and vanity; are taught to be proud and petulant, delicate and fantastic, humorous and inconstant, 'tis not strange that the ill effects of this conduct appear in all the future actions of our lives. And seeing it is ignorance, either habitual or actual, which is the cause of all sin, how are they like to escape *this*, who are bred up in *that?* That therefore women are unprofitable to most, and a plague and dishonour to some men is not much to be regretted on account of the *men*, because 'tis the product of their own folly, in denying them the benefits of an ingenuous and liberal education, the most effectual means to direct them into, and to secure their progress in the ways of virtue.

For that ignorance is the cause of most feminine vices, may be instanced in that pride and vanity which is usually imputed to us, and which, I suppose if thoroughly sifted, will appear to be some way or other, the rise and original of all the rest. These, tho' very bad weeds, are the product of a good soil; they are nothing else but generosity degenerated and corrupted. A desire to advance and perfect its being, is planted by God in all rational natures, to excite them hereby to every worthy and becoming action; for certainly, next to the grace of God, nothing does so powerfully restrain people from evil and stir them up to good, as a generous temper. And therefore to be ambitious of perfections is no fault, tho' to assume the glory of our excellencies to ourselves, or to glory in such as we really have not, are. And were women's haughtiness expressed in disdaining to do a mean and evil thing, would they pride themselves in somewhat truly perfective of a rational nature, there were no hurt in it. But then they ought not to be denied the means of examining and judging what is so; they should not be imposed on with tinsel ware. If by reason of a false light, or undue medium, they choose amiss, theirs is the loss, but the crime is the deceiver's. She who rightly understands wherein the perfection of her nature consists, will lay out her thoughts and industry in the acquisition of such perfections: but she who is kept ignorant of the matter, will take up with such objects as first offer themselves, and bear any plausible resemblance to what she desires; a show of advantage being sufficient to render them agreeable baits, to her who wants judgement and skill to discern between reality and pretence. From whence it easily follows, that she who has nothing else to value her self upon, will be proud of her beauty, or money, and what that can purchase, and think herself mightily obliged to him, who tells her she has those perfections which she naturally longs for. Her inbred self-esteem and desire of good, which are degenerated into pride and mistaken self-love, will easily open her ears to whatever goes about to nourish and delight them; and when a cunning designing enemy from without, has drawn over to his party these traitors within, he has the poor unhappy person at his mercy, who now very glibly swallows down his poison, because 'tis presented in a golden cup, and credulously hearkens to the most disadvantageous proposals, because they come attended with a seeming esteem. She whose vanity makes her swallow praises by the wholesale, without examining whether she deserves them, or from what hand they come, will reckon it but gratitude to think well of him who values her so much, and think she must needs be merciful to the poor despairing lover whom her charms have reduced to die at her feet. Love and honour are what every one of us naturally esteem; they are excellent things in themselves and very worthy our regard, and by how much the readier we are to embrace whatever resembles them, by so much the more dangerous it is that these venerable names should be wretchedly abused and affixed to their direct contraries, yet this is the custom of the world: and how can she possibly detect the fallacy, who has no better notion of either than what she derives from plays and romances? How can she be furnished with any solid principles whose very instructors are froth and emptiness? Whereas women, were they rightly educated, had they obtained a well-informed and discerning mind; they would be proof against all those batteries; see through and scorn those silly artifices which are used to ensnare and deceive them. Such a one would value herself only on her virtue, and consequently be most chary of what she esteems so much. She would know, that not what others *say*, but what she her self *does*, is the true commendation and the only thing that exalts her; the loudest encomiums being not half so satisfactory, as the calm and secret plaudit of her own mind, which moving on true principles of honour and virtue, would not fail on a review of it self to anticipate that delightful eulogy she shall one day hear. . . .

Thus ignorance and a narrow education lay the foundation of vice, and imitation and custom rear it up. Custom, that merciless torrent that carries all before it, and which indeed can be stemmed by none but such as have a great deal of prudence and a rooted virtue. For 'tis but decorous that she who is not capable of giving better rules, should follow those she sees before her, least she only change the instance and retain the absurdity. 'Twould puzzle a considerate person to account for all that sin and folly that is in the world (which certainly has nothing in it self to recommend it) did not custom help to solve the difficulty. For virtue without question has on all accounts the pre-eminence of vice; 'tis abundantly more pleasant in the act, as well as more advantageous in the consequences, as anyone who will but rightly use her reason, in a serious reflection on her self and the nature of things, may easily perceive. 'Tis custom, therefore, that tyrant custom, which is the grand motive to all those irrational choices which we daily see made in the world, so very contrary to our present interest and pleasure, as [well] as to our future. We think it an unpardonable mistake not to do as our neighbours do, and part with our peace and pleasure as well as our innocence and virtue, merely in compliance with an unreasonable fashion. And having inured ourselves to folly, we know not how to quit it; we go on in vice, not because we find satisfaction in it, but because we are unacquainted with the joys of virtue.

Add to this the hurry and noise of the world, which does generally so busy and pre-engage us, that we have little time and less inclination to stand still and reflect on our own minds. Those impertinent amusements which have seized us, keep their hold so well, and so constantly buzz about our ears, that we cannot attend to the dictates of our reason, nor to the soft whispers and winning persuasives of the divine spirit, by whose assistance were we disposed to make use of it, we might shake off these follies and regain our freedom. But alas! to complete our misfortunes, by a continual application to vanity and folly, we quite spoil the contexture and frame of our minds, so loosen and dissipate, that nothing solid and substantial will stay in them. By an habitual inadvertancy we render ourselves incapable of any serious and improving thought, till our minds themselves become as light and frothy as those things they are conversant about. To all which if we further add the great industry that bad people use to corrupt the good, and that unaccountable backwardness that appears in too many good persons, to stand up for and propagate the piety they profess; (so strangely are things transposed, that virtue puts on the blushes which belong to vice, and vice insults with the authority of virtue!) and we have a pretty fair account of the causes of our non-improvement.

When a poor young lady is taught to value herself on nothing but her clothes, and to think she's very fine when well accoutred; when she hears say, that 'tis wisdom enough for her to know how to dress her self, that she may become amiable in his eyes, to whom it appertains to be knowing and learned; who can blame her if she lay out her industry and money on such accomplishments, and sometimes extends it farther than her misinformer desires she should? When she sees the vain and the gay, making parade in the world and attended with the courtship and admiration of the gazing herd, no wonder that her tender eyes are dazzled with the pageantry, and wanting judgement to pass a due estimate on them and their admirers, longs to be such a fine and celebrated thing as they! What tho' she be sometimes told of another world, she has however a more lively perception of this, and may well think, that if her instructors were in earnest when they tell her of *hereafter*, they would not be so busied and concerned about what happens *here*. She is, it may be, taught the principles and duties of religion, but not acquainted with the reasons and grounds of them, being told 'tis enough for her to believe; to examine why, and wherefore, belongs not to her. And therefore, though her piety may be tall and spreading, yet because it wants foundation and root, the first rude temptation overthrows and blasts it, or perhaps the short-lived gourd decays and withers of its own accord. But why should she be blamed for setting no great value on her soul, whose noblest faculty, her understanding, is rendered useless to her? Or censured for relinquishing a course of life, whose prerogatives she was never acquainted with, and though highly reasonable in itself, was put upon the embracing it with as little reason as she now forsakes it? For if her religion itself be taken up as the mode of the country, 'tis no strange thing that she lays it down again in conformity to the fashion. Whereas she whose reason is suffered to display itself, to inquire into the grounds and motives of religion, to make a disquisition of its graces and search out its hidden beauties; who is a Christian out of choice, not in conformity to those among whom she lives; and cleaves to piety, because 'tis her wisdom, her interest, her joy, not because she has been accustomed to it; she who is not only eminently and unmovably good, but able to give a reason *why* she is so, is too firm and stable to be moved by the pitiful allurements of sin, too wise and too well bottomed to be undermined and supplanted by the strongest efforts of temptation. Doubtless a truly Christian life requires a clear understanding as well as regular affections, that both together may move the will to a direct choice of good and a steadfast adherence to it. For tho' the heart may be honest, it is but by chance that the will is right if the understanding be ignorant and cloudy. And what's the reason that we sometimes see persons unhappily falling off from their piety, but because 'twas their affections, not their judgement, that inclined them to be religious? Reason and truth are firm and immutable; she who bottoms on them is on sure ground, humour and inclination are sandy foundations, and she who is swayed by her affections more than by her judgement, owes the happiness of her soul in a great measure to the temper of her body; her piety may perhaps blaze high but will not last long. For the affections are various and changeable, moved by every object, and the last comer easily undoes whatever its predecessor had done before. Such persons are always in extremes; they are either violently good or quite cold and indifferent, a perpetual trouble to themselves and others, by indecent raptures, or unnecessary scruples; there is no beauty and order to their lives, all is rapid and unaccountable; they are now very furious in such a course, but they cannot well tell why, and anon as violent in the other extreme. Having more heat than light, their zeal outruns their knowledge, and instead of representing piety as it is in itself, the most lovely and inviting thing imaginable, they expose it to the contempt and ridicule of the censorious world. Their devotion becomes ricketed, starved, and contracted in some of its vital parts, and disproportioned and over-grown in less material instances; whilst one duty is over-done to commute for the neglect of another, and the mistaken person thinks the being often on her knees, atones for all the miscarriages of her conversation: not considering that 'tis in vain to petition for those graces which we take no care to practise, and a mockery to adore those perfections we run counter to, and that the true end of all our prayers and external observances is to work our minds into a truly Christian temper, to obtain for us the empire of our passions, and to reduce all irregular inclinations, that so we may be as like God in purity, charity, and all his imitable excellencies, as is consistent with the imperfection of a creature.

And now having discovered the disease and its cause, 'tis proper to apply a remedy. Single medicines are too weak to cure such complicated distempers; they require a full dispensatory; and what good would a good woman refuse to do, could she hope by that to advantage the greatest part of the world, and improve her sex in knowledge and true religion? I doubt not, Ladies, but that the age, as bad as it is, affords very many of you who will readily embrace whatever has a true tendency to the glory of God and your mutual edification, [the opportunity] to revive the ancient spirit of piety in the world and to transmit it to succeeding generations. I know there are many of you who so ardently love God, as to think no time too much to spend in his service, nor anything too difficult to do for his sake; and bear such a hearty good will to your neighbours, so to grudge no prayers or pains to reclaim and improve them. I have therefore no more to do but to make the proposal, to prove that it will answer these great and good ends, and then 'twill be easy to obviate the objections that persons of more wit than virtue may happen to raise against it.

Now as to the proposal, it is to erect a monastery, or if you will (to avoid giving offence to the scrupulous and injudicious, by names which tho' innocent in themselves, have been abused by superstitious practices), we will call it a *religious retirement*, and such as shall have a double aspect, being not only a retreat from the world for those who desire that advantage, but likewise, an institution and previous discipline, to fit us to do the greatest good in it; such an institution as this (if I do not mightily deceive my self) would be the most probable method to amend the present and improve the future age. For here, those who are convinced of the emptiness of earthly enjoyments, who are sick of the vanity of the world and its impertinencies, may find more substantial and satisfying entertainments, and need not be confined to what they justly loath. Those who are desirous to know and fortify their weak side, first do good to themselves, that hereafter they may be capable of doing more good to others; or for their greater security are willing to avoid temptation, may get out of that danger which a continual stay in view of the enemy, and the familiarity and unwearied application of the temptation may expose them to; and gain an opportunity to look into themselves, to be acquainted at home and no longer the greatest strangers to their own hearts. Such as are willing in a more peculiar and undisturbed manner, to attend the great business they came into the world about, the service of God and improvement of their own minds, may find a convenient and blissful recess from the noise and hurry of the world. A world so cumbersome, so infectious, that although through the grace of God and their own strict watchfulness, they are kept from sinking down into its corruptions, 'twill however damp their flight to heaven, hinder them from attaining any eminent pitch of virtue.

You are therefore, Ladies, invited into a place where you shall suffer no other confinement, but to be kept out of the road of sin: you shall not be deprived of your grandeur, but only exchange the vain pomps and pageantry of the world, empty titles and forms of state, for the true and solid greatness of being able to despise them. You will only quit the chat of insignificant people for an ingenious conversation; the froth of flashy wit for real wisdom; idle tales for instructive discourses. The deceitful flatteries of those who under pretence of loving and admiring you, really served their *own* base ends, for the seasonable reproofs and wholesome counsels of your hearty well-wishers and affectionate friends; which will procure you those perfections your feigned lovers pretended you had, and kept you from obtaining. No uneasy task will be enjoined you, all your labour being only to prepare for the highest degrees of that glory, the very lowest of which is more than at present you are able to conceive, and the prospect of it sufficient to out-weigh all the pains of religion, were there any in it, as really there are none. All that is required of you, is only to be as happy as possibly you can, and to make sure of a felicity that will fill all the capacities of your souls! . . .

We have hitherto considered our retirement only in relation to religion, which is indeed its *main*, I may say its *only* design; nor can this be thought too contracting a word, since religion is the adequate business of our lives, and largely considered, takes in all we have to do, nothing being a fit employment for a rational creature, which has not either a *direct* or *remote* tendency to this great and *only* end. But because, as we have all along observed, religion never appears in its true beauty, but when it is accompanied with wisdom and discretion, and that without a good understanding, we can scarce be *truly*, but never *eminently* good; being liable to a thousand seductions and mistakes (for even the men themselves, if they have not a competent degree of knowledge, are carried about with every wind of doctrine). Therefore, one great end of this institution shall be, to expel that cloud of ignorance which custom has involved us in, to furnish our minds with a stock of solid and useful knowledge, that the souls of women may no longer be the only unadorned and neglected things. It is not intended that our *religious* should waste their time, and trouble their heads about such unconcerning matters as the vogue of the world has turned up for learning; the impertinency of which has been excellently exposed by an ingenious pen,* but busy themselves in a serious inquiry after *necessary* and *perfective* truths, something which it *concerns* them to know, and which tends to their real interest and perfection, and what that is the excellent author just now mentioned will sufficiently inform them. Such a course of study will neither be too troublesome nor out of the reach of a female virtuoso; for it is not intended she should spend her hours in learning *words* but *things*, and therefore no more languages than are necessary to acquaint her with useful authors. Nor need she trouble her self in turning over a great number of books, but take care to understand and digest a few well-chosen and good ones. Let her but obtain right ideas, and

---

* Mr. Nor. *Conduct of Human Life*. [Mary Astell's note. She is referring to John Norris, *Reflections upon the Conduct of Human Life* (London, 1691). In 1705, Astell published a work entitled *Letters Concerning the Love of God, Between the Author of the Proposal to the Ladies and Mr. John Norris*.]

be truly acquainted with the nature of those objects that present themselves to her mind, and then no matter whether or no she be able to tell what fanciful people have said about them, and thoroughly to understand Christianity as professed by the Church of England, will be sufficient to confirm her in the truth, though she have not a catalogue of those particular errors which oppose it. Indeed a learned education of the women will appear so unfashionable, that I began to startle at the singularity of the proposition, but was extremely pleased when I found a late ingenious author† (whose book I met with since the writing of this) agree with me in my opinion. For speaking of the repute that learning was in about 150 years ago, "It was so very modish (says he) that the fair sex seemed to believe that Greek and Latin added to their charms; and Plato and Aristotle untranslated, were frequent ornaments of their closets. One would think by the effects, that it was a proper way of educating them, since there are no accounts in history of so many great women in any one age, as are to be found between the years 15 and 1600."

For since God has given women as well as men intelligent souls, why should they be forbidden to improve them? Since he has not denied us the faculty of thinking, why should we not (at least in gratitude to him) employ our thoughts on himself, their noblest object, and not unworthily bestow them on trifles and gaieties and secular affairs? Being the soul was created for the contemplation of truth as well as for the fruition of good, is it not as cruel and unjust to preclude women from the knowledge of the one as from the enjoyment of the other? Especially since the will is blind, and cannot choose but by the direction of the understanding; or to speak more properly, since the soul always *wills* according as she understands, so that if she understands amiss, she wills amiss. And as exercise enlarges and exalts any faculty, so through want of using it becomes cramped and lessened; if therefore we make little or no use of our understandings, we shall shortly have none to use; and the more contracted and unemployed the deliberating and directive power is, the more liable is the elective to unworthy and mischievous options. What is it but the want of an ingenious education that renders the generality of feminine conversations so insipid and foolish and their solitude so insupportable? Learning is therefore necessary to render them more agreeable and useful in company, and

† Mr. Wotton's *Reflections upon Antient and Modern Learning* [Mary Astell's note. She is referring to William Wotton's book, published in 1694.]

to furnish them with becoming entertainments when alone, that so they may not be driven to those miserable shifts, which too many make use of to put off their time, that precious talent that never lies on the hands of a judicious person.

Sarah Fyge Egerton (fl. 1700)

Sarah Fyge Egerton, also sometimes known as "Mrs. Sarah Field," remains for the most part a mystery. No particulars of her birth, parentage, or childhood are extant, except for a remark she makes in a poem indicating that she had begun writing poetry at a very early age. Apparently her versifying was not well received: though the poem in question was "without design of publication writ," it nevertheless "did fatal prove,/And robbed me of a tender father's love."

In 1700 Egerton contributed three poems to a volume entitled *The Nine Muses. Or, Poems Written by Nine Several Ladies upon the Death of the Late Famous John Dryden, Esq.* The "Muses" who collaborated in this venture were Mary de la Rivière Manley, Mary Pix, Susanna Centlivre, Lady Sarah Pierce (or Piers), and Catherine Trotter (later Cockburn), in addition to Egerton, who signed herself successively "Mrs. S.F.," "Mrs. J.E.," and "Mrs. L.D." Egerton's poems were later reprinted in the volume she published in 1706, under the title *Poems upon Several Occasions.* Both Mary Pix and Susanna Centlivre contributed commendatory verses. Egerton and Mary de la Rivière Manley had quarreled the summer before when Manley had visited her in Buckinghamshire.[1]

1. Paul Bunyan Anderson, "Mistress Delariviere Manley's Biography," *Modern Philology* 33 (1935–36): 271.

Poems upon Several Occasions. London, 1706.

[Poems prefacing this edition:]

To Mrs. S.F. on Her Poems

Oh! say what happy Muse informs thy lyre,
Or do the sacred Nine, thy breast inspire;

That thus we see in each judicious line,
Nature and art in beauteous order shine,
The numbers easy and the thoughts divine.
No more let haughty man with fierce disdain,
Despise the product of a female brain,
But read thy works, there view thy spacious mind,
Thy reason clear, thy fancy unconfined;
And then be just to thy immortal fame,
And with due honours celebrate thy name.
In thy harmonious strains at once admire,
Orinda's judgement, and Astrea's fire.
Many are in poetic annals found,
Whose brows with never fading laurels bound,
For some one grace were by Apollo crowned:
Of generous friendship, this composed her song,
And that with love still charmed the listening throng.
Another in philosophy excells,
And pleasing wonders tunefully reveals;
But thou alone on every theme can'st write,
That task was left for thy superior wit.

                                        J.H.

To Mrs. S.F. on Her Poems

Hail to Clarinda, dear Euterpe hail,
Now we shall conquer, now indeed prevail;
Clarinda will her charming lines expose,
And in her strength we vanquish all our foes.
To these triumphant lays, let each repair,
A sacred sanction to the writing fair;
Mankind has long upheld the learned sway,
And tyrant custom forced us to obey.
Thought art and science did to them belong,
And to assert our selves was deemed a wrong,
But we are justified by thy immortal song:
Come ye bright nymphs a lasting garland bring,
In never fading verse, Clarinda's praises sing;
Read o're her works, see how genuine nature fires,
Observe the sweetness which her pen inspires.

From thence grow wise, from thence your thoughts improve
Here's judgement piercing sense and softer love;
To idle gaieties true wit prefer,
Strive all ye thinking fair, to copy her.

                                           M.P. [Mary Pix]

To Mrs. S.F. on Her Incomparable Poems.

Thou champion for our sex go on and show
Ambitious man what womankind can do
In vain they boast of large scholastic rules,
Their skill in arts and labour in the schools.
What various tongues and languages acquired,
How famed for policy, for wit admired;
Their solid judgement in philosophy,
The metaphysics, truths, and poetry,
Since here they'll find themselves outdone by thee.
Thy matchless thoughts, and flowing numbers sweet,
And lofty flights, in just conjunction meet;
Thy mighty genius can each subject trace,
The best can equal and to none give place.
Sappho the great, whom by report we know,
Would yield her laurels were she living now,
And strait turn chaste, to gain a friend of you:
Of you! to whom we all obedience pay,
And at your feet our humble tribute lay,
Whilst all around, your beams dart like the God of day;
We bask with pleasure in your glorious shine,
And read and wonder at your verse divine.

                                    S.C. [Susanna Centlivre]

To the Lady Cambell, with a Female Advocate.

Go, fatal book, yet happy at the last,
Since in so fair, so kind a hand thou'rt placed,
(That such a trifle, e'er should be so graced.)
But your desires, which are to me commands,
Can charm what e'er you please out of my hands;
I rather than neglect obliging you,
Expose my follies, to your nice view;

But hope your goodness, will one smile bestow,
On what my tender infant muse did do.
Scarce fourteen years, when I the piece begun,
And in less time than fourteen days 'twas done;
Without design of publication writ,
And innocence supplies the want of wit.
But ah! my poetry, did fatal prove,
And robbed me of a tender father's love;
(I thought that only men, who writ for fame,
Or sung lewd stories, of unlawful flame,
Were punished for, their proud or wanton crime.
But children too, must suffer if they'll rhyme:)
The present is but mean, which you receive,
Yet cost me more, than all the world can give,
That which I would, with life itself retrieve.
But Madam, if your goodness condescend,
And one kind minute, on this trifle spend;
It will complete my happiness at last,
And recompense for all my sorrows past.

The Liberty

Shall I be one of those obsequious fools,
That square their lives, by custom's scanty rules;
Condemned forever, to the puny curse,
Of precepts taught, at boarding-school, or nurse,
That all the business of my life must be,
Foolish, dull, trifling, formality.
Confined to a strict magic complaisance,
And round a circle, of nice visits dance,
Nor for my life beyond the chalk advance:
The Devil censure, stands to guard the same,
One step awry, he tears my ventrous fame.
So when my friends, in a factious vein,
With mirth and wit, a while can entertain;
Tho' ne'er so pleasant, yet I must not stay,
If a commanding clock, bids me away:
But with a sudden start, as in a fright,

I must be gone indeed 'tis after eight.
Sure these restraints, with such regret we bear,
That dreaded censure, can't be more severe,
Which has no terror, if we did not fear;
But let the bug-bear, timerous infants fright,
I'll not be scared, from innocent delight:
Whatever is not vicious, I dare do,
I'll never to the idol custom bow,
Unless it suits with my own humour too,
Some boast their fetters, of formality,
Fancy they ornamental bracelets be,
I'm sure they're gyves,* and manacles to me.
To their dull fulsome rules, I'd not be tied,
For all the flattery that exalts their pride:
My sex forbids, I should my silence break,
I lose my jest, cause women must not speak.
Mysteries must not be, with my search prophaned,
My closet not with books, but sweet-meats crammed,
A little china, to advance the show,
My prayer book, and seven champions, or so.
My pen, if ever used, employed must be,
In lofty themes of useful housewifery,
Transcribing old recipes of cookery:
And what is necessary 'mongst the rest,
Good cures for agues, and a cancered breast,
But I can't here, write my *Probatum est.*
My daring pen, will bolder sallies make,
And like my self, an unchecked freedom take;
Not chained to the nice order of my sex,
And with restraints my wishing soul perplex:
I'll blush at sin, and not what some call shame,
Secure my virtue, slight precarious fame.
This courage speaks me, brave 'tis surely worse,
To keep those rules, which privately we curse:
And I'll appeal, to all the formal saints,
With what reluctance they endure restraints.

* Fetters.

The Emulation

Say tyrant custom, why must we obey,
The impositions of thy haughty sway;
From the first dawn of life, unto the grave,
Poor womankind's in every state, a slave.
The nurse, the mistress, parent and the swain,
For love she must, there's none escape that pain;
Then comes the last, the fatal slavery,
The husband with insulting tyranny
Can have ill manners justified by law;
For men all join to keep the wife in awe.
Moses who first our freedom did rebuke,
Was married when he writ the Pentateuch;
They're wise to keep us slaves, for well they know,
If we were loose, we soon should make them, so.
We yield like vanquished kings whom fetters bind,
When chance of war is to usurpers kind;
Submit in form; but they'd our thoughts control,
And lay restraints on the impassive soul:
They fear we should excell their sluggish parts,
Should we attempt the sciences and arts.
Pretend they were designed for them alone,
So keep us fools to raise their own renown;
Thus priests of old their grandeur to maintain,
Cried vulgar eyes would sacred laws prophane.
So kept the mysteries behind a screen,
There homage and the name were lost had they been seen:
But in this blessed age, such freedom's given,
That every man explains the will of Heaven;
And shall we women now sit tamely by,
Make no excursions in philosophy,
Or grace our thoughts in tuneful poetry?
We will our rights in learning's world maintain,
Wit's empire, now, shall know a female reign;
Come all ye fair, the great attempt improve,
Divinely imitate the realms above:
There's ten celestial females govern wit,
And but two Gods that dare pretend to it;

And shall these finite males reverse their rules,
No, we'll be wits, and the men must be fools. . . .

[Dedication: To Charles, Lord Halifax,]

My Lord,
    Was not your affability and condescension, as conspicuous as your other
graces, I durst not presume on your protection of these trifles, some of the
first attempts of my unskilful muse. Most of the copies being writ, ere I
could write seventeen; long they lay in a neglected silence, and ne'er
designed to disturb the world; but an unlucky accident forced them to the
press, not giving time for that examination and correction, which might
have made them, (tho' a smaller) yet more worthy offering. My zeal for
your Lordship's name has ever been so great, I could not persuade my self
to pass by this opportunity, of acknowledging it to the world. . . . I hope
your Lordship is of my opinion, that where the circumstances do not make
love a crime, the confessing of it can be none. Besides, our sex is confined
to so narrow a sphere of action, that things of greater consequence seldom
fall within our notices; so that love seems the only proper theme (if any
can be so) for a woman's pen, especially at the age they were writ in; and
some of them were done at the request of friends, without any other
warmth than that of my officious muse. Excuses and encomiums are, I
think, the common business of dedications; but I have too many faults to
proceed on the first, and your Lordship too many excellencies to dare
venture on the latter. . . . These poems (except those on Mr. Dryden)
tho' writ long since, I offer to your Lordship with all their pristine bloom,
unsullied by a vulgar touch, not handed round the town for opinion and
amendments; but just snatched from their recluse in all their native rudeness and simplicity, presume for shelter from your hospitable hand. They
were never abroad before, nor e'er seen but by my own sex, some of which
have favour'd me with their compliments, and I was too much a woman to
refuse them. But, my Lord, I detain you from their ingenious lines, which
I hope will make some atonement, at least, for the ambition of publicly
owning my value for your Lordship, and for begging your protection.

Lady Mary Chudleigh (1656–1710)

Lady Mary Chudleigh was born Mary Lee in Devonshire, during the Interregnum, and married a local squire, Sir George Chudleigh. She was, it appears, bitterly disappointed in both marriage and husband, and consoled herself with literary pursuits. Lady Mary was first moved to venture into print by the much-discussed sermon on the necessity of wifely obedience delivered by the Reverend John Sprint. The sermon excited so much animosity among women that the reverend decided to defend himself by publishing the text, remarking in the preface that his villany had been much exaggerated by his "waspish accusers," and adding that he had "not met with one woman among all my accusers whose husband is able to give her the character of a dutiful and obedient wife."

Lady Mary Chudleigh answered the Reverend Mr. Sprint in a long poem entitled *The Ladies' Defence; or, "The Bride-Woman's Counseller" Answer'd* (1701). In a verse dialogue between Melissa, who speaks for the author, Sir John Brute, a misogynist, Sir William Loveall, a "defender" of women, and the offending parson, Sprint, Lady Chudleigh attacks the "slavery" of marriage. She also derides the customs that keep women ignorant and ridicules the men who are more comfortable for their being so.

After publishing *The Ladies Defence*, Lady Chudleigh brought out *Poems upon Several Occasions* in 1703, and followed with *Essays upon Several Subjects* in 1710.

The Ladies' Defence; or, "The Bride-Woman's Counseller"
Answer'd. London, 1701.

Preface to the Reader.

The book which has been the occasion of the ensuing poem, was presented to me by its author, of whom, notwithstanding he has been pleased to treat us with the utmost severity and neglect, I think my self obliged in justice to say, that he is a person of learning. What his reasons were for using us so roughly, I know not; perhaps he did it to let us see his wit, who has had the ill fortune to converse with women of ungovernable tempers, whose passions have got the ascendant of their reason; such I think cannot be too harshly treated, and the greatest kindness that can be done 'em, is to bring 'em (if 'tis possible) to the knowledge of themselves, and their duty, and by showing them their faults, endeavour to depress those towering imaginations. But 'tis hard that all should suffer for the failures and indescretions of some; that those who are willing to give up themselves entirely to the conduct of reason, who make it their study to live according to the strictest rules of virtue, and are so far from indulging themselves in their follies, that they esteem reproofs as the greatest favours that can be shown 'em, and are contented that all mankind should be judges of their actions; whom passions cannot bias, nor interest tempt, nor ill usage provoke to do or say any thing unworthy of themselves, should be ranked with criminals, and have no deference paid 'em: 'tis for their sakes alone I have made the following remarks. I have done it by way of dialogue, and those expressions which I thought would be indecent in the mouth of a Reverend Divine, are spoken by Sir John Brute, who has all the extraordinary qualifications of an accomplished husband; and to render his character complete, I have given him the religion of a wit, and the good humour of a critic. I am afraid the clergy will accuse me of atheism for making Sir John speak so irreverently of them; but before they condemn me, I beg 'em to be so just as to consider, that I do not speak my own thoughts, but what one might rationally suppose a man of his character will say on such occasions: and to prevent their having any misapprehensions of me, I do assure 'em, that for all such of their order as are pious and ingenuous men, whose conversations are instructive, and whose lives are conformable to those holy truths they teach, none can have a higher veneration than I: and if such as these find any thing in my poem that they dislike, they will oblige me in letting me know it, and I promise 'em I will retract it. Had he treated us with a little more respect, and instead of the surly sourness of a cynic, expressed himself with the good humour of an English man, and soft and endearing mildness of a Christian, I should have thought my self obliged to have returned him thanks for his instructions. That we are generally less knowing, and less rational than the men, I cannot but acknowledge; but I think 'tis oftener owing to the illness of our education, than the weakness of our capacities. The learned F. Malebranch says, " 'Tis in a certain temperature of the largeness and agitation of the animal spirits, and conformity with the fibers of the brain, that the strength of parts consists," and he tells us, that women are sometimes blessed with that just temperature, and are learned, couragious, and capable of every thing; and instead of that nauseous jargon, and those impertinent stories with which our maids usually entertain us in our younger years, taught the languages of the schools, and accustomed to the reading of histories, and books of morality; and did our husbands treat us with that kindness, that sincerity, I will not say with that respect, for fear that should be thought too much for a wife, but only with that common civility which is due to strangers, they would meet with a grateful return, and have much less reason to complain. Would the men do me the honour to take my advice, I am confident they would for the future have less occasion to complain. First, I would have them be more judicious in their choice, and prefer virtue and good sense, before either riches, beauty or quality; these, joined with an agreeable humour, will make them happier than the greatest affluence of wealth, or than all the charms of a lovely face; and if 'tis their good fortune to meet with such; I would in the second place persuade 'em to treat them with all that affection and tenderness which they deserve, and leave entirely to their management the affairs of the kitchen, and those other little concerns of the family which seem to be below their inspection. And lastly, I would have them look upon [their wives] as friends, as persons fit to be confided in, and trusted with their designs, as such whose interest is inseparably united with theirs: by such methods as these, they would not only win their love, but preserve it, and engage 'em to a reciprocal esteem; and when once they have secured their affection, they need not doubt of their obedience; the desire to please will render the most difficult commands easy. Should I give a particular answer to each paragraph, I should not only tire the reader's patience, but my own, for which reason I intend only to take notice of some very remarkable things, such as his saying, we make it our business before we are married to lay snares for hearts, and imprint, come love me, in the pleasantness of our looks, in the neatness of our dress, in the discretion of our words, in the obligingness of our deportment. Now what can be vainer than to think, that while the men are admirers of themselves, and aim at nothing but their own satisfaction, the women should be wholly destitute of self-love, and do nothing to please themselves; or that pleasantness, vivacity and cheerfulness, which are the effects of an internal joy and tranquility of mind, should continue when the cause ceases? Perhaps before they were married, they had nothing to discompose them, no cares to disturb their thoughts, no unkindness to resent, nothing to pall their delights; but now the case may be altered; they may meet with a thousand discouragements, with troubles capable of altering the gayest temper. . . .

There is one thing which I think does more contribute to the unhappiness of the married state, than any of those which he has mentioned, and that is, parents forcing their children to marry contrary as they please; and they think it below them to consult their satisfaction: 'tis no matter what their thoughts are, if the fathers like, 'tis enough: and is it rational enough to suppose, that such matches can ever be fortunate? If the men were prudent, they will carry it civilly to their wives; and the women if they are discreet, will be obsequious and respectful to their husbands, but there cannot be that friendship, that tenderness, that unity of affection which ought to be in that sacred state. I could say much more on so copious a subject, but I fear I have already wearied my reader, to whose trouble I will not add, by making trifling apologies for what I have written: the liberty I take, I am willing to give, and the ingenious author may, if he pleases, animadvert as freely on my book, as I have done on his. . . .

[A dialogue between Sir John Brute, Sir William Loveall, Melissa, and a Parson.]

Sir John. Welcome, thou brave defender of our right;
'Till now, I thought you knew not how to write:
Dull heavy morals did your pens employ;
And all your business was to pall our joy:
With frightful tales our ears you still did grate,
And we with awful reverence heard you prate;
Heard you declaim on vice, and blame the times,
Because we impudently shared your crimes;
Those darling sins you wholly would engross:
And when disturbed, and fretting at your loss,
With whining tomes, and a pretended zeal,
Saw you the rancour of your mind reveal:
'Till now, none of your tribe [was] ever kind,
Good humour is alone to you confined;
You, who against those terrours of our lives,
Those worst of plagues, those furies called our wives,
Have showed your anger in a strain divine,
Resentment sparkles in every line.

Sure you've the fate of wretched husbands met,
And 'tis your own misfortune you regret;
You could not else with such a feeling sense
Expatiate on each fault, and blazon each offence. . . .

Parson: Not led by passion, but by zeal inspired,
I've told the women what's of them required:
Showed them their duty in the clearest light,
Adorned with all the charms that could invite:
Taught them their husband to obey and please,
And to their humours sacrifice their ease:
Give up their reason, and their wills resign,
And every look, and every thought confine.
Sure, this, detraction you can't justly call?
'Tis kindly meant, and addressed to all.

Melissa: Must men command, and we alone obey,
As if designed for arbitrary sway?
Born petty monarchs, and like Homer's Gods,
See all subjected to their haughty nods?
Narcissus-like, you your own graces view,
Think none deserve to be admired but you:
Your own perfections you adore,
And think all others despicably poor. . . .
But unto us is there no deference due?
Must we pay all, and look for none from you?
Why are not husbands taught as well as we;
Must they from all restraints, all laws be free?
Passive obedience you've to us transferred,
And we must drudge in paths where you have erred:
That antiquated doctrine you disown;
'Tis now your scorn, and fit for us alone.

Parson: Love and respect, are, I must own, your due,
But not 'till there's obedience paid by you:
Submission, and a studious care to please,
May give a right to favours great as these:
But if subjection is by you denied,
You'll fall the unpitied victims of your pride:
We then all husband justly may appear,
And talk, and frown, 'till we have taught [you] fear.

Sir John: Yes, as we please, we may your wives chastise,
'Tis the prerogative of being wise:
They are but fools, and must as such be used.
Heaven! how I blush to see our power abused:
To see men dote upon a female face,
And all the manly roughness of their sex disgrace! . . .
I loved [my wife], 'till to her I was confined,
But who can long to what's his own be kind?
Melissa: There spoke the husband; all the fiend revealed:
Your passion utters what's by most concealed.
O that my sex safe infidels would live,
And no more credit to your flatteries give.
Mistrust your vows, despise your little arts,
And keep a constant guard upon their hearts.
Unhappy they, who by their duty led,
Are made the partners of a hated bed;
And by their fathers' avarice or pride,
To empty fops, or nauseous clowns are tied;
Or else constrained to give up all their charms
Into an old ill-humoured husband's arms,
Who hugs his bags, and never was inclined
To be to aught besides his money kind.
On that he dotes, and to increase his wealth,
Would sacrifice his conscience, ease and health,
Give up his children, and devote his wife,
And live a stranger to the joys of life.
Who's always positive in what is ill,
And still a slave to his imperious will:
Averse to anything he thinks will please,
Still sick, and still in love with his disease:
With fears, with discontent, with envy cursed,
To all uneasy, and himself the worst. . . .
Parson: Why all this rage? we merit not your hate,
'Tis you alone disturb the marriage state.
If to your Lords you strict allegiance paid,
And their commands submissively obeyed,
If like wise eastern slaves with trembling awe
You watched their looks, and made their will your law,

You would both kindness and protection gain,
And find your duteous care was not all in vain. . . .
If we are cruel, [women] have made us so;
Whatever they suffer, to themselves they owe:
Our love on their obedience does depend,
We will be kind, when they no more offend.

Melissa: Of our offenses who shall judges be?

Parson: For that great work Heaven has commissioned me. . . .
I'll prove your duty from the law divine,
Celestial truth in my discourse shall shine. . . .
Unhappy Eve unto her ruin led,
Tempted by pride, on the bright poison fed.
Then to her thoughtless husband gave a part,
He ate, seduced by her bewitching art.
And 'twas but just that for so great a fault
She should be to a strict subjection brought:
So strict, her thoughts should no more be her own,
But all subsurvient made to him alone. . . .
With all your patience, all your toil and art,
You scarce can keep the surly husband's heart.
Your kindness hardly can esteem create. . . .
If you would live as it becomes a wife,
And raise the honour of a married life,
You must the useful art of wheedling try,
And with his various humours still comply.
Admire his wit, praise all that he does do,
And when he's vexed, do you be pettish too;
When he is sad, a cloudy aspect wear,
And talk to him with a dejected air:
When rage transports him, be as mad as he,
And when he's pleased, be easy, gay and free.
You'll find this method will effectual prove,
Enhance your merit, and secure his love. . . .
And now [addressing the gentlemen] if you dare try a married state,
You'll have no reason to accuse your fate,
Since I have told 'em, if they'll be good wives,
They must submit, and flatter all their lives.
You, who already drag the nuptial chain,
Will now have no occasion to complain,

Since they beyond their sphere no more will tower,
But for the future own your sovereign power:
And being endued by this advice of mine,
To you their sense and liberty resign:
Turn fools and slaves, that they the more may please. . . .
Melissa: 'Tis hard we should be by the men despised,
Yet kept from knowing what would make us prized:
Debarred from knowledge, banished from the schools,
And with the utmost industry bred fools.
Laughed out of reason, jested out of sense,
And nothing left but native innocence:
Then we are told we are incapable of wit,
And only for drudgeries fit,
Made slaves to serve their luxury and pride,
And with innumerable hardships tried. . . .
Sir William: Had you the learning you so much desire,
You, sure, would nothing, but yourselves admire:
All our addresses would be then in vain,
And we no longer in your hearts should reign:
Sighs would be lost, and ogles cast away,
You'd laugh at all we do, and all we say.
No courtship then durst by the beaux be made
To anything above a chamber maid. . . .
Then blame us not if we our interest mind,
And would have knowledge to ourselves confined,
Since that alone pre-eminence does give,
And robbed of it we should unvalued live.
While you are ignorant, we are secure,
A little pain will your esteem procure.
Nonsense well clothed will pass for solid sense,
And well pronounced, for matchless eloquence,
Boldness for learning, and a foreign air,
For nicest breeding, with the admiring fair.
Sir John: By heaven, I wish 'twere by the laws decreed,
They never more should be allowed to read. . . .
Women were not for this province made,
And should not our prerogative invade;
What e'er they know should be from us conveyed:

We their preceptors and their guides should prove,
And teach them what to hate, and what to love. . . .

Sir William: Madam, since we none of your beauty share,
You should content yourselves with being fair:
That is a blessing, much more great, than all
That we can wisdom, or can science call.
Such beauteous faces, such bewitching eyes,
Who would not more than musty authors prize? . . .

Melissa: Beauty's a trifle merits not my care.
I'd rather Aesop's ugly visage wear,
Joined with his mind, than be a fool, and fair.
Brightness of thought, and an extensive view
Of all the wonders nature has to show;
So clear, so strong, and so enlarged a sight
As can pierce through the gloomy shades of night. . . .
But do not think 'tis an ambitious heat,
To you I'll leave the being rich and great:
Yours be the fame, the profit and the praise;
We'll neither rob you of your vines, nor Bays:
Nor will we to dominion once aspire;
You shall be chief, and still yourselves admire.
The tyrant man may still possess the throne,
'Tis in our minds that we would rule alone.
Those unseen empires give us leave to sway,
And to our reason private homage pay:
Our struggling passion within bounds confine,
And to our thoughts their proper tasks assign,
This, is the use we would of knowledge make.
You quickly would the good effects partake.
Our conversations it would soon refine,
And in our words, and in our actions shine:
And by a powerful influence on our lives,
Make us good friends, good neighbours and good wives. . . .
But you our humble suit will still decline;
To have us wise was never your design:
You'll keep us fools, that we may be your jest;
They who know least, are ever treated best.
If we do well, with care it is concealed;
But every errour, every fault's revealed:

While to each other you still partial prove,
Can see no failures, and even vices love. . . .
'Tis we alone hard measure still must find;
But spite of you, we'll to ourselves be kind:
Your censures slight, your little tricks despise,
And make it our whole business to be wise.
The mean, low trivial cares of life disdain,
And read and think, and think and read again,
And on our minds bestow the utmost pain.
Our souls with strictest morals we'll adorn,
And all your little arts of wheedling scorn,
Be humble, mild, forgiving, just and true,
Sincere to all, respectful unto you,
While as becomes you, sacred truths you teach,
And live those sermons you to others preach.
With want of duty none shall us upbraid,
Where e'er 'tis due, it shall be nicely paid.
Honour and love we'll to our husbands give,
And ever constant and obedient live:
If they are ill, we'll try by gentle ways
To lay those tempests which their passions raise;
But if our soft submissions are in vain,
We'll bear our fate, and never once complain.
Unto our friends the tenderest kindness show,
Be wholly theirs, no separate interest know:
With them their dangers and their suff'rings share,
And make their persons, and their fame our care.
The poor we'll feed, to the distressed be kind,
And strive to comfort each afflicted mind.
Visit the sick, and try their pains to ease;
Not without grief the meanest wretch displease:
And by a goodness as diffused as light,
To the pursuit of virtue all invite.
Thus will we live, regardless of your hate,
Till re-admitted to our former state;
Where, free from the confinement of our clay
In glorious bodies we shall bask in day,
And with enlightened minds new scenes survey.

Scenes, much more bright than any here below,
And we shall then the whole of nature know;
See all her springs, her secret turnings view,
And be as knowing, and as wise as you.
With generous spirits of a make divine,
In whose blessed minds celestial virtues shine,
Whose reason, like their station, is sublime,
And who see clearly through the mists of time,
Those puzzling glooms where busy mortals stray,
And still grope on, but never find their way.

Poems upon Several Occasions, London, 1703.

To the Ladies

Wife and servant are the same,
But only differ in the name:
For when that fatal knot is tied,
Which nothing, nothing can divide.
When the word *obey* has said,
And man by law supreme has made,
Then all that's kind is laid aside,
And nothing left but state and pride:
Fierce as an eastern prince he grows,
And all his innate rigour shows:
Then but to look, to laugh, or speak,
Will the nuptial contract break.
Like mutes she signs alone must make,
And never any freedom take:
But still be governed by a nod,
And fear her husband as her God:
Him still must serve, him still obey,
And nothing act, and nothing say,
But what her haughty Lord thinks fit,
Who with the power, has all the wit.
Then shun, oh! shun that wretched state,
And all the fawning flatterers hate.

Value yourselves, and men despise,
You must be proud, if you'll be wise.

To Clorissa

1.

To your loved bosom pleased Marissa flies;
That place where sacred friendship gives a right,
And where ten thousand charms invite.
Let others power and awful greatness prize;
Let them exchange their innocence and fame
For the dear purchase of a mighty name:
Let greedy wretches hug their darling store,
The tempting product of their toils adore,
And still with anxious souls, desire and grasp at more:
While I disdain to have my bliss confined
To things which fortune can bestow, or take,
To things so foreign to the mind,
And which no part of solid pleasure make:
Those joys of which I am possessed,
Are safely lodged within my breast,
Where like deep waters, undisturbed they flow,
And as they pass, a glassy smoothness show:
Unmoved by storms, or by the attacks of fate,
I envy none, nor wish a happier state.

2.

When all alone in some belov'd retreat,
Remote from noise, from business, and from strife,
Those constant cursed attendants of the great;
I freely can with my own thoughts converse,
And clothe them in ignoble verse,
'Tis then I taste the most delicious feast of life:
There, uncontrolled I can my self survey,
And from observers free,
My intellectual powers display.
And all the opening scenes of beauteous nature see:
Form bright ideas, and enrich my mind,
Enlarge my knowledge, and each error find;

Inspect each action, every word dissect,
And on the failures of my life reflect:
Then from my self, to books, I turn my sight,
And there, with silent wonder and delight,
Gaze on the instructive venerable dead. . . .

Anne Finch, Countess of Winchilsea (1661–1720)

Anne Kingsmill was born into an old and respected family in Hampshire. Both parents died when she was still very young, leaving her under the care of a stepfather. In 1683 she went to court as a maid of honor to Mary of Modena. There she met Heneage Finch and, in 1684, married him. She was twenty-three, but preferred to record her age on the marriage license as "about eighteen."

The Finches were exiled from court with the departure of James II, and wandered about without financial resource for a time before receiving an invitation from Heneage's nephew, the Earl of Winchilsea, to settle at the family estate in Kent. After his nephew's death in 1712, Heneage inherited the estate and title, and became the lord of Eastwell. Though they were no longer attached to the Kentish countryside out of financial necessity, the Earl and Countess of Winchilsea had become increasingly fond of the pleasures of rural life and chose to remain in semiretirement. The Earl took great pride in his wife's literary accomplishments, and together they established a lively literary coterie at Eastwell Park.

London society regarded Lady Winchilsea's poetic accomplishments with less enthusiasm than her husband and friends. She was pilloried savagely in a satire called *Three Hours after Marriage*, produced at Drury Lane Theatre in January 1717. It appeared under the name of "Gay," but was commonly known to have been jointly written with Pope. Lady Winchilsea, under the guise of Phoebe Clinket, made her entrance in an ink-stained dress, with pens stuck in her hair. She was accompanied by a maid carrying a desk strapped to her back, ready in case her mistress should be inspired to versify.

Phoebe Clinket is portrayed as hungry for publicity to further her literary career, but the real Lady Winchilsea left much of her work unpublished, printing only one volume of verse, *Miscellany Poems on Several Occasions, Written by a Lady* (1713) in her lifetime.

Miscellany Poems on Several Occasions, Written by a Lady.
London, 1713.

To Mr. F Now Earl of W. *
Who Going Abroad, Had Desired Ardelia† to Write Some Verses upon
Whatever Subject She Thought Fit, Against His Return, in the Evening
Written in the Year 1689

No sooner, Flavio, was you gone,
But, your injunction thought upon,
   Ardelia took the pen;
Designing to perform the task,
Her Flavio did so kindly ask,
   Ere he returned again.

Unto Parnassus strait she sent,
And bid the messenger, that went
   Unto the Muses' court,
Assure them, she their aid did need,
And begged they'd use their utmost speed,
   Because time was short.

The hasty summons was allow'd;
And being well-bred, they rose and bow'd,
   And said, they'd post away;
That well they did Ardelia know,
And that no female's voice below
   They sooner would obey:

That many of that rhyming train,
On like occasions, sought in vain
   Their industry t'excite;
But for Ardelia all they'd leave:
Thus flatt'ring can the Muse deceive.
   And wheedle us to write.

* Mr. Finch, now Earl of Winchilsea.
† The Countess of Winchilsea's "literary" name.

Yet, since there was such haste requir'd;
To know the subject was desir'd,
　　On which they must infuse;
That they might temper words and rules,
And with their counsel carry tools,
　　As country-doctors use.

Wherefore to cut off all delays,
'Twas soon reply'd, a husband's praise
　　(Tho' in these looser times)
Ardelia gladly would rehearse
A husband's, who indulging her verse,
　　And now required her rhymes.

A husband! echo'd all around:
And to Parnassus sure that sound
　　Had never been sent;
Amazement in each face was read,
In haste th'affrighted sisters fled,
　　And unto council went.

Erato cried, since Grizel's‡[sic] days,
Since Troy-town pleased, and Chivey-chace[sic],*
　　No such design was known;
And 'twas their business to take care,
It reached not to the public ear,
　　Or got about the town. . . .

The Introduction

Did I, my lines intend for public view,
How many censures, would their faults persue,
Some would, because such words they do affect,
Cry they're insipid, empty, uncorrect.
And many, have attained, dull and untaught
The name of wit, only by finding fault.
True judges, might condemn their want of wit,
And all might say, they're by a woman writ.

‡ Patient Griselda, model wife.
* "Chevy Chase," a ballad.

Alas! a woman that attempts the pen,
Such an intruder on the rights of men,
Such a presumptuous creature, is esteemed,
The fault, can by no virtue be redeemed.
They tell us, we mistake our sex and way;
Good breeding, fashion, dancing, dressing, play
Are the accomplishments we should desire,
To write, or read, or think or to inquire
Would cloud our beauty, and exhaust our time,
And interrupt the conquests of our prime;
Whilst the dull manage, of a servile house
Is held by some, our utmost art, and use.

Sure 'twas not ever thus, nor are we told
Fables of women that excelled of old. . . .
How are we fall'n, fall'n by mistaken rules?
And education's, more than nature's fools,
Debarred from all improvements of the mind,
And to be dull, expected and designed;
And if some one would soar above the rest,
With warmer fancy, and ambition pressed,
So strong, th' opposing faction still appears,
The hopes to thrive, can ne're outweigh the fears,
Be cautioned then my Muse, and still retired;
Nor be despised, aiming to be admired;
Conscious of wants, still with contracted wing,
To some few friends, and to thy sorrows sing;
For groves of Laurel, thou wert never meant;
Be dark enough thy shades, and be thou there content.

The Unequal Fetters

Could we stop the time that's flying
  Or recall it when 'tis past
Put far off the day of dying
  Or make youth for ever last
To love would then be worth our cost.

But since we must lose those graces
    Which at first your hearts have won
And you seek for in new faces
    When our spring of life is done
It would but urge our ruin on.

Free as nature's first intention
    Was to make us, I'll be found
Nor by subtle man's invention
    Yield to be in fetters bound
By one that walks a freer round.

Marriage does but slightly tie men
    Whilst close prisoners we remain
They the larger slaves of Hymen
    Still are begging love again
At the full length of their chain.

The Preface

Beaumont in the beginni[n]g of a copy of verses to his friend Fletcher (upon the ill success of his faithful shepherdess) tells him,

I know too well! that no more, than the man
That travels through the burning deserts, can
When he is beaten with the raging sun,
Half smothered in the dust, have power to run
From a cool river, which himself doth find,
E're he be slacked; no more can he, whose mind
Joys in the Muses, hold from that delight,
When nature, and his full thoughts, bid him write.

And this indeed, I not only find true by my own experience, but have also too many witnesses of it against me, under my own hand in the following poems; which though never meriting more than to be once read, and then carelessly scattered or consumed, are grown by the partiality of some of my friends, to the formidable appearance of a volume, though but in manuscript, and have been solicited to a more daring manifestation, which I shall ever resist, both from the knowledge of their incapacity of bearing a public trial; and also, upon recalling to my memory, some of the first lines I ever writ, which were part of an invocation of Apollo, whose wise and limited answer to me, I did there suppose to be

> I grant thee no pretence to Bays,
> Nor in bold print do thou appear;
> Nor shalt thou reach Orinda's praise,
> Though all thy aim, be fixed on her.

And tho' I have still avoided the confident producing [of] anything of mine in that manner, yet have I come too near it, and been like those imperfect penitents, who are ever relenting, and yet ever returning to the same offences. For I have writ, and exposed my uncorrect rhymes, and immediately repented; and yet have writ again, and again suffered them to be seen; tho' at the expense of more uneasy reflections, till at last (like them) wearied with uncertainty, and irresolution, I rather choose to be hardened in an error, than to be still at the trouble of endeavouring to overcome it: and now, neither deny myself the plesure of writing, or any longer make a mystery of that to my friends and acquaintance, which does so little deserve it; tho' it is still a great satisfaction to me, that I was not so far abandoned by my prudence, as out of a mistaken vanity, to let any attempts of mine in poetry, show themselves whilst I lived in such a public place as the court, where everyone would have made their remarks upon a versifying maid of honour; and far the greater number with prejudice, if not contempt. And indeed, the apprehension of this, had so much weaned me from the practice and inclination to it, that had not an utter change in my condition and circumstances, removed me into the solitude and secu-rity of the country, and the generous kindness of one that possessed the most delightful seat in it, invited him, from whom I was inseparable, to partake of the pleasures of it, I think I might have stopped ere it was too late, and suffered those few compositions I had then by me, to have sunk into that oblivion, which I ought to wish might be the lot of all that have succeeded them. But when I came to Eastwell,† and could fix my eyes only upon objects naturally inspiring soft and poetical imaginations, and found the owner of it so indulgent to that art, so knowing in all the rules of it, and at his pleasure, so capable of putting them in practice; and also most obligingly favourable to some lines of mine that had fallen under his Lordship's perusal, I could no longer keep within the limits I had pre-scribed my self, nor be wisely reserved, inspite of inclination, and such

† The Earl of Winchilsea's estate near Wye, Kent.

powerful temptations to the contrary. Again I engage my self in the service of the Muses, as eagerly as if

> From their new worlds, I know not where,
> Their golden Indies in the air—

they could have supplied the material losses, which I had lately sustained in this. And now, whenever I contemplate all the several beauties of this park, allowed to be (if not of the universal yet) of our British world, infinitely the finest,

> A pleasing wonder through my fancy moves,
> Smooth as her lawns, and lofty as her groves.
> Boundless my genius seems, when my free sight,
> Finds only distant skies to stop her flight.
> Like mighty Denham's, then, methinks my hand,
> Might bid the landskip, in strong numbers stand,
> Fix all its charms, with a poetic skill,
> And raise its fame, above his Cooper's hill.

This, I confess, is what in itself it deserves; but the unhappy difference is that he, by being a real poet, could make that place (as he says) a Parnassus to him; whilst I, that behold a real Parnassus here, in that lovely hill, which in this park bears that name, find in my self so little of the poet, that I am still restrained from attempting a description of it in verse, tho' the agreeableness of the subject, has often prompted me most strongly to it.

But now, having pleaded an irresistible impulse as my excuse for writing, which was the chief design of this preface, I must also express my hopes of escaping all suspicion of vanity, or affectation of applause from it; since I have in my introduction, delivered my sincere opinion that when a woman meddles with things of this nature,

> So strong, the opposing faction still appears,
> The hopes to thrive, can ne're outweigh the fears.

And, I am besides sensible that poetry has been of late so explained, the laws of it being put into familiar languages, that even those of my sex, (if they will be so presumptuous as to write) are very accountable for their transgressions against them. For what rule of Aristotle, or Horace is there

that has not been given us by Rapin,‡ Despreaux,* Dacier,† my Lord
Roscommon, etc.? What has Mr. Dryden omitted, that may lay open the
very mysteries of this art? And can there any where be found a more
delightsome, or more useful piece of poetry, than that,

correct Essay,
Which so repairs, our old Horatian way.

If then, after the perusal of these, we fail, we cannot plead any want, but
that of capacity, or care, in both of which I own myself so very defective,
yet whenever any things of mine escape a censure, I always attribute it to
the good nature or civility of the reader; and not to any merit in the
poems, which I am satisfied are so very imperfect, and uncorrect, that I
shall not attempt their justification.

For the subjects, I hope they are at least inoffensive; tho' sometimes
[they treat] of love; [as] for keeping within those limits which I have
observed, I know not why it should be more faulty, to treat of that passion,
than of any other violent excursion, or transport of the mind. Though I
must confess, the great reservedness of Mrs. Philips‡ in this particular,
and the praises I have heard given her upon that account, together with
my desire not to give scandal to the most severe, has often discouraged me
from making use of it, and given me some regret for what I had writ of
that kind, and wholly prevented me from putting the *Aminta* of Tasso
into English verse, from the verbal translation that I procured out of the
Italian, after I had finished the first act extremely to my satisfaction; and
was convinced, that in the original, it must be as soft and full of beauties,
as ever anything of that nature was; but there being nothing mixed with it,
of a serious morality, or usefulness, I sacrificed the pleasure I took in it, to
the more solid reasonings of my own mind; and hope by so doing to have
made an attonement, to my gravest readers, for the two short pieces of
that pastoral, (taken from the French), the songs, and other few lighter
things, which yet remain in the following sheets.

As to lampoons, and all sorts of abusive verses, I ever so much detested
both the underhanded dealing and uncharitableness which accompanies
them, that I never suffered my small talent, to be that way employed;

‡ Nicolas Rapin (1540–1608), a poet of the school of Ronsard.
* Nicolas Boileau-Despréaux (1636–1711), the French writer usually referred to as
"Boileau."
† Mme. Dacier, née Anne Lefebvre (c. 1654–1720), a learned Hellenist and Latinist.
‡ Katherine Philips.

though the facility of doing it, is too well known to many, who can but make two words rhyme; and there wants not some provocation often, either from one's own resentments, or those of others, to put such upon it, as are any way capable of that mean sort of revenge. The only copy of mine that tends towards this, is the letter to Ephelia, in answer to an invitation to the town; but, as that appears to have been long written [i.e. written earlier], by the mention made of my Lord Roscommon under the name of Piso, given to him first in a panegyric of Mr. Waller's, before his Art of Poetry; so I do declare, that at the time of composing it, there was no particular person meant by any of the disadvantageous characters; and the whole intention of it, was in general to expose the censorious humour, foppishness and coquetterie that then prevailed. And I am so far from thinking there is any ill in this, that I wish it oftener done, by such hands as might sufficiently ridicule, and wean us from those mistakes in our manners, and conversation.

Plays, were translated by our most virtuous Orinda; and mine, tho' originals, I hope are not less reserved. The *Queen of Cyprus*, I once thought to have called the *Triumphs of Love and Innocence;* and doubted not but the latter part of the title, would have been as aptly applied as the former. *Aristomenes* is wholly tragical, and if it answer my intention, moral and inciting to virtue. What they are as to the performance, I leave to the judgement of those who shall read them; and if any one can find more faults than I think to be in [them], I am much mistaken. I will only add, that when they were composed, it was far from my intention ever to own them, the first was for my own private satisfaction, only an essay whether I could go through with such a piece of poetry. The other, I was led to, by the strong impressions, which some wonderful circumstances in the life of Aristomenes, made upon my fancy; and chiefly the sweetness of his temper, observable in it, wrought upon me; for which reason, though it may be I did not so poeticaly, I chose rather to represent him good, than great; and pitched upon such parts of relation, and introduced such additional circumstances of my own, as might most illustrate that, and show him to be (as declared by the Oracle) the best of men. I know not what effect they will have upon others, but I must acknowledge, that the giving some interruption to those melancholy thoughts which possessed me, not only for my own, but much more for the misfortunes of those to whom I owe all immaginable duty, and gratitude, was so great a benefit, that I have reason to be satisfied with the undertaking, be the performance never

so inconsiderable. And indeed, an absolute solitude (which often was my
lot) under such dejection of mind, could not have been supported, had I
indulged myself (as was too natural to me) only in the contemplation of
present and real afflictions, which I hope will plead my excuse, for turning
them for relief, upon such as were imaginary, and relating to persons no
more in being. I had my end in the writing, and if they please not those
who still take the pains to peruse them, it will be a just accusation to my
weakness, for letting them escape out of their concealment; but if attended with a better success, the satisfaction any friend of mine, may take
in them, will make me think my time past, not so unprofitably bestowed,
as otherwise I might; and which I shall now endeavour to redeem, by
applying myself to better employments, and when I do write, to choose
my subjects generally out of divinity or from moral and serious occasions;
which made me place them last, as capable of addition; for when we have
run through all the amusements of life, it will be found, that there is but
one thing necessary; and they only wise, who choose the better part. But
since there must be also some relaxation, some entertaining of the spirits,

> Whilst life by fate is lent to me,
> Whilst here below, I stay,
> Religion, my sole business be,
> And poetry, my play.

The Apology

'Tis true I write and tell me by what rule
I am alone forbid to play the fool
To follow through the Groves a wand'ring Muse
And fained ideas for my pleasures choose
Why should it in my pen be held a fault
Whilst Mira paints her face, to paint a thought
Whilst Lamia to the manly Bumper flys
And borrowed spirits sparkle in her eyes
Why should it be in me a thing so vain
To heat with poetry my colder brain
But I write ill and there-fore should forbear
Does Flavia cease now at her fortieth year
In ev'ry place to let that face be seen
Which all the town rejected at fifteen

Each woman has her weakness; mind *[sic]* indeed
Is still to write tho' hopeless to succeed
Nor to the men is this so easy found
Ev'n in most works with which the wits abound
(So weak are all since our first breach with Heav'n)
There's less to be applauded than forgiven.

Elizabeth Singer Rowe (1674–1737)

Elizabeth Singer Rowe was born on September 11, 1674, at Ilchester, Somerset. Her father, a Nonconformist minister, had first met her mother while in prison for his religious beliefs—she was then engaged in the charitable practice of calling on prisoners. Elizabeth's mother died while she was still quite young, however, and she was brought up by her adoring father. Though he gave her a rigorous religious education, he also encouraged her early interest in music, drawing, and poetry, hiring masters to teach her in those disciplines. By the age of twelve, she was writing verse with great enthusiasm, and at twenty-two published a volume entitled *Poems on Several Occasions, Written by Philomena* (1696). The work was introduced by a friend named Elizabeth Johnson, who protested that men "would monopolise sense," and furthermore deny women learning, "nor so much as wit must be allowed us, but all overruled by the tyranny of the prouder sex. . . ." She goes on to argue for women's innate capacities, citing precedents for feminine literary achievement in Sappho, Anna van Schurman, Katherine Philips ("Orinda"), and Aphra Behn. This strongly feminist preface closes by reaffirming that the verses that followed had indeed been written "by a young lady . . . whose name had been prefixed had not her own modesty absolutely forbidden it."

Though anonymous, the work was widely known to belong to Elizabeth Singer, and she developed a large circle of admirers, including Lord Weymouth, Bishop Ken, Dr. Isaac Watts, and Matthew Prior, who proposed marriage and was turned down by her. In 1708 she fell in love with a man thirteen years her junior, and married him the next year. Like her father, Thomas Rowe stood in awe of Elizabeth's literary abilities, and gave her versifying great support and encouragement. He himself had been a child prodigy, a brilliant student in the classics, and a well-known scholar even in his early twenties. The marriage was apparently an extremely happy one, but lasted only five years. When Thomas Rowe died in 1715 of consumption, Elizabeth Singer Rowe retired to the country, devot-

ing herself to grief, prayer, literary work, and a voluminous correspondence. Her earlier enthusiasm for poetry was overshadowed by
works with a religious underpinning. She was particularly taken with
the question of death; her *Friendship in Death, in Twenty Letters
from the Dead to the Living* (1728) underwent several editions in
her lifetime, and many more into the nineteenth century.

After her death in 1737, Mrs. Rowe's *Miscellaneous Works in
Prose and Verse* were published in two volumes, with an account of
her life written by her brother-in-law, Theophilius Rowe, and her
husband's verses printed in an appendix.

Poems on Several Occasions, Written by Philomena. London, 1696.

Verses to the Author, Known Only by Report, and by Her Poems.

No—'tis in vain—attempt not to persuade!
They were not, could not be by woman made:
Each thought so strong, so finished every line,
All o'er we see so rich a genius shine;
O more than man, we cry, O workmanship divine!
Courtly thy style as Waller's! clear, and neat,
Not Cowley's sense more beautiful, or great:
Num'rous the verse, as Dryden's flowing strain,
Smooth as the Thames, yet copious as the man.
   But when the author Royal Mary mourns,
Or in soft fires for gay Orestes burns,
Again, our sex's pride is undeceived:
A soul so soft in man yet never lived.
In vain, alas! in vain our fate we shun;
We read, and sigh, and love, and are undone:
Circean charms, and female arts we prove,
Transported all to some new world of love.
Now our ears tingle, and each thick-drawn breath
Comes hard, as in the agonies of death:
Back to the panting heart the purple rivers flow,
Our swimming eyes to see, our feet unlearn to go:
In every trembling nerve, a short-lived palsy reigns,
Strange fevers boil our blood, yet shudder through our veins.

Tyrannous charmer hold! our sense, our souls restore!
Monopolise not love, nor make the world adore!
Can heavenly minds be angry! can she frown?
What thunders has one eager thought pulled down?
Diana thus by the bold hunter found,
Instead of darts, shot angry blushes round.
O Goddess spare—all white as Cypria's Dove
Is thy untarnished soul, and loves as angels love;
Honour and virtue each wild wish repell,
And doubly sink 'em to their native Hell.
Saints may by thee, their holiest thoughts refine,
And Vestal Virgins dress their souls by thine.
Sure none but thee such passion can restrain;
None ever loved like thee, and loved in vain.
What age can equal, what historian find
Such tenderness, with so much duty joined?
Sappho and Behn reformed, in thee revive,
In thee we see the chaste Orinda live.
Thy works express thy soul, we read thee there,
Not thine own pencil draws more like, or fair.
As flowers steal unobserved from nature's bed,
And silent sweets around profusely shed,
So you in secret shades unknown, unseen
Commence at once a Muse, and heroine.
Yet you're in vain unknown, in vain would shroud
That sun, which shines too bright t'endure a cloud.
    Prepare then for that fame which you despise!
But when you're seen, still hide, O hide your eyes!
Love virtue, and adorn it! still let's see
Such wit and beauty joined with piety. . . .

To the Reader:

    The occasion of this preface, is to give the world some account of the
author of these poems, as far as I am permitted to do it: an employment I
the more willingly choose, because our sex has some excuse for a little
vanity, when they have so good reason for it, and such a champion among
themselves, as not many of the other can boast.

We are not unwilling to allow mankind the brutal advantages of strength; they are superior to ours in force, they have custom on their side, and have ruled, and are like to do so; and may freely do it without disturbance or envy; at least they should have none from us, if they could keep quiet among themselves. But when they would monopolise sense too, when neither that, nor learning, nor so much as wit must be allowed us, but all overruled by the tyranny of the prouder sex; nay, when some of them will not let us say our souls are our own, but would persuade us we are no more reasonable creatures than themselves, or their fellow-animals; we then must ask their pardons if we are not yet so completely passive as to bear all without so much as a murmur. We complain, and we think with reason, that our fundamental constitutions are destroyed; that here is a plain and an open design to render us mere slaves, perfect Turkish wives, without properties, or sense, or souls; and are forced to protest against it, and appeal to all the world, whether these are not notorious violations on the liberties of freeborn Englishwomen? This makes the meekest worm amongst us all, ready to turn again when we are thus trampled on; But alas! What can we do to right ourselves? Stingless and harmless as we are, we can only kiss the foot that hurts us. However, sometimes it pleases Heaven to raise up some brighter genius than ordinary to succor a distressed people; an Epaminondas in Thebes; a Timoleon for Corinth; (for you must know we read Plutarch, now he is translated) and a Nassau for all the world: nor is our defenceless sex forgotten! We have not only Bonducas and Zenobias; but Sapphos and Daciers; Schurmans, Orindas, and Behns, who have humbled the most haughty of our antagonists, and made them do homage to our wit, as well as to our beauty. It is true, their mischievous and envious sex have made it their utmost endeavours to deal with us, as Hannibal was served at Capua, and to corrupt that virtue which they can no otherwise overcome; and sometimes they prevailed: but, if some angels fell, others remained in their innocence and perfection, if there were not also some addition made to their happiness and glory, by their continuing steadfast. Angels love; but they love virtuously, and reasonably, and neither err in the object, nor the manner: and if all our poetesses had done the same, I wonder what our enemies could have found out to have objected against us. However, here they are silenced; and I dare be bold to say, that whoever does not come extremely prejudiced to these Poems, will find in them that vivacity of thought, that purity of language, that softness and delicacy in the love-part, that strength and majesty of numbers almost everywhere, especially on heroical subjects, and that clear and unaffected love to virtue; that height of piety and warmth of devotion in the Canticles, and other religious pieces, which they will hardly find exceeded in the best authors on those different kinds of writing, much less equalled by any single writer.

And now I have nothing more, I think, lies upon my hands, but to assure the reader, that they were actually writ by a young lady, (all, but some of the answers, as is well known to many persons of Quality and worth) whose name had been prefixed, had not her own modesty absolutely forbidden it.

The way of thinking and writing is all along the same, only varying with the subject; and the whole a mixture, so very agreeable, that unless Philaret and my self, who have the honour to be her friends, and who persuaded her to publish this specimen, are very partial, it is more than probable, they will meet with so favourable a reception with the pious and ingenious reader, that we may ere long prevail with her to oblige the world with some others, no way inferior to these.

Elizabeth Johnson

Harding's-Rents,
May 10th, 1696

To a Friend, Who Persuades me to leave the Muses:

Forego the charming Muses! No, in spite
Of your ill-natured prophecy I'll write;
And for the future paint my thoughts at large,
I waste no paper at the hundred's charge:
I rob no neighbouring geese of quills, nor slink,
For a collection, to the church for ink:
Beside, my Muse is the most gentle thing
That ever yet made an attempt to sing:
I call no lady punk,* nor gallants fops,
Nor set the married world an edge for ropes;
Yet I'm so naturally inclined to rhyming,
That undesigned, my thoughts burst out a chiming;
My active genius will by no means sleep,
Pray let it then its proper channel keep.

* Whore.

I've told you, and you may believe me too,
That I must this, or greater mischief do:
And let the world think me inspired, or mad,
I'll surely write whilst paper's to be had;
Since heaven to me has a retreat assigned,
That would inspire a less harmonious mind.
All that a poet loves I have in view,
Delightsome hills, refreshing shades, and pleasant valleys too;
Fair spreading meadows clothed with lasting green,
And sunny banks with gliding streams between,
Gay as Elysium, in a lover's dream,
Or Flora's mansion, seated by a stream,
Where free from sullen cares I live at ease,
Indulge my Muse, and wishes, as I please,
Exempt from all that looks like want or strife,
I smoothly pass along the plains of life:
Thus fate conspires; which way then can I move?
Besides, my friend, I'm veh'mently in love,
This truth there's not a willow sprig but knows,
In whose sad shade I breathe my watchful woes.
But why for these slight reasons do I pause,
When I've a cogent one at hand, *Because!*
And that my muse may take no counter spell,
I fairly bid the boarding-school farewell:
No young impertinent shall here intrude,
And coax me from this blissful solitude.
Spite of her heart, my Dame shall damn no more
Great Sedley's plays, tho' never look'd 'em o'er;
Affront my novels, no, nor in a rage,
Force Dryden's lofty products from the stage,
Whilst all the rest of the melodious crew,
With the whole system of Athenians too,
For study's sake, out of the window flew.
But I to church shall fill her train no more,
And walk as if I sojourned by the hour.
To dancing master I have bid adieu,
Fall off, and on, be hanged, and Coopee too
Thy self for me, my cap'ring days are o'er,

Th' inspired Bacchanals I'll act no more.
Eight notes must for another treble look,
In burlesque to make faces by the book.
My darling pencil, and japanning† too,
And pretty Cupid in the glass, Adieu!
And since the dearest friends that are must part,
Old governess farewell, with all my heart.
Now welcome peaceful shades and murm'ring springs,
And welcome all th' inspiring tender things,
That please my genius, suit my make and years,
Unburdened yet with all but lover's cares.

The Female Passion

I.

A thousand great resolves, as great
    As reason could inspire,
I have commenced; but ah! how soon
    The daring thoughts expire!

II.

Honour and pride I've often roused,
    And bid 'em bravely stand,
But ere my charming foe appears,
    They cowardly disband.

III.

One dart from his insulting eyes,
    Eyes I'm undone to meet,
Throws all my boasting faculties
    At the loved tyrant's feet.

IV.

In vain, alas! 'tis all in vain,
    To struggle with my fate;
I'm sure I ne'er shall cease to love,
    Much less can e'er I hate!

† A decorative art frequently taught at schools for young ladies.

V.

Against relentless destiny,
Hopeless to overcome,
Not Sisyphus more sadly strives
With his eternal doom.

To Strephon

To me his sighs, to me are all his vows,
But there's my Hell, the depth of all my woes,
We burn alike, but O! the distant bliss,
A view of that my greatest torment is;
Accurst, ambition, grov'ling interest,
Such hated crimes as yet did never rest
Within my soul, must now unjustly keep
Me from my heaven! would they may sink as deep,
As that black chaos whence they sprung, and leave
Those mortals wretched which they now deceive.

THE FEMALE WITS

Mary Pix (1666–1720?)
Catherine Trotter Cockburn (1679–1749)
Mary de la Rivière Manley (1663–1724)

In 1696 three new women playwrights made their debuts on the English stage. They all paid tribute to Aphra Behn, and were evidently encouraged in their "bold attempt" by the undeniable fact of her success. All of the new playwrights, like Aphra, speak of their entry into the world of the theater (in the capacity of authors) in the same terms of military warfare that Aphra Behn used. One feature is new, however: they all acknowledge mutual support and inspiration. All wrote verses in praise of the others, that were printed in the first pages preceding the plays. Clearly, the fact that there were other contemporary women writers taking the same risk, as well as precedents in the past, is important to these women, even though they continue to express some of the same doubts and insecurities that their predecessors did. Catherine Trotter (later Cockburn) published her play anonymously, but did not bother to keep secret the fact that she was the author.

The presumption of these three young women was punished by a lampoon called *The Female Wits*. Mary de la Rivière Manley was ridiculed in the character of Marsilia, a vain "poetess that admires her own works." Mary Pix is portrayed as a fat fool in the character of Mrs. Wellfed; and Catherine Trotter is represented by Calista, a pretentious, absurd, "learned" lady.

The mild, frequently apologetic words "to the reader" hardly seem to justify the attack they incited. I have reproduced a few of them, along with brief biographical accounts of their authors.

Mary Pix was born in 1666, the daughter of the Reverend Roger Griffith, a country vicar in Oxfordshire. She married a London merchant, George Pix, at eighteen, shortly after her father died. Mary was thirty when her first play, *Ibrahim, the Thirteenth Emperor of the Turks: A Tragedy*, was staged. In the next four years, three more plays and a novel by her were published. All of them appeared under her own name, but the fourth play was published anonymously. A contemporary chronicler of the theater attributes at least two more anonymous plays to her.

Ibrahim, the Thirteenth Emperor of the Turks: A Tragedy. London, 1696.

Dedication
To the Honourable Richard Minghall, of Bourton, Esq.

Sir,

That sweetness of temper I have had the happiness to discover in the honour of your company in the first place, and your favourable opinion of my play in the next, gives me encouragement to claim your protection.

I am often told, and always pleased when I hear it, that the work's not mine; but oh I fear your closet view will too soon find out the woman, the imperfect woman there. The story was true, and the action gave it life; for I should be very rude not to own each maintained their character beyond my hopes. Then that pretty ornament, the ingenious dialogue, these might divert you at the theatre, but these avail not me; the reading may prove tiresome as a dull repeated tale: yet I have still recourse to what I mentioned first, your good nature, that I hope will pardon and accept it. I only wish my self mistress of eloquence, rhetoric, all the perfections of the pen, that I might worthily entertain Mr. Minchall.

Your noble family has been long the glory of my native country, and you are what I think no other nation equals, a true English Gentleman, kind to the distressed, a friend to all. I dare not proceed—my weakness would too plainly appear in aiming at a character which I can never reach: therefore, I conclude, once more asking your pardon, and leave to subscribe myself,

Sir,

Your most humble
and obliged servant,
Mary Pix

Born in 1679, Catherine Trotter was only four when her father, a naval commander, died at sea and left the family in financial distress. Her mother was a relative of the Duke of Lauderdale, however, so the family had access to court circles and was granted a small pension by Queen Anne. Catherine, the youngest daughter, taught herself to read and write French, and was instructed in Latin and logic by a tutor. From a very early age, she wrote poetry, and by the time she was seventeen had written her first play, *Agnes de Castro, A Tragedy. Written by a Young Lady.* She wrote four more plays in the next few years, then dropped out of the theater altogether. Her interests shifted to philosophy, and in 1702 she anonymously published a defense of Locke's theories. A few years later, Catherine Trotter married Mr. Cockburn and gave up literature for the next two decades, later writing of this time: "Being married in 1708, I bid adieu to the muses, and so wholly gave myself up to the cares of a family, and the education of my children, that I scarce knew there was any such thing as books, plays, or poems stirring in Great Britain." In 1726 Mrs. Cockburn returned once again to print in a second defense of Mr. Locke, and in 1739 wrote some *Remarks upon some Writers in the Controversy concerning the Foundation of Moral Duty and Moral Obligation.*

Here is the young Catherine Trotter, however, introducing her first play:

Agnes de Castro, A Tragedy. Written by a Young Lady. London, 1696.

Dedication
To the Right Honourable Charles, Earl of Dorset and Middlesex.

My Lord,

This little offspring of my early Muse was first submitted to your lordship's judgement, whether it should be stiffled in the birth, or preserved to try its fortune in the world; and since 'tis from your sentence it has ventured thus far, it now claims a sort of title to your Lordship's protection, which it could not have the least pretence to from its own merit. But 'tis your Lordship's character to encourage all great attempts, though unsuccessful: this was indeed a bold one for a woman at my years, but I would not offer my little experience, as a reason to be pardoned for not acquitting my self well, (for I think the incapacity of producing anything better, a very ill excuse for exposing a foolish thing) if the same inconsidering youth might not excuse the rashness of the undertaking; and I shall be much less pardonable, if the next I bring upon the stage has not a better title to the favour of the town. This seems to promise another attempt, which should not be expected from one who conceals her name, to shun that of poetress. I wish I could separate them here, for then I should be proud to own myself to the world, with all respect,

My Lord,

Your Lordship's most obliged,

and most humble servant.

To the Author of Agnes de Castro

Orinda, and the fair Astrea gone,
Not one was found to fill the vacant throne:
Aspiring man had quite regained the sway,
Again had taught us humbly to obey;
Till you (nature's third start, in favour of our kind)
With stronger arms, their empire have disjoined,
And snatched a laurel which they thought their prize,
Thus conqueror, with your wit, as with your eyes.
Fired by the bold example, I would try
To turn our sex's weaker destiny.
O! How I long in the poetic race,
To loose the reins, and give their glory chase;
For thus encouraged, and thus led by you,
Methinks we might more crowns than theirs subdue.

Dela Manley
[Mary de la Rivière Manley]

The third of the "triumvirate of female wits" was Mary de la Rivière Manley. Though she was born into a good family (April 7, 1663), the future wit's upbringing was rather more casual than not, since her mother died while she was quite young and Mary's father, Sir Roger, took little interest in her. The father, too, died when Mary was in her mid-twenties, leaving her a small inheritance. A cousin who was twenty years her senior proposed marriage, and was accepted.

At the birth of their first child, John Manley announced the existence of another wife, a circumstance which invalidated his more recent marriage to cousin Mary. Having spent her small fortune, John Manley vanished, leaving Mary and her baby to their own devices. Here Mary Manley drops from sight for a number of years, until in 1696 she resurfaces, publishing a volume of *Letters written by Mrs. Manley,* and staging two plays: *The Royal Mischief* and *The Lost Lover,* both comedies. The first was printed with encomiums from Mary Pix and Catherine Trotter, and both were introduced by prefaces in which Mary Manley testified to "the prejudice against our sex" in literary matters.

The Royal Mischief. London, 1696.

To Mrs. Manley.

By the Author of Agnes de Castro. *
Th' attempt was brave, how happy your success,
The men with shame our sex with pride confess;
For us you've vanquished, though the toil was yours;
You were our champion, and the glory ours.
Well you've maintained our equal right in fame,
To which vain man had quite engrossed the claim;
I knew my force too weak, and but assayed
The borders of their empire to invade;
I incite a greater genius to my aid:
The war begun you generously pursued;

* Catherine Trotter (later Cockburn).

Our title cleared, nor can a doubt remain,
Unless in which you'll greater conquest gain,
The comic, or the loftier tragic strain.
The men always o'ercome will quit the field,
Where they have lost their hearts, the laurel yield.

To Mrs. Manley, upon Her Tragedy Called The Royal Mischief.

As when some mighty hero first appears,
And in each act excells his wanting years;
All eyes are fixed on him, each busy tongue
Is employed in the triumphant song:
Even pale envy hangs her dusky wings,
Or joins with brighter fame, and hoarsely sings;
So you the unequalled wonder of the age,
Pride of our sex, and glory of the stage;
Have charmed our hearts with your immortal lays,
And tuned us all with everlasting praise.
You snatch laurels with undisputed right,
And conquer when you but begin to fight;
Your infant strokes have such Herculean force,
Your self must strive to keep the rapid course;
Like Sappho charming, like Afra† eloquent,
Like chaste Orinda, sweetly innocent:
But no more, to stop the reader were a sin,
Whilst trifles keep from the rich store within.

                                      Mary Pix

To the Reader

I should not have given my self and the town the trouble of a preface if
the aspersions of my enemies had not made it necessary. I am sorry those
of my own sex are influenced by them, and receive any character of a play
upon trust, without distinguishing ill nature, envy and detraction in the
representor.

The principal objection made against this tragedy is the warmth of it, as
they are pleased to call it; in all writings of this kind, some particular
passion is described, as a woman I thought it policy to begin with the

† Aphra Behn.

softest, and which is easiest to our sex. Ambition, &c., were too bold for the first flight; all would have condemned me if venturing on another I had failed, when gentle love stood ready to afford an easy victory, I did not believe it possible to pursue him too far, or that my laurel should seem less graceful for having made an entire conquest.

Leonora, in the double discovery, and part of *Aureng-Zebe*, have touches as full of natural fire as possible. I am amazed to know the boxes can be crowded, and the Ladies sit attentively, and unconcerned, at the Widow Lackitt, and her son Daniel's dialect, yet pretend to be shocked at the meaning of blank verse, for the words can give no offence; the shutting of the scene I judged modester (as being done by a creature of the princess), than in any terms to have had both the lovers agree before the audience, and then retire, as resolving to perform articles; the pen should know no distinction. I should think it but an indifferent commendation to have it said she writes like a woman: I am sorry to say there was a Princess more wicked than Homais. Sir John Chardin's *Travels into Persia*, whence I took the story, can inform the reader, that I have done her no injustice, unless it were in punishing her at the last; which the historian is silent in. Bassima's severer virtue should incline my audience to bestow the same commendation which they refuse me; for her rival's contrary character.

I do not doubt when the Ladies have given themselves the trouble of reading, and comparing it with others, they'll find the prejudice against our sex, and not refuse me the satisfaction of entertaining them, nor themselves the pleasure of Mrs. Barry, who by all that saw her, is concluded to have exceeded that perfection which before she was justly thought to have arrived at; my obligations to her were the greater, since against her own approbation, she excelled and made the part of an ill woman, not only entertaining, but admirable.

The Lost Lover. London, 1696.

The Preface

This comedy by the little success it met with in the acting, has not at all deceived my expectations; I had ever so great a distrust, and so impartial an opinion, that nothing but the flattery of my friends (and them, one would imagine, men of too much sense to be so grossly mistaken, and without whose persuasion I never designed publishing of it) could in the least have held me in suspense of its good or evil fortune: and to confess my faults, I own it an unpardonable one, to expose, after two years' reflection, the follies of seven days, (for barely in that time this play was wrought) and my self so great a stranger to the stage, that I had lived buried in the country, and in the six foregoing years, had actually been but twice at the house. The better half was cut; they say, 'thas suffered by it, tho' they told me, 'twas possible to have too much of a good thing, but I think never too little of an ill.

That knowledge I had of the town was the gentle part, which does not always afford diverting characters; my design in writing was only to pass some tedious country hours, not imagining I should be so severely repaid. I now know my faults, and will promise to mend them by the surest way, not attempting to repeat them.

I am now convinced writing for the stage is no way proper for a woman, to whom all advantages but mere nature, are refused; if we happen to have a genius to poetry, it presently shoots to a fond desire of imitation. Tho' to be lamely ridiculous, mine was indulged by my flatterers, who said nothing could come from me unentertaining: like a hero not contented with applause from lesser conquests, I find my self not only disappointed of my hopes of greater, but even to have lost all the glory of the former. Had I confined my sense, as before, to some short song of Phillis, a tender billet, and the freedom of agreeable conversation, I had still preserved the character of a witty woman.

Give me leave to thank the well-natured town for damning me so suddenly; they would not suffer me to linger in suspense, nor allow me any degrees of mortification; neither my sex, dress, music and dancing, could allow it a three day's reprieve, nor the modesty of the play itself, prevail with the ladies to espouse it: here I should most justly reproach my self, if I did not make all due acknowledgements for Sir Thomas Skipwith's civility, his native generosity, and gallantry of temper, took care nothing on his part should be wanting to make it pleasing.

Once more, my offended judges, I am to appear before you, once more in possibility of giving you the like damning satisfaction; there is a tragedy of mine rehearsing, which 'tis too late to recall, I consent it meet with the same fortune: 'twill for ever rid me of a vanity too natural to our sex, and make me say with a Grecian hero, "I had been lost, if I had not been lost."

They object the verses wrote by me before *Agnes de Castro*, where, with poetic vanity I seemed to think my self a champion for our sex; some of my witty critics make a jest of my proving so favourable an enemy, but let me tell them, this was not designed a consequence of that challenge, being writ two years before, and cannot have a smaller share in their esteem than mine: after all, I think my treatment much severer than I deserved; I am satisfied the bare name of being a woman's play damned it beyond its own want of merit. I will conclude with Dionysius, "That Plato and philosophy have taught me to bear so great a loss (even of fame) with patience."

Prologue.

The first adventurer for her fame I stand,
The curtain's drawn now by a lady's hand,
The very name you'll cry bodes impotence,
To fringe and tea they should confine their sense,
And not outstrip the bounds of providence.
I hope then critics, since the case is so,
You'll scorn to arm against a worthless foe,
But curb your spleen and gall, and trial make,
How our fair warrior gives her first attack.
    Now all ye chattering insects straight be dumb,
The men of wit and sense are hither come;
Ask not this mask to sup, nor that to show
Some face more ugly than a fifty beau,
Who, if our play succeeds, will surely say,
Some private lover helped her on her way,
As female wit were barren like the moon,
That borrows all her influence from the sun.
    The sparks and beaus will surely prove our friends,
For their good breeding must make them commend
What *billet doux* so e're a lady sends.
She knew old threadbare topics would not do,
But beaus *[sic]* a species thinks itself still new,
And therefore she resolved to copy you.

After the staging of her two plays in 1696, Mary de la Rivière Manley disappeared from the literary world for nine years. In 1705 she ended her silence with the publication of *The Secret History of*

Queen Zarah. This was followed a few years later by a volume entitled *Secret Memoirs and Manners of Several Persons of Quality of Both Sexes. From the New Atalantis, an Island in the Mediterranean* (1709). The narrator of this "fiction" was Aphra Behn, returned to earth as "Astrea," who is invisibly touring the country along with her companions "Fame" and "Virtue." Their guide, "Intelligence," relates the secret histories of everyone they meet—thus allowing Mrs. Manley to introduce, under a thin fictional disguise, all sorts of scandalous particulars, both political and personal. Her "characters" were immediately recognized, and Mrs. Manley was arrested along with the publisher and printer. She took all the responsibility upon herself in court, however, and the others were released. Manley spent three months in prison before being discharged. Her book, in the meantime, had met with enormous success. She published three more volumes without further hindrance from the authorities, and appended a *Key* at the end of the fourth volume of the sixth edition for the benefit of those few readers who may have missed some of the allusions.

In 1714 Manley published a romanticized autobiography, entitled *The Adventures of Rivella; or, The History of the Author of the Atalantis.* The purported author, an English knight named Sir Charles Lovemore, recounts the life and adventures of Mrs. Manley in a conversation with his friend the Chevalier D'Aumont.

The fact that Mrs. Manley had been seduced, betrayed, and abandoned to poverty as a young woman unquestionably made the loss of her "reputation" less of a consideration that it necessarily had to be for other women. She did pay a certain price for her public image as a scandalous woman; on the other hand, it provided her with a freedom few other women of her generation enjoyed.

The Adventures of Rivella; or, The History of the Author of the Atalantis. With Secret Memoirs and Characters of Several Considerable Persons Her Contemporaries. London, 1714.

The History of Rivella.

There are so many things praise, and yet blame-worthy, in Rivella's conduct, that as her friend, I know not well how with a good grace, to repeat, or as yours, to conceal, because you seem to expect from me an impartial history. Her virtues are her own, her vices occasioned by her misfortunes; and yet as I have often heard her say, If she had been a man, she had been without fault: but the charter of that sex being much more confined than ours, what is not a crime in men is scandalous and unpardonable in woman, as she herself has very well observed in divers places, throughout her own writings.

Her person is neither tall nor short; from her youth she was inclined to fat; whence I have often heard her flatterers liken her to the Grecian Venus. It is certain, considering that disadvantage, she has the most easy air that one can have; her hair is of a pale ash-color, fine, and in a large quantity. I have heard her friends lament the disaster of her having had the smallpox in such an injurious manner, being a beautiful child before that distemper; but as that disease has now left her face, she has scarce any pretence to it. Few, who have only beheld her in public, could be brought to like her; whereas none that became acquainted with her, could refrain from loving her. I have heard several wives and mistresses accuse her of fascination: they would neither trust their husbands, lovers, sons, nor brothers with her acquaintance upon terms of the greatest advantage. Speak to me of her eyes, interrupted the Chevalier, you seem to have forgot that index of the mind; is there to be found in them, store of those animating fires with which her writings are filled? Do her eyes love as well as her pen? You reprove me very justly, answered the Baronet, Rivella would have a good deal of reason to complain of me, if I should silently pass over the best feature in face. In a word, you have your self described them: nothing can be more tender, ingenious and brillant with a mixture so languishing and sweet, when love is the subject of the discourse, that without being severe, we may very well conclude, the softer passions have their predominancy in her soul.

How are her teeth and lips, spoke the Chevalier? Forgive me, dear Lovemore, for breaking in so often upon your discourse; but kissing being the sweetest leading pleasure, 'tis impossible a woman can charm without a good mouth. Yet, answered Lovemore, I have seen very great beauties please, as the common witticism speaks, "in spite of their teeth": I do not find but love in the general is well natured and civil, willing to compound for some defects, since he knows that 'tis very difficult and rare to find true symmetry and all perfections in one person: red hair, out-mouth, thin and livid lips, black broken teeth, coarse ugly hands, long thumbs, ill-formed dirty nails, flat, or very large breasts, splay feet; which together makes a frightful composition, yet divided amongst several, prove no allay to the strongest passions: but to do Rivella justice, till she grew fat, there was not I believe any defect to be found in her body: her lips admirably coloured; her teeth small and even, a breath always sweet; her complexion fair and fresh; yet with all this you must be used to her before she can be thought thoroughly agreeable. Her hands and arms have been publicly celebrated; it is certain, that I never saw any so well turned; her neck and breasts have an established reputation for beauty and colour: her feet small and pretty. Thus I have run through whatever custom suffers to be visible to us; and upon my word, Chevalier, I never saw any of Rivella's hidden charms.

Pardon me this once, said D'Aumont, and I assure you, dear Sir Charles, I will not hastily interrupt you again: "What humour is she of? Is her manner gay or serious? Has she wit in her conversation as well as her pen? What do you call wit, answered Lovemore? If by that word, you mean a succession of such things as can bear repetition, even down to posterity? How few are there of such persons, or rather none indeed, that can be always witty? Rivella speaks things pleasantly; her company is entertaining to the last; no woman except one's mistress wearies one so little as her self. Her knowledge is universal; she discourses well, and agreeably upon all subjects, bating* a little affectation, which nevertheless becomes her admirably well; yet this thing is to be commended in her, that she rarely speaks of her own writings, unless when she would expressly ask the judgement of her friends, insomuch that I was well pleased at the character a certain person gave her (who did not mean it much to her advantage) that one might discourse seven years together with Rivella, and never find out from herself, that she was a wit, or an author. . . .

I was in the country when the two first volumes of the *Atalantis* were published, and did not know who was the author, but came to town just as the Lord S——d had granted a warrant against the printer and publisher: I went as usual, to wait upon Rivella, whom I found in one of her heroic strains; she said she was glad I was come, to advise her in a business of very great importance; she had as yet consulted with but one friend, whose counsel had not pleased her; no more would mine, I thought, but did not interrupt her; in conclusion she told me that her self was author of the *Atalantis*, for which three innocent persons were taken up and would be ruined with their families; that she was resolved to surrender herself into the messenger's hands, whom she heard had the Secretary of State's war-

* Excepting.

rant against her, so to discharge those honest people from their imprisonment: I stared upon her and thought her directly mad; I began with railing at her books; the barbarous design of exposing people that never had done her any injury; she answered me she was become *misanthrope*, a perfect Timon, or man-hater; all the world was out of humour with her, and she with all the world, more particularly a faction who were busy to enslave their Sovereign, and overturn the Constitution; that she was proud of having more courage than had any of our sex,† and of throwing the first stone, which might give a hint for other persons of more capacity to examine the defects, and vices of some men who took a delight to impose upon the world, by the pretence of public good, whilst their true design was only to gratify and advance themselves. As to exposing those who had never injured her, she said she did no more by others, than had done by her (i.e.) tattle of frailties; the town had never shown her any indulgence, but on the contrary reported tenfold against her in matters of which she was wholly innocent; whereas she did but take up old stories that all the world had long since reported, having ever been careful of glancing against such persons who were truly virtuous, and who had not been very careless of their own actions.

Rivella grew warm in her defence, and obstinate in her design of surrendering her self a prisoner: I asked her how she would like going to Newgate? She answered me very well; since it was to discharge her conscience; I told her all this sounded great, and was very heroic, but there was a vast difference between real and imaginary sufferings: she had chose to declare herself of a party most supine, and forgetful of such who served them; that she would certainly be abandoned by them, and left to perish and starve in prison. The most severe critics upon Tory writings, were Tories themselves, who never considering the design or honest intention of the author, would examine the performance only, and that too with as much severity as they would an enemy's, and at the same time value themselves upon their being impartial, tho' against their friends: then as to gratitude or generosity, the Tories did not come up to the Whigs, who never suffered any man to want encouragement and rewards if he were never so dull, vicious or insignificant, provided he declared himself to be for them; whereas the Tories had no general interest, and consequently no particular, each person refusing to contribute towards the benefit of the whole; and when it should come to pass (as certainly it would) that she perished

† I.e., the masculine sex.

thro' want in a goal,‡ they would sooner condemn her folly, than pity her sufferings; and cry: "she may take it for her pains. Who bid her write? What good did she do? Could not she sit quiet as well as her neighbours, and not meddle her self about what did not concern her?"

Rivella was startled at these truths, and asked me, what then would I have her do? I answered that I was still at her service, as well as my fortune: I would wait upon her out of England, and then find some means to get her safe into France, where the Queen, that was once to have been her mistress, would doubtless take her into her own protection; she said the project was a vain one, that lady being the greatest bigot in nature to the Roman church, and she was, and ever would be, a Protestant, a name sufficient to destroy the greatest merit in that court. I told her I would carry her into Switzerland, or any country that was but a place of safety, and leave her there if she commanded me; she asked me in a hasty manner, as if she demanded pardon for hesitating upon the point, what then would become of the poor printer, and those two other persons concerned, the publishers, who with their families all would be undone by her flight? That the misery I had threatened her with, was a less evil than doing a dishonourable thing. I asked her if she had promised those persons to be answerable for the event? She said no, she had only given them leave to say, if they were questioned, "they had received the copy from her hand!" I used several arguments to satisfy her conscience that she was under no farther obligation, especially since the profit had been theirs; she answered it might be so, but she could not bear to live and reproach her self with the misery that might happen to those unfortunate people. Finding her obstinate, I left her with an angry threat, of never beholding her in that wretched state, into which she was going to plunge her self.

Rivella remained immovable in a point which she thought her duty, and accordingly surrendered herself, and was examined in the Secretary's office. They used several arguments to make her discover who were the persons concerned with her in writing her books; or at least from whom she had received information of some special facts, which they thought were above her own intelligence. Her defence was with much humility and sorrow, for having offended, at the same time denying that any persons were concerned with her, or that she had a farther design than writing for her own amusement and diversion in the country, without intending particular reflections or characters. When this was not believed,

‡ Jail.

and the contrary urged very home to her by several circumstances and likenesses, she said then it must be inspiration, because knowing her own innocence she could account for it no other way. The Secretary replied upon her, that inspiration used to be upon a good account, and her writings were stark naught; she told him, with an air full of penitence, that might be true, but it was as true, that there were evil angels as well as good; so that nevertheless what she had wrote might still be by inspiration.

Not to detain you any longer, dear attentive D'Aumont, the gathering clouds beginning to bring night upon us, this poor lady was close shut up in the messengers hands from seeing or speaking to any person, without being allowed pen, ink and paper; where she was most tyrannically and barbarously insulted by the fellow and his wife who had her in keeping, tho' doubtless without the knowledge of their superiors; for when Rivella was examined, they asked her if she was civilly used? She thought it below her to complain of such little people, who when they stretched authority a little too far, thought perhaps that they served the intention and resentments, tho' not the commands of their masters; and accordingly chose to be inhuman, rather than just and civil.

Rivella's counsel sued out her *Habeas Corpus* at the Queen's Bench-Bar in Westminster Hall; and she was admitted to bail. Whether the persons in power were ashamed to bring a woman to her trial for writing a few amorous trifles purely for her own amusement, or that our laws were defective, as most persons conceived, because she had served herself with romantic names, and a feigned scene of action? But after several times exposing her in person to walk cross the Court before the bench of Judges, with her three attendants, the printer and both the publishers; the Attorney General at the end of three or four terms dropped the prosecution, though not without a very great expense to the defendants, who were however glad to compound with their purses for their heinous offence, and the notorious indiscretion of which they had been guilty.

There happened not long after, a total change in the Ministry, the persons whom Rivella had disobliged being removed, and consequently her fears dissipated; upon which that native gaiety and good humour so sparkling and conspicuous in her, returned; I had the hardest part to act, because I could not easily forego her friendship and acquaintance, yet knew not very well how to pretend to the continuance of either, considering what I had said to her upon our last separation the night before her imprisonment: finding I did not return to wish her joy with the rest of her friends upon her enlargement, she did me the favour to write to me, assuring me that she very well distinguished that which a friend out of the greatness of his friendship did advise, and what a man of honour could be supposed to endure, by giving advice wherein his friend or himself must suffer, and that since I had so generously endeavoured her safety at the expense of my own character, she would always look upon me as a person whom nothing could taint but my friendship for her. I was ashamed of the delicacy of her argument, by which since I was proved guilty, tho' the motives were never so prevalent, still my honour was found defective, how perfect soever my friendship might appear.

Rivella had always the better of me at this argument, and when she would insult me, never failed to serve her self with that false one, success; in return, I brought her to be ashamed of her writings, saving that part by which she pretended to serve her country, and the ancient constitution; (there she is a perfect bigot from a long untainted descent of loyal ancestors, and consequently immoveable) but when I would argue with her the folly of a woman's disobliging any one party, by a pen equally qualified to divert all, she agreed my reflection was just, and promised not to repeat her fault, provided the world would have the goodness to forget those she had already committed, and that henceforward her business should be to write of pleasure and entertainment only, wherein party should no longer mingle; but that the Whigs were so unforgiving they would not advance one step towards a coalition with any Muse that had once been so indiscreet to declare against them. She now agrees with me, that politics is not the business of a woman, especially of one that can so well delight and entertain her readers with more gentle pleasing themes, and has accordingly set her self again to write a tragedy for the stage. If you stay in England, dear Chevalier, till next winter, we may hope to entertain you from thence, with whatever Rivella is capable of performing in the dramatic art.

Susannah Centlivre (c. 1670–1723)

Susannah Freeman was born into a family of Dissenters who had been ruined at the Restoration. No record of her birthplace has been found, but one contemporary speculates that she may have been born in Ireland, where her father fled at the Restoration, then later returned to a small village named Holbeach, in Lincolnshire, on The Wash. Susannah's mother is said to have died when she was quite young. Her father remarried, then died when she was nine, leaving her under the direction of a stepmother. This circumstance, apparently, was an unhappy one. There are a number of differing accounts of Susannah's escape from her stepmother—one biographer has it that she ran away at fourteen with little money and no resources, but was found (in tears) sitting by the roadside by a "Gentleman from the University of Cambridge afterwards well known in the polite and literary world."[1] Said "Gentleman" [Anthony Hammond, Esq.] dressed Susannah in boy's clothes and introduced her into the university as his "Cousin Jack." The two young "Gentlemen" spent two very agreeable months together, until Hammond concluded that they were attracting too much notice and sent her on her way with a letter of introduction to useful persons and a gold purse.

The story reads very much like the plot of one of the romantic novels popular then, but it is also not inconsistent with what we know of Mrs. Centlivre's character, nor with the "gay adventures" of her youth that all the contemporary witnesses refer to. Subsequent "gay adventures" included marriage at sixteen to a Mr. Fox, who "bore her off in triumph from a cloud of rivals"[2] (but died shortly thereafter), and a second marriage to an army officer named Mr. Carroll. This marriage lasted only a little more than a year, as Mr. Carroll was killed in a duel. Sometime before, during, or between marriages, Susannah had joined a company of strolling players. She was particularly fond of playing male parts.

Susannah Centlivre first appeared in print as "Mrs. Carroll," contributing a series of "literary" letters to a volume brought out by

Sam Briscoe, on May 11, 1700, under the title, *Familiar and Courtly Letters, Written by Monsieur Voiture to Persons of the Greatest Honour, Wit, and Quality of Both Sexes in the Court of France. Made English by Mr. Dryden, Mr. Wycherley.* Mrs. Carroll chose to call herself "Astrea" and her correspondent "Celadon," no doubt as a tribute to Aphra Behn, who had earlier used those "poetic" names. In one letter, Mrs. Carroll wishes she could write with the "genius" of Mrs. Aphra Behn, or "Orinda." She had, however, already chosen to follow the scandalous precedent of the former.

Susannah Centlivre's first play, *The Perjured Husband: or, The Adventures of Venice, a Tragedy,* was acted in the fall of 1700. It met with a fair degree of success, and her second effort, *The Beau's Duel: or, A Soldier for the Ladies,* was produced in June 1702 at Lincoln's Inn Fields. By December of that year, a third play, *The Stolen Heiress: or The Salamanca Doctor Outplotted,* was on the boards. Centlivre's first play had been printed with her name on the title page; the third not only appeared anonymously, but the prologue even attempted to disguise the author's sex. In a preface to a later play *(The Platonick Lady,* 1707), Centlivre explains that pressures from her booksellers, the audience, and the actors themselves forced her to the expedient of concealing her identity, and consequently the fact that she was a woman.

Despite the opposition she describes, Centlivre enjoyed a quite successful, long, and productive career: like Aphra Behn, she wrote seventeen plays in seventeen years (and possibly more). Nearly all of them were acted at the time they were written, and several continued to be revived for more than a hundred years.

After years of literary independence, Susannah Freeman Fox Carroll married the Queen's cook, Joseph Centlivre, in 1707. The fact that she was no longer obliged to write "for bread," however, did not lessen the steady stream of plays and poems that issued from her pen until her death in 1723.

1. John Wilson Bowyer, *The Celebrated Mrs. Centlivre* (Durham, 1952), p. 8.

2. *A List of All the Dramatic Authors, with Some Account of their Lives; and of All the Dramatic Pieces Ever Published in the English Language to the Year 1747* (London, 1747), quoted in Bowyer, op. cit., p. 12.

The Perjured Husband: or, The Adventures of Venice, A Tragedy.
London, 1700.

To the Reader

I should not trouble my reader with a preface, if Mr. Collier* had taught manners to masks, sense to beaux, and good nature to critics, as well as morality to the stage; the first are sure to envy what they can't equal, and condemn what they don't understand; the beaux usually take a greater liberty with our sex than they would with their own, because there's no fear of drawing a duel upon their hands; the latter are a sort of rude splenatic men, that seldom commend any thing but what they have had a hand in. These snarling sparks were pleased to carp at one or two expressions, which were spoken in an aside by one of the inferior characters in the drama; and without considering the reputation of the persons in whose mouths the language is put, condemn it strait for loose and obscure. Now (with submission to better judges) I cannot believe that a prayer-book should be put into the hands of a woman, whose innate virtue won't secure her reputation; nor is it reasonable to expect a person, whose inclinations are always forming projects to the dishonour of her husband, should deliver her commands to her confident in the words of a psalm. I heartily wish that those that find fault with the liberty of my style, would be pleased to set a pattern to the town, by retrenching some of their debaucheries, for modesty thrives best by example. Modest language from the truly virtuous is expected, I mean such as will neither act ill, nor suffer ill to be acted: it is not enough that Lucy says she's honest, in having denied the brutal part; whoever thinks virtue centers in that, has a wrong notion of it; no, virtue is a tender plant, which cannot live in tainted ground; virtue is what the air of flattery cannot blast, nor the vile sordid dross of gain poison; and she that can withstand these two shocks may be styled truly virtuous. I ask my reader's pardon for my bluntness, but I hope none of my sex so qualified will condemn me for exposing the vices of the seeming religious.

I fear there is but too many hit by the character of Signora Pizalta; I wish for the sake of the reverse party there were fewer, or they better

* Jeremy Collier, author of *A Short View of the Immorality and Profaneness of the English Stage* (London, 1698).

known, since the malicious world are so apt to judge of people's inclinations by the company they keep: which is sometimes authentic but not
always an infallible rule. I shall say little in justification of the play, only
desire the reader to judge impartially, and not condemn it by the shortness
of its life, since the season of the year ne're promised much better success.
It went off with general applause; and 'tis the opinion of some of our best
judges, that it only wanted the addition of good actors, and a full town, to
have brought me a sixth night, there having been worse plays within this
twelve-month approved of.

The Platonick Lady. London, 1707.

*To all the Generous Encouragers of Female Ingenuity, this Play is Humbly
Dedicated:*

Gentlemen and Ladies;
  My Muse chose to make this universal address, hoping, among the
numerous crowd, to find some souls great enough to protect her against
the carping malice of the vulgar world; who think it a proof of their sense,
to dislike everything that is writ by women. I was the more induced to this
general application, from the usage I have met on all sides.
  A play secretly introduced to the house, whilst the author remains unknown, is approved by every body: the actors cry it up, and are in expectation of a great run; the bookseller of a second edition, and the scribbler of
a sixth night. But if by chance the plot's discovered, and the brat found
fatherless, immediately it flags in the opinion of those that extolled it
before, and the bookseller falls in his price, with this reason only: *It is a
woman's.* Thus they alter their judgement, by the esteem they have for
the author, tho' the play is still the same. They ne'er reflect, that we have
had some male-productions of this kind, void of plot and wit, and full as
insipid as ever a woman's of us all.
  I can't forbear inserting a story which my bookseller, that printed my
Gamester told me, of a spark that had seen my *Gamester* three or four
times, and liked it extremely: having bought one of the books, asked who
the author was; and being told, a woman, threw down the book, and put
up his money, saying, he had spent too much after it already, and was sure
if the town had known that, it would never have run ten days. No doubt

this was a wit in his own eyes. It is such as these that rob us of that which inspires the poet, praise. And it is such as these made him that printed my comedy called, *Love's Contrivance; or, Medcin [sic] Malgre Lui*, put two letters of a wrong name to it; which tho' it was the height of injustice to me, yet his imposing on the town turned to account with him; and thus passing for a man's, it has been played at least a hundred times.

And why this wrath against the women's works? Perhaps you'll answer, because they meddle with things out of their sphere: But I say, no; for since the poet is born, why not a woman as well as a man? Not that I would derogate from those great men who have a genius, and learning to improve that genius: I only object against those ill-natured critics, who wanting both, think they have a sufficient claim to sense, by railing at what they don't understand. Some have armed themselves with resolution not to like the plays they paid to see; and if in spite of spleen they have been pleased against their will, have maliciously reported it was none of mine, but given me by some gentleman. Nay, even my own sex, which should assert our prerogative against such detractors, are often backward to encourage a female pen.

Would these professed enemies but consider what examples we have had of women that excelled in all arts; in music, painting, poetry; also in war: nay, to our immortal praise, what empresses and queens have filled the world? What cannot England boast from women? The mighty Romans felt the power of Boadicea's arm; Eliza made Spain tremble; but Anne, the greatest of the three, has shook the man that aimed at universal sway. After naming this miracle, the glory of our sex, sure none will spitefully cavil at the following scenes, purely because a woman writ 'em. This I dare venture to say in their behalf, there is a plot and story in them, I hope will entertain the reader; which is the utmost ambition of,

Gentlemen and Ladies,

Your most obedient and humble servant.

Mary Davys (b. 1674)

Little is known about Mary Davys's early life, except that she was a native of Ireland. She married Peter Davys, headmaster of the free school attached to St. Patrick's in Dublin, and a friend of Dean Swift. When her husband died in 1698, Mary Davys moved first to York and then to Cambridge, where she supported herself by keeping a coffee-house and, when she could, by writing plays and novels. Writing in 1725, she alluded to the difficulty a woman alone encountered keeping herself afloat by these means, testifying that she herself had been "left to her own endeavours for twenty-seven years together." There is rather pathetic reference to Mrs. Davys in Swift's *Journal to Stella*, February 21, 1712/13. The Dean mentions that he has "been writing a letter to Mrs. Davis at York. She took care to have a letter delivered for me at Lord Treasurer's; for I would not own one she sent by post. She reproaches me for not writing to her these four years; and I have honestly told her it is my way never to write to those whom I am never likely to see, unless I can serve them, which I cannot her, &c., Davis, the schoolmaster's widow."

Mrs. Davys's first play, *The Northern Heiress, or the Humours of York, a Comedy*, was performed at the New Theatre in Lincoln's Inn Fields, in 1716. In 1724 she published a novel, entitled *The Reformed Coquet, or the Memoirs of Amoranda*. In 1725 a two-volume edition of her *Works* (published and unpublished) appeared. She continued to publish occasionally until 1756, after which there is no further record of her life or work.

Works. London, 1725.

To the Ladies of Great Britain:

At a time when the town is so full of masquerades, operas, new plays, conjurors, monsters, and feigned devils, how can I, Ladies, expect you to throw away an hour upon the less agreeable amusements my coquet can give you? But she who has assurance to write, has certainly the vanity of expecting to be read. All authors see a beauty in their own compositions, which perhaps nobody else can find; as mothers think their own offspring amiable, how deficient soever nature has been to them. But whatever my faults may be, my design is good, and hope you British Ladies will accordingly encourage it.

If I have here touched a young lady's vanity and levity, it was to show her how beautiful she is without those blots, which certainly stain the mind, and stamp deformity where the greatest beauties would shine, were they banished. I believe everybody will join with my opinion, that the English ladies are the most accomplished women in the world; that, generally speaking, their behaviour is so exact, that even envy itself cannot strike at their conduct: but even your selves must own, that there are some few among you of a different stamp, who change their gold for dross, and barter the highest perfections for the lowest weaknesses. Would but this latter sort endeavour as much to act like angels, as they do to look like them, the men, instead of reproaches, would heap them with praises, and their cold indifference would be turned to idolatry. But who can forsake a fault, 'till they are convinced they are guilty? Vanity is a lurking subtle thief, that works itself insensibly into our bosoms, and while we declare our dislike to it, know not 'tis so near us; everybody being (as a witty Gentleman has somewhere said) provided with a racket to strike it from themselves. . . .

Ladies, your most devoted,
and most obedient,
Humble servant,
Mary Davys.

The Preface

Idleness has so long been an excuse for writing, that I am almost ashamed to tell the world it was that, and that only, which produced the following sheets. Few people are so inconsiderable in life, but they may at some time do good; and tho' I must own my purse is (by a thousand misfortunes) grown wholly useless to everybody, my pen is at the service of the public, and if it can but make some impression upon the young unthinking minds of some of my own sex, I shall bless my labour, and reap an unspeakable satisfaction: but as I have addressed them in another place, I shall say no more of them here. I come now to the worthy Gentlemen of Cambridge, from whom I have received so many marks of favour on a thousand occasions, that my gratitude is highly concerned how to make a due acknowledgement. . . . They knew [the author of this book] to be a relict* of one of their brotherhood [the clergy], and one, who (unless poverty be a sin) never did anything to disgrace the gown; and for those reasons encouraged all her undertakings.

But as this book was writ at Cambridge, I am a little apprehensive some may imagine the Gentlemen had a hand in it. It would be very hard, if their humanity to me, should bring an imputation to themselves so greatly below their merit, which I can by no means consent to; and do therefore assure the world, I am not acquainted with one member of that worthy and learned society of men, whose pens are not employed in things infinitely above anything I can pretend to be the author of: so that I only am accountable for every fault of my book; and if it has any beauties, I claim the merit of them too. Tho' I cannot but say, I did once apply myself to a young genius for a preface, which he seemed to decline, and I soon considered the brightness of his pen would only eclipse the glimmering light of my own; so I called back my request. . . .

Perhaps it may be objected against me, by some more ready to give reproach than relief, that as I am the relict of a clergyman, and in years, I ought not to publish plays, &c. But I beg of such to suspend their uncharitable opinions, till they have read what I have writ, and if they find anything there offensive either to God or Man, anything either to shock their morals or their modesty, 'tis then time enough to blame. And let them farther consider, that a woman left to her own endeavours for twenty-seven years together, may well be allowed to catch at any opportunity for that bread, which they that condemn her would very probably deny to give her.

The Northern Heiress, or the Humours of York, a Comedy. London, 1717.

The Prologue

A female muse, from northern clime, this day
Presents upon the stage her first-born play.
What she expects, to all but her's unknown:

* Widow.

She sure can never hope to please this town.
Learning she'as none, so can have no supplies
From ancient books, but on her self relies.
How weak support, you poets know, whose brains
Having at last produced, with mighty pains,
Pieces in which not one rule was forgot
Of all that mighty Aristotle wrote;
Nature in all the characters observed,
And time and place to nicety preserved.
Yet for all this ill-natured critics' spite,
Have scarcely let them live 'till their third night.
Beside, she wants those helps that some have got,
Who take from French or Spanish plays their plot,
From others' works judiciously can glean
The choicest flowers to adorn their barren scene.
Could she do this, she then perhaps might please
An audience, and do it too with ease.
Alas! She knows no languages but one;
And what she gives you here, is all her own.
From her own sex something she may expect;
'Tis women's duty women to protect.
For pity, ladies, let her not despair,
But kindly take the suppliant to your care;
Let her from you but some small favour find,
The men will be out of good manners kind.

Penelope Aubin (fl. 1720)

Very few particulars of Penelope Aubin's life are a matter of record, except that she was a prolific writer of novels, a highly successful public speaker (whom the public paid to hear), and a devout Roman Catholic. Though she regarded novels principally as "entertainment," Aubin also felt compelled to shape characters and outcome after a moral design: in order, as she said, "to encourage virtue, and excite us to heroic actions. . . ." She felt this distinguished her from the "careless and loose" style of the other female authors, "my contemporaries, whose lives and writings have, I fear, too great a resemblance."

Though for the most part Penelope Aubin chose to ignore the fact of her sex in the words to the reader that prefaced her works, and consequently eschewed any mention of the difficulties or contradictions that other women discussed at such length, she does not wish to be classified as a "professional," and is careful to state that "I do not write for bread." At the same time, she cannot resist telling the reader that, according to the booksellers, her "novels sell tolerably well."

It may be that Aubin's avowed moral purpose in writing freed her from the constant need to apologize for the act of publication, but whatever the reason, her attitude toward authorship seems far less caught up in the kind of guilt, anguish, or equivocation that earlier women writers manifested.

Among Penelope Aubin's works are *The Life of Madame de Beaumont* (1721), *The Life of Charlotta DuPont* (1723), *The Strange Adventures of the Count de Vinevil* (1721), and *The Life and Adventures of the Lady Lucy* (1726).

The Life of Charlotta DuPont. London, 1723.

Dedication
To My Much Honoured Friend, Mrs. Rowe.

Madam,

I have long waited an opportunity to give some public testimony of the esteem and respect I have for you. The friendship you and Mr. Rowe have shown to me and my dead friend, have laid me under the greatest obligations to love and value you; but your particular merit has doubly engaged me to honour you. In you I have found all that is valuable in our sex; and without flattery, you are the best wife, the best friend, the most prudent, most humble, and most accomplished woman I ever met withal. I am charmed with your conversation, and extremely proud of your friendship. The world has often condemned me for being too curious, and, as they term it, partial in my friendships; but I am of Horace's mind, and take no pleasure in variety of acquaintance and conversation: two or three persons of worth and integrity are enough to make life pleasant. I confess I have little to recommend me to such, except the grateful sense I have of the honour they do me, and the love I bear their virtues; and I account it my good fortune to have found such friends, amongst whom I esteem you in the first rank. I need say nothing of Mr. Rowe, but that he has such excellencies as prevailed with you, who are an admirable judge, and endowed with as much sense and virtue as any woman living, to prefer him before all the rest of mankind: and your choice is sufficient to speak his merit. May heaven prolong your lives, and continue your felicity, that your friends may long enjoy you, and the world be bettered by your examples. You act as your learned father taught, and are in all kinds an honour to the ancient noble families from whence you are descended. Forgive this rapture; my zeal transports me when you are the subject of my thoughts; and I had almost forgot to entreat the favour of you to accept the little present I here make of the adventures of a lady, whose life was full of the most extraordinary incidents. I hope it will agreeably entertain you at a leisure hour, and I assure you I dedicate it to you with the utmost respect and affection, and am, Madam,

Your most sincere friend,
and devoted humble servant,
Penelope Aubin

The Preface

Gentlemen and Ladys,

The Court being removed to the other side of the water, and beyond the sea, to take the pleasures this town and our dull island cannot afford; the greater part of our nobility and Members of Parliament retired to Hanover or their country-seats, where they may supinely sit, and with pleasure reflect on the great things they have done for the public good, and the mighty toils they have sustained from sultry days and sleepless nights, unraveling the horrid plot: whilst these our great patriots enjoy the repose of their own consciences, and reap the fruits of their labours, and enlarged* prisoners freed from stone walls, and jailors taste the sweets of liberty; I believed something new and diverting would be welcome to the town, and that the adventures of a young lady, whose life contains the most extraordinary events that I ever heard or read of, might agreeably entertain you at a time when our newspapers furnish nothing of moment. The story of Madam Charlotta duPont, I had from the mouth of a gentleman of integrity, who related it as from his own knowledge. I have joined some other histories to hers, to embellish, and render it more entertaining and useful, to encourage virtue, and excite us to heroic actions, which is my principal aim in all I write; and this I hope you will rather applaud than condemn me for. The kind reception you have already given the trifles I have published, lay me under an obligation to do something more to merit your favour. Besides, as I am neither a statesman, courtier, or modern great man or lady, I cannot break my word without blushing, having ever kept it as a thing that is sacred: and I remember I promised in my preface to the Count de Vineville, to continue writing if you dealt favourably with me. My booksellers say, my novels sell tolerably well. I had designed to employ my pen on something more serious and learned; but they tell me, I shall meet with no encouragement, and advise me to write rather more modishly, that is, less like a Christian, and in a style careless and loose, as the custom of the present age is to live. But I leave that to the other female authors my contemporaries, whose lives and writings have, I fear, too great a resemblance.† My design in writing, is to employ my leisure hours to some advantage to myself and others; and I shall forbear publishing any work of greater price and value than these, till

* Released.
† Mary Manley, Susannah Centlivre, etc.

times mend, and money again is plenty in England. Necessity may make wits, but authors will be at a loss for patrons and subscribers whilst the nation is poor. I do not write for bread, nor am I vain or fond of applause; but I am very ambitious to gain the esteem of those who honour virtue, and shall ever be,

Their devoted humble servant,
Penelope Aubin

Eliza Haywood (1693?–1756)

Eliza Fowler was the daughter of a small shopkeeper in London. She married the Reverend Valentine Haywood before she was twenty, but in 1721 ran away with her two children and set up housekeeping on her own. After a brief flirtation with the theater, in the capacity of both actress and playwright, she began writing novels. These were hugely successful: one of her earliest, *Love in Excess, or the Fatal Enquiry,* had already gone into its fifth edition by 1724. More often than not, the subject of these fictions was the constant threat to virtue women of character were exposed to. Though the outcome of the story left "virtue" intact, the assaults thereon were so salacious that Mrs. Haywood acquired a reputation as scandalous as that of Mrs. Manley. She continued to write at an almost industrial rate, however, since she was poorly paid for the novels that sold so well. By the time she died, Haywood had published more than seventy books.

In 1728 Pope heaped scorn on Eliza Haywood in the *Dunciad,* calling her a "shameless scribbler," among other insults. His attack may have caused her some difficulty with her publisher, since for a time after that she chose to publish her work anonymously. In 1744 she founded a periodical for ladies, called the *Female Spectator.* In the twenty-four monthly issues that were published, the "editorial committee"—purportedly made up of Mrs. Haywood, editor in chief, and three other ladies—addressed issues of concern to their sex. Women wrote in with questions or replies to matters discussed in earlier issues of the periodical.

The Female Spectator. London, 1744–46.

When first myself and assistants set about this undertaking, we agreed to lay down certain rules to be observed among us, in order to preserve that harmony, which is necessary should exist in all societies, whether composed of a great or small number—one of the most material of which is to devote two evenings in every week to the business we have engaged in. In the first of these meetings we communicate to each other what intelligence we receive, and consider on what topics we shall proceed. In the second, we lay our several productions on the table, which being read over, everyone has the liberty of excepting against, or censuring whatever she disapproves; nothing being exhibited to the public without the joint concurrence of all. The rendezvous is kept at my lodgings, and I give strict orders, that no person whatever shall be admitted to interrupt our consultations; but you may as well attempt to exclude the lightning, as the impertinence of some people . . . they come galloping to repeat everything they see or hear of. . . .

We were beginning to lament the misfortunes our sex frequently fall into through want of those improvements we are, doubtless, capable of, when a letter, left for us at our publishers, was brought in, which happening to be on that subject, cannot anywhere be more properly inserted than in this place.

To the Female Spectator

Ladies,

Permit me to thank you for the kind and generous talk you have undertaken in endeavouring to improve the minds and manners of our unthinking sex; it is the noblest act of charity you could exercise in an age like ours, where the sense of good and evil is almost extinguished, and people desire to appear more vicious than they really are, that so they may be less unfashionable. This humour, which is too prevalent in the female sex, is the true occasion of many evils and dangers to which they are daily exposed: no wonder men of sense disregard us, and the dissolute triumph over that virtue they ought to protect!

Yet, I think, it would be cruel to charge the ladies with all the errors they commit; it is most commonly the fault of a wrong education, which makes them frequently do amiss, while they think they not only act innocently but uprightly; it is therefore only the men, and the men of understanding too, who, in effect, merit the blame of this, and are answerable for all the misconduct we are guilty of. Why do they call us *silly women*, and not endeavour to make us otherwise? God and Nature has endued them with means, and *custom* has established them in power of rendering over minds such as they ought to be; how ungenerous is it then to give us a wrong turn, and then despise us for it!

The Mahomedans, indeed, enslave women, but them they teach to believe their inferiority will extend to eternity; but our case is even worse than this, for while we live in a free country, and are assured from our excellent Christian principles refined pleasures which last to immortality, our minds, our better parts, are wholly left uncultivated, and, like a rich soil neglected, bring forth nothing but noxious weeds.

There is, undoubtedly, no sexes in souls, and we are as able to receive and practise the impressions, not only of virtue and religion, but also those sciences which the men engross to themselves, as they can be: surely our bodies were not form'd by the great Creator out of the finest mold, that our Souls might be neglected like the coarsest of the clay!

O! Would too imperious, and too tenacious man, be so just to the world as to be more careful of the education of those females to whom they are parents or guardians! Would they convince them in their infancy that dress and show are not the essential of a fine lady, and that true beauty is scated in the mind; how soon should we see our sex retrieve the many virtues which false taste had buried in oblivion! Strange infatuation! To refuse us what would so much contribute to their own felicity! Would not themselves reap the benefit of our amendment? Should we not be more obedient daughters, more faithful wives, more tender mothers, more sincere friends, and more valuable in every other station of life?

But, I find, I have let my pen run a much greater length than I at first intended. If I have said anything worthy of your notice, or what you think the truth of the case, I hope you will mention this subject in some of your future essays; or if you find I have any way err'd in my judgement, to set me right will be the greatest favour you can confer on,

Ladies, your constant reader,
and humble servant,
Cleora

Hampton Court,
January 12, 1744/5.

After thanking this lady for the favour of her obliging letter, we think it our duty to congratulate her on being one of those happy few who have been blessed with that sort of education which she so pathetically laments the want of in the greatest part of our sex.

Those men are certainly guilty of a great deal of injustice who think that all the learning becoming a woman is confined to the management of her family; that is, to give orders concerning the table, take care of her children in their infancy, and observe that her servants do not neglect their business. All this no doubt is very necessary, but would it not be better if she performs those duties more through principle than custom? And will she be less punctual in her observance of them, after she becomes a wife, for being perfectly convinced, before she is so, of the reasonableness of them, and why they are expected from her?

Many women have not been inspired with the least notion of even those requisites in a wife, and when they become so, continue the same loitering, lolloping, idle creatures they were before; and then the men are ready enough to condemn those who had the care of their education.

Terrible is it, indeed for the husband, especially if he be a tradesman, or gentleman of small estate, who marries with a woman of this stamp; whatever fortune she brings will immediately run out, and 'tis well if all his own does not follow. Even persons of the highest rank in life will suffer greatly both in their circumstances and peace of mind, when she, who ought to be the mistress of the family, lives in it like a stranger, and perhaps knows no more of what those about her do than an alien.

But supposing her an excellent oeconomist, in every respect what the world calls a notable woman, methinks the husband would be yet infinitely happier were she endued with other good qualities as well as a perfect understanding in household affairs: the governess of a family, or what is commonly called house-keeper, provided she be honest and careful, might discharge this trust as well as a wife; but there is, doubtless, somewhat more to be expected by a man from that woman whom the ceremony of marriage has made part of himself: she is, or ought to be, if qualified for it, the repository of his dearest secrets, the moderator of his fiercer passions, the softner of his most anxious cares, and the constantly cheerful and entertaining companion of his more unbended moments.

To be all this she must be endued with a consumate prudence, a perfect evenness of temper, an unshaken fortitude, a gentle affable behaviour, and a sprightly wit. The foundation of these virtues must be indeed in nature, but nature may be perverted by ill customs, or, if not so, still want many embellishments from education, without which, however valuable in itself, it would appear rude and barbarous to others, and lose more than half the effect it ought to have. . . .

We all groan under the curse entailed upon us for the transgression of Eve.

Thy desire shall be to thy husband, and he shall rule over thee.

But we are not taught enough how to lighten this burden, and render ourselves such as would make him ashamed to exert that authority, he thinks he has a right to, over us.

Were that time which is taken up in instructing us in accomplishments, which, however taking at first sight, conduce little to our essential happiness, employed in studying the rules of wisdom, in well informing us what we are, and what we ought to be, it would doubtless inspire those, to whom we should happen to be united, with a reverence which would not permit them to treat us with that lightness and contempt, which, though some of us may justly enough incur, often drives not only such, but the most innocent of us, to extravagancies that render ourselves, and those concerned with us equally miserable.

Why then, Cleora says, do the men, who are and will be the sole arbitrators in this case, refuse us all opportunities of enlarging our minds, and improving those talents we have received from God and Nature; and which, if put in our power to exert in a proper manner, would make no less their own happiness than our glory?

They cry, of what use can learning be to us, when custom, and the modesty of our sex, forbids us to speak in public places? 'Tis true that it would not befit us to go into the pulpit, nor harangue at the bar; but this is a weak and trifling argument against our being qualified for either, since all men who are so were never intended for the service of the Church, nor put on the long robe; and by the same rule therefore the sons as well as daughters of good families should be bred up in ignorance.

Knowledge is a light burden, and, I believe, no one was ever the worse for being skilled in a great many things, tho' he might never have occasion for any of them.

But of all kinds of learning the study of philosophy is certainly the most pleasant and profitable: it corrects all the vicious humours of the mind, and inspires the noblest virtues; it enlarges our understanding; it brings us acquainted with ourselves, and with everything that is in Nature. . . .

Many examples have there been of ladies who attained to very great perfection in this sublime and useful science; and doubtless the number had been greatly increased but for the discouragement our sex meets with, when we aim at anything beyond the needle.

The world would infallibly be more happy than it is, were women more knowing than they generally are; and very well worth the while of those who have the interest of the female part of their family at heart, to instruct them early in some of the most necessary rudiments of philosophy. All those little follies now ascribed to us, which indeed, we but too much incur the censures of, would then vanish, and the dignity of human nature shine forth in us, I will venture to say, with, at least, as much splendour as in the other sex. . . .

I cannot, however, take leave of this subject without answering one objection which I have heard made against learning in our sex, which is, that the polite studies take us off from those that are more necessary, tho' less ornamental.

I believe many well-meaning people may be deceived into this opinion, which, notwithstanding, is very unjust: those improvements which I have mentioned, sublime as they are, will never be of prejudice to our attending to those lower occupations of life, which are not to be dispensed with except in those of the great world. They will rather, by making a woman more sensible than she could otherwise be, of what is either her duty, or becoming in her to do, that she will be doubly industrious and careful, not to give any excuse for reproaches, either from her own conscience, or the tongues of those who would suffer by her transgression.

In a word, it is entirely owing to a narrow education that we either give our husbands room to find fault with our conduct, or that we have leisure to pry too scrutinously into theirs—happy it would be for both, were this almost sole cause of all our errors once reformed; and I am not without some glimmerings of hope that it will one day be so.

The ladies themselves, methinks, begin to seem sensible of the injustice which has long been done them, and find a vacuum in their minds, which, to fill up, they, of their own accord, invented the way of sticking little pictures on cabinets, screens, dressing-tables, and other little pieces of chamber-furniture, and then varnishing them over to look like one piece of painting;* and now they have got into the art of turning ivory into whatever utensils they fancy. . . .

If the married ladies of distinction begin the change, and bring learning into fashion, the younger will never cease soliciting their parents and

* Japanning.

guardians for the means of following it, and every toilet in the kingdom will be loaded with materials for beautifying the mind more than the face of the owner.

The objection, therefore, that I have heard made by some men, that learning would make us too assuming, is weak and unjust in itself, because there is nothing would so much cure us of those vanities we are accused of, as knowledge. . . .

O but, say they, learning puts the sexes too much on an equality, it would destroy that implicit obedience which it is necessary the women should pay to our commands: if once they have the capacity of arguing with us, where would be our authority!

Now will I appeal to any impartial reader, even among the men if this very reason for keeping us in subjection does not betray an arrogance and pride in themselves, yet less excusable than that which they seem so fearful of our assuming. . . .

Modesty is the characteristic of our sex; it is indeed the mother of all those graces for which we can merit either love or esteem: sweetness of behaviour, meekness, courtesy, charity in judging others, and avoiding all that will not stand the test of examination in ourselves, flow from it: it is the fountainhead, as well as the guardian of our chastity and honour, and when it is once thrown off, every other virtue grows weak, and by degrees, is in danger of being wholly lost; she who is possessed of it can be guilty of no crime, but she who forfeits it is liable to fall into all.

How far is it consistent with that decent reserve, or even that softness so becoming in womankind, I leave anyone to judge who has been witness in what manner some ladies come into public assemblies: they do not walk but straddle; and sometimes run with a kind of frisk and jump; throw their enormous hoops almost in the faces of those who pass by them; stretch out their necks, and roll their eyes from side to side, impatient to take the whole company at one view; and if they happen to see any one dresses less exactly according to the mode, than themselves, presently cry out, *"Antiquity to perfection!—A picture of the last age!"* then burst into a laugh, loud enough to be heard at two or three furlongs distant, happy if they can put the unfortunate object of their ridicule out of countenance. Can such behaviour pass upon the world for modesty, good-manners, or good-nature?

I do not pretend to say that all ladies who give themselves an air of boldness, merely because it is the fashion, are guilty of anything which may arraign their chastity: many may be innocent in fact who are not in show. . . .

Far be it from me to debar my sex from going to those public diversions, which, at present, make so much noise in the town: none of them but may be enjoyed without prejudice, provided they are frequented in a reasonable manner, and behaved at with decency: it is the immoderate use, or rather the abuse of anything, which renders the partaking it a fault. What is more agreeable than freedom in conversation, yet when it extends to levity and wantonness, what more contemptible and odious!

Bibliography and Suggestions for Additional Reading

I have included here an expanded list of women who published during the seventeenth century, whose texts either did not provide sufficient interest for the questions under examination, or were simply excluded because space was limited. I have also listed sources which shed light on aspects of women's education, social lives, sexuality, legal position, material circumstances, religious experience, etc.

Abbot, Elizabeth. *The Apprehension and Execution of E. Abbot.* London, 1608.
Abbott, Margaret. *A Testimony Against the False Teachers.* N.p. 1659.
Academy of Complements, The. London, 1640.
Account of Marriage, An. London, 1672.
Account of the Fund for the Relief of the Widows. London, 1673.
Adams, Mary. *The Ranters Monster.* London, 1652.
Ady, Thomas. *A Perfect Discoverie of Witches.* London, 1661.
Agrippa, Henry Cornelius. *Female Pre-eminence; or, The Dignity and Excellency of That Sex.* London, 1670.
———. *The Glory of Women; or A Looking-glasse.* London, 1652.
Allen, Hannah. *Satan: His Method and Malice Baffled.* London, 1683.
[Allestree, Richard.] *The Gentleman's Calling.* London, 1660.
———. *The Government of the Tongue.* Oxford, 1674.
———. *The Ladies Calling.* Oxford, 1673, reprinted 1675.
———. *The Whole Duty of Man.* London, 1658, reprinted 1695.
Ames, Richard. *The Female Fire-Ships.* London, 1691.
———. *The Folly of Love; or, An Essay.* London, 1691.
Anatomy of a Woman's Tongue, The. London, 1638.
Andrewe, Thomas. *The Unmasking of a Feminine Machiavell.* London, 1604.
Anger, Jane. *Jane Anger Her Protection for Women.* London, 1589.
Answer to the Character of an Exchange-Wench, An. London, 1675.
Ape-Gentlewoman, or The Character of an Exchange-Wench, The. London, 1675.
Art of Making Love: or, Rules for the Conduct of Ladies and Gallants in Their Amours, The. London, 1676.
Ascham, Roger. *The Scholemaster.* London, 1570.

Askew, Anne. *The First Examination of the Worthy Servant of God, Maistres Anne Askew.* London, 1548.

Astell, Mary. *Some Reflections upon Marriage.* London, 1706.

————. *A Serious Proposal to the Ladies for the Advancement of Their True and Greatest Interest.* London, 1694.

Athenian Mercury, The. Vols. 1–6. London, 1691–93.

Aubin, Penelope. *The Life and Adventures of the Lady Lucy.* London, 1726.

————. *The Life of Charlotta DuPont.* London, 1723.

————. *The Life of Madame de Beaumont.* London, 1721.

————. *The Strange Adventures of the Count de Vinevil.* London, 1721.

Austin, William. *Haec Homo, Wherein the Excellency of the Creation of Women Is Described.* London, 1637.

Avery, Elizabeth. *Scripture-prophecies Opened.* London, 1647.

A[ylett], R[obert]. *A Wife, Not Ready-made, but Bespoken.* London, 1653.

B., A. *A Letter of Advice Concerning Marriage.* London, 1676.

B., F. *The Office of the Good House-wife.* London, 1672.

Barker, Jane. *Entertaining Novels.* London, 1715.

————. *A Patch-work Screen for the Ladies, or Love and Virtue Recommended.* London, 1723.

————. *Poetical Recreations.* London, 1688.

————. "Political Poems." B.L., Add. Mss. 21, 621.

B[arksdale], C[lement]. *A Letter Touching a College of Maids.* London, 1675.

Baron and Feme: A Treatise of Law and Equity Concerning Husbands and Wives. London, 1700.

Bastwick, Susannah. *To the High Court of Parliament.* London, 1654.

Batchelor's Answer to the Maid's Complaint, The. London, 1675.

Batchelor's Directory, The. London, 1694.

Batchiler, John. *The Virgins Pattern.* London, 1661.

[Bateman, Susanna.] *I Matter Not How I Appear to Man.* London, 1657.

[Bathurst, Elizabeth.] *An Expostulatory Appeal to the Professors.* London, 1680.

————. *The Sayings of Women.* London, 1683.

————. *Truth Vindicated.* London, 1691.

Beale, Mary. "Correspondence," B.L., Harl. Ms. 6828.

Behn, Aphra. *The Dutch Lover.* London, 1673.

————. *The Forced Marriage.* London, 1671.

————. *The Lucky Chance.* London, 1686.

————. *Sir Patient Fancy.* London, 1686.

————. *Works.* 6 Vols. Edited by Montague Summers. London, 1915.

Bell, Susanna. *The Legacy of a Dying Mother to Her Children.* London, 1673.

Biddle, Hester. *The Trumpet of the Lord God.* London, 1662.

————. *Wo to Thee City of Oxford.* London, 1655.

Boothby, Frances. *Marcelia.* London, 1670.

Brathwaite, Richard. *Art Asleep Husband? A Boulster Lecture.* London, 1640.

————. *The English Gentlewoman.* London, 1631, reprinted 1641.

Breton, Nicholas. *The Good and the Badde: or, A Description of the Worthies and Unworthies of This Age.* London, 1616.

————. *The Will of Wit . . . The Fourth Discourse, The Praise of Virtuous Ladies and Gentlewomen.* London, 1606.

Brief Anatomie of Women: Being an Invective, A. London, 1653.

Brinsley, John. *A Looking-glass for Good Women.* London, 1645.

Broad-side Against Marriage, A. London, 1675.

Brown, Thomas. *Letters from the Dead to the Living and from the Living to the Dead.* London, 1702.

Burch, Dorothy. *A Catechism of the Several Heads.* London, 1646.

C., J. *An Elegy upon the Death of the Most Incomparable Mistress Katherine Philips.* London, 1664.

C., S. *The Life of Lady Halket.* Edinburgh, 1701.

Camfield, Benjamin. *A Consolatory Discourse for the Support of Distressed Widows.* London, 1690.

C[arey], Lady E[lizabeth]. *The Tragedie of Mariam, the Faire Queen of Jewry.* London, 1613.

Cary, Mary. *The Little Horns Doom.* London, 1651.

————. *A New and More Exact Map or Description of the New Jerusalem's Glory.* London, 1651.

————. *The Resurrection of the Witnesses.* London, 1648.

————. *A Word in Season.* London, 1647.

Case of the Poor Widows, The. N.p. 1685.

Catherine (Parr), Queen. *The Lamentation of a Sinner.* London, 1547.

————. *Prayers or Meditacions.* London, 1545.

Caution for Scolds, A. London, 1685–88.

Cavendish, Margaret, Duchess of Newcastle. *Letters of Margaret Lucas to Wm. Cavendish, Duke of Newcastle.* London, 1956.

————. *The Life of the Thrice Noble, High and Puisant Prince William Cavendish, Duke, Marquess, and Earl of Newcastle.* London, 1667.

————. *Natures Pictures Drawn by Fancies Pencil.* London, 1656.

————. *Observations upon Experimental Philosophy.* London, 1666.

————. *Orations of Divers Sorts.* London, 1662.

————. *Philosophical Fancies.* London, 1653.

————. *Philosophical Letters.* London, 1664.

————. *The Philosophical and Physical Opinions.* London, 1655.

————. *Playes.* London, 1668.

————. *Poems and Fancies.* London, 1653.

————. *Sociable Letters.* London, 1664.

————. *The Worlds Olio.* London, 1655.

Cellier, Elizabeth. *The Ladies Answer to That Busiebody.* Oxford, 1670.

————. *Maddam Cellier's Answer to the Pope's Letter.* Oxford, 1680.

————. *Malice Defeated.* Oxford, 1680.

————. *Mistress Cellier's Lamentation.* Oxford, 1681.

————. *To Dr. . . . An Answer to His Queries Concerning the College of Midwives.* London, 1687–88.

Centlivre, Susannah. *Works.* 3 vols. London, 1761.

Certain Precepts Left by a Father to His Son and a Man of Eminent Note in this Kingdom. London, 1615.

Challenge; or the Female War, The. London, 1697.

Challenge Sent by a Young Lady, The. London, 1697.

Chamberlayne, Edward. *An Academy or College; Wherein Young Ladies and Gentlewomen May at a Very Moderate Expense Be Educated.* London, 1671.

Character of the Beaux, The. London, 1696.

Character of a Town Gallant. London, 1675.

Character of a Town-Mistress, The. London, 1675.

Cheevers, Sarah. *The Justification of the Independent Churches of Christ.* London, 1641.

————. *A New-Yeares Gift, or A Brief Exhortation.* London, 1645.

————. *To All People upon the Face of the Earth; A Sweet Salutation.* London, 1663.

Chudleigh, Mary. *Essays upon Several Subjects.* London, 1710.

————. *The Ladies' Defence; or, "The Bride-Woman's Counseller" Answer'd.* London, 1701.

————. *Poems upon Several Occasions.* London, 1703.

City-Dames Petition, in Behalf of the Long-Afflicted, but Well-Affected Cavaliers, The. London, 1647.

Clark, Margaret. *The True Confession of Margaret Clark.* London, 1680.

————. *Warning for Servants.* London, 1680.

Clarkstone, Bessie. *The Conflict in Conscience.* Edinburgh, 1631.

Cleaver, Robert. *Bathsheba's Instructions to her Son Lemuel.* London, 1614.

————. *A Godlie Forme of Household Government.* London, 1598.

Clifford, A., ed. *Tixall Letters; or The Correspondence of the Astor Family . . . During the Seventeenth Century.* 2 Vols. London, 1815.

Cockburn, Catherine [Trotter]. *The Works of . . . Theological, Moral, Dramatic and Poetical.* Edited by Thomas Birch. 2 Vols. London, 1751.

Codrington, Robert. *The Second Part of Youth's Behaviour; or, Decency in Conversation Amongst Women.* London, 1664.

Coke, Mary. *Letters and Journals of Lady Mary Coke.* Edited by I. A. Home. Edinburgh, 1889–96.

Collins, Anne. *Divine Songs and Meditacions.* London, 1653.

Concina, Leonora, Marchioness. *The Teares of the Marshall D'Ancres Wife, Shed for the Death of Her Husband.* London, 1617.

Conway, Anne Finch, Viscountess. *Letters.* Edited by Marjorie Hope Nicholson. London, 1930.

————. *The Principles of the Most Ancient and Modern Philosophy.* Amsterdam, 1690, Reprinted London, 1692.

Cooke, Frances. *Mistress Cooke's Meditations.* Cork, 1650.

Cornwallis, Jane Meautys, Lady. *Private Correspondence, 1613–1644.* Edited by Lord Braybrooke. London, 1842.

[Cotton, Pricilla.] *To the Priests and People of England, We Discharge Our Consciences.* London, 1655.

Court of Good Counsell. Wherein to Get Downe the True Rules, How a Man Should Choose a Good Wife from a Bad, The. London, 1607.

[Crouch, Nathaniel.] *Female Excellency, or The Ladies Glory.* London, 1688.

Culpeper, Nicholas. *A Directory for Midwives.* London, 1651.

D., J. *A Sermon Preached at the Funeral of . . . Lady Mary Armyne.* 1676.

Dalton, James. *A Strange and True Relation of a Young Woman Possest with the Devil.* London, 1647.

Davys, Mary. *Works.* 2 Vols. London, 1725.

Dawson, Thomas. *The Good Huswife's Jewel.* London, 1610.

Day, Martin. *A Mirror for Modesty.* London, 1621.

Declaration of the Maids of the City of London, A. London, 1659.

Defoe, Daniel. *An Essay upon Projects.* London, 1697.

"Description of a Poetress, The." B.L., Harl. Ms. 6913.

Dialogue Between Two Young Ladies, A. London, 1696.

Diary of Lady Ann Clifford, 1616–1619, The. Edited by Vita Sackville-West. London, 1923.

Dillingham, William. *A Sermon at the Funeral of the Lady Elizabeth Alston.* London, 1677.

Discourse of Women, A. London, 1662.

A Discoverie of Six Women Preachers . . . in Middlesex, Kent. London, 1641.

Douglas, Anne, Countess of Morton. *The Countess of Morton's Daily Exercise.* London, 1666.

Douglas, Lady Eleanor. *The Blasphemous Charge Against Her.* N.p. 1649.

———. *The Bride's Preparation.* London, 1644.

———. *I Am the First, and the Last.* N.p. 1644/5.

———. *A Prophesy of the Last Day.* 1645.

Dowriche, Anne. *The French Historie.* London, 1589.

[Duncon, John.] *The Holy Life and Death of . . . Letice, Vi-countess of Falkland.* N.p. 1653.

Dutchess of Monmouth's Lamentation, The. London, 1683.

Dutchess of Portsmouth's Farewell, The. London, 1685.

Egerton, Sarah Fyge. *Poems upon Several Occasions.* London, 1706.

[Elson, Mary.] *A Tender and Christian Testimony to Young People.* London, 1685.

English Midwife Enlarged, The. London, 1682.

Essay in Defence of the Female Sex, An. London, 1696.

[Evelyn, Mary.] *The Ladies Dressing Room Unlock'd.* London, 1700.

———. *Mundus Muliebris.* London, 1690.

Examination and Tryall of Margaret Fell, The. London, 1664.

F., S. *The Female Advocate: or, An Answer to a Late Satyr Against the Pride, Lust and Inconstancy of Woman.* London, 1686.

Fage, Mary. *Fame's Roule.* London, 1637.

Fair Warning to Murderers of Infants: Being an Account of the Tryal . . . of Mary Goddenough. London, 1692.

Fanshawe, Lady Ann. *Memoirs.* London, 1907.

F[arnworth], R[ichard]. *A Woman Forbidden to Speak in the Church.* London, 1654.

Fearon, Jane. *Universal Redemption.* London, 1698.

Featherstone, Sarah. *Living Testimonies.* London, 1689.

Fell, Margaret. *The Citie of London Reprov'd.* London, 1660.

―――. *The Daughter of Sion Awakened.* London, 1677.

―――. *A Spirit Moving in the Women Preachers.* London, 1646.

―――. *Women's Speaking Justified.* London, 1666, reprinted 1667.

Fell, Sarah. *Household Account Book.* Edited by Norman Penney, Cambridge, 1920.

The Female Advocate, or A Plea for the Just Liberty of the Tender Sex, and Particularly of Married Women, Being Reflections on a Late Rude and Disingenuous Discourse Delivered by Mr. John Sprint, in a Sermon at a Wedding. London, 1700.

Female Hector, The. London, 1663.

Female Wits, The. London, 1697.

Ferne-seede, Margaret. *The Arraignment and Burning of Margaret Ferne-seede, for the Murther of Her Husband.* London, 1608.

Fiennes, Celia. *Through England on a Side Saddle in the Time of William and Mary.* London, 1888.

Finch, Anne, Countess of Winchilsea. *Miscellany Poems on Several Occasions, Written by a Lady.* London, 1713.

―――. *Poems.* Edited by Myra Reynolds. Chicago, 1903.

Fox, George. *The Woman Learning in Silence.* London, 1656.

―――. *This Is an Encouragement to All Womens-meetings.* London, 1676.

Freke, Mrs. Elizabeth. *Diary, 1671–1714.* Cork, 1913.

G., E. *A Prodigious & Tragicall History of the Arraignment, Tryall, Confession . . . of Six Witches.* N.p. 1652.

Gargill, Ann. *A Brief Discovery of That Which Is Called the Popish Religion.* London, 1656.

―――. *A Warning to All the World.* London, 1656.

Gauden, John. *A Discourse of Artifical Beauty.* London, 1662.

Giffard, Lady Martha. *Martha, Lady Giffard, Her Life and Correspondence (1664–1722).* Edited by Julia G. Longe. London, 1911.

Gilman, Anne. *An Epistle to Friends.* London, 1662.

Gossips Braule, The. 1655.

Gossips Meeting, The. N.p., n.d.

Gotherson, Dorothea. *To All That Are Unregenerated.* London, 1661.

Gouge, William. *Of Domesticall Duties.* London, 1622.

[Gough, John.] *The Academy of Complements.* London, 1684.

Gould, Robert. *Love Given O're: or, A Satyr Against the Pride, Lust, and Inconstancy, &c. of Woman.* London, 1682.

―――. *A Satyrical Epistle to the Female Author of a Poem Called Sylvia's Revenge.* London, 1691.

Great News from a Parliament of Women. N.p., 1684.

Grey, Elizabeth, Countess of Kent. *A Choice Manual.* London, 1653.

Grey, Lady Jane. *The Life, Death, and Actions of.* London, 1615.

Grymeston, Elizabeth. *Miscelanea, Meditations, Memoratives.* London, 1604.

H., T. *A Looking-Glasse for Women*. London, 1644.

Haec-Vir: Or, The Womanish Man: Being an Answere to a Late Booke Intituled Hic-Mulier. London, 1620.

Halkett, Lady Ann. *Autobiography*. Edited by J. Gough Nichols. London, 1875.

Hall, Anne. *A Brief Representation and Discovery*. London, 1649.

Hannay, Patrick. *A Happy Husband or Directions for a Maid to Chuse Her Mate*. London, 1618.

Harcourt, Anne. *The Diary of Lady Anne Harcourt, 1649–1661*. Edited by E. W. Harcourt. Vol. 1. Oxford, 1880.

Harley, Lady Brilliana. *Letters*. Edited by T. T. Lewis.

Hatton. *Correspondence of the Family of Hatton, 1601–1704*. Edited by E. M. Thompson. 2 Vols. London, 1878.

Haywood, Eliza. *The Female Spectator*. London, 1744–46.

Heale, William. *An Apologie for Women*. Oxford, 1609.

Henshaw, Anne. *To the Parliament of the Commonwealth . . . the Humble Petition of*. London, 1654.

[Heydon, John.] *Advice to a Daughter in Opposition to the Advice to a Son*. London, 1658.

———. *The Ladies' Champion*. London, 1660.

Heywood, Thomas. *A Curtaine Lecture*. London, 1637.

———. *The General History of Women*. London, 1657.

Hic Mulier: Or, The Man-Woman: Being a Medicine to Cure the Coltish Disease of the Staggers in the Masculine-Feminines of Our Times. London, 1620.

Hoby, Lady Margaret. *Diary, 1599–1605*. Edited by Dorothy M. Meads. New York, 1930.

Holden, Mary. *The Woman's Almanack for . . . 1688*. London, 1688.

Hooton, Elizabeth. *To the King and Both Houses of Parliament*. London, 1670.

[Hopton, Susannah.] *Daily Devotions*. London, 1673.

[Howe, John.] *A Funeral Sermon on the Death of . . . Mistress Judith Harmond*. London, 1696.

———. *A Funeral Sermon on the Decease of . . . Mistress Margaret Baxter*. London, 1681.

Howgill, Mary. *A Remarkable Letter of*. N.p. 1657.

———. *The Vision of the Lord of Hosts*. London, 1662.

Humours, and Conversations of the Town, The. London, 1693.

Husbands' Authority Unveiled, The. London, 1650.

Hutchinson, Lucy. *Memoirs of the Life of Col. Hutchinson*. Edited by James Sutherland. Oxford, 1973.

Ivie, Thomas. *Alimony Arraign'd*. N.p. 1654.

James, Elinor. *The Case Between a Father and His Children*. London, 1682.

———. *Mrs. James' Advice to the Citizens of London*. N.p. 1688.

James I. *Basilikon Doron, or His Majesties' Instruction to His Dearest Son, Henry the Prince*. London, 1603.

Jesserson, Susanna. *A Bargain for Bachelors*. London, 1675.

Jinner, Sarah. *An Almanack or Prognostication for Women*. London, 1658.

Joceline, Elizabeth. *The Mother's Legacie to Her Unborn Child*. London, 1624.

Killigrew, Anne. *Poems.* London, 1686.
Ladies Dictionary, The. London, 1694.
Ladies Mercury, The. London, 1693.
Ladies Remonstrance, The. London, 1659.
Lanyer, Emilia. *Salve Deus Rex Judaeorum.* London, 1611.
Lawes Resolutions of Womens Rights, The. London, 1632.
[Lead, Jane.] *The Ascent to the Mount of Vision.* N.p. 1699.
Leigh, Dorothy. *The Mother's Blessing.* London, 1616.
Letter Concerning the College of Midwives, A. Oxford, 1688.
Letters and Poems in Honour of . . . Margaret, Dutchess of Newcastle. London, 1676.
Life and Death of Mrs. Mary Frith, The. London, 1662.
Lilburne, Elizabeth. *To the Chosen and Betrusted Knights . . . the Humble Petition of.* London, 1646.
Lincoln, Countess of. *The Countesse of Lincoln's Nurserie.* Oxford, 1622.
Livingston, Helen, Countess of Linlitgow. *The Confession and Conversion of.* Edinburgh, 1629.
Maid's Prophecies, The. London, 1648.
Major, Elizabeth. *Honey on the Rod.* London, 1656.
Makin, Bathsua. *An Essay to Revive the Antient Education of Gentlewomen in Religion, Manners, Arts and Tongues.* London, 1673.
Manley, Mary de la Rivière. *The Adventures of Rivella; or, The History of the Author of the Atlantis.* London, 1714.
———. *Letters Written by Mrs. Manley.* London, 1696.
———. *The Lost Lover.* London, 1696.
———. *The Royal Mischief.* London, 1696.
Marriage Promoted. In a Discourse. London, 1690.
M[arsin], M. *The Womens Advocate.* London, 1683.
Martyn, William. *Youths Instruction.* London, 1612.
Masham, Lady Damaris. *A Discourse Concerning the Love of God.* London, 1696.
———. *Occasional Thoughts in Reference to a Vertuous or Christian Life.* London, 1705.
Melville, Elizabeth. *A Godlie Dreame.* Edinburgh, 1606.
Meriton, George. *Immorality, Debauchery, and Profaneness Exposed.* London, 1698.
Mid-wives Just Petition, The. London, 1643.
Modesty Triumphing Over Impudence. London, 1680.
Mordaunt, Elizabeth Carey, Viscountess. *The Private Diary of Elizabeth, Viscountess Mordaunt.* Duncairn, 1856.
Munda, Constantia. *The Worming of a Mad Dogge: or, A Soppe for Cerberus the Jaylor of Hell. No Confutation but a Sharp Redargution of the Bayter of Women.* London, 1617.
Murell, John. *The Ladies Practice; or, A Plain and Easy Direction for Ladies and Gentlewomen.* London, 1621.
Neville, Henry. *News from the New Exchange; or The Commonwealth of Ladies.* London, 1649.

New Academy of Complements, The. London, 1669.

Niccholes, Alexander. *A Discourse of Marriage and Wiving.* London, 1615.

Now or Never: or, A New Parliament of Women. London, 1656.

Osborne, Dorothy. *Letters.* Edited by G. C. Moore Smith. Oxford, 1928.

Osborne, Francis. *Advice to a Son.* Oxford, 1656.

Overbury, Thomas. "A Wife." In *The Overburian Characters.* Edited by W. J. Paylor. Oxford, 1936.

Overton, Mary. *To the Right Honourable, the Knights . . . the Humble Appeal.* London, 1647.

Owen, Jane. *An Antidote Against Purgatory.* N.p. 1634.

"Oxinden Correspondence," B.L., Additional Mss. 28,001–3.

————. *The Oxinden and Peyton Letters, 1642–1670.* Edited by Dorothy Gardiner, London, 1937.

Parliament of Women, The. London, 1646.

Parr, Susanna. *Susanna's Apologie Against the Elders.* Oxford, 1659.

P[eachum], H[enry]. *The Compleat Gentleman.* London, 1661.

P[ennyman], M[ary]. *Something Formerly Writ.* London, 1676.

[Philips, Joan.] *Female Poems on Several Occasions, Written by Ephelia.* London, 1679.

Philips, Judith. *The Brideling, Sadling and Ryding, of a Rich Churle in Hampshire.* London, 1595.

P[hilips], K[atherine]. *Letters from Orinda to Poliarchus.* London, 1705.

————. *Poems.* London, 1664, reprinted 1669.

————. *Pompey,* London, 1663.

Pix, Mary. *Ibrahim, the Thirteenth Emperor of the Turks: A Tragedy.* London, 1696.

————. *The Innocent Mistress.* London, 1697.

————. *The Spanish Wives.* London, 1696.

Polwhele, Elizabeth. *The Frolicks, or The Lawyer Cheated.* (1671) Edited by Judith Milhous and Robert D. Hume. Ithaca, N.Y., 1977.

Poole, Elizabeth. *An Alarum of War.* London, 1649.

Pope, Mary. *Behold, Here Is a Word.* London, 1649.

Powell, Thomas. *Tom of All Trades.* London, 1631.

Primrose, Diana. *A Chaine of Pearle.* London, 1630.

Prologue and Epilogue to a Play Acted by Women Only. London, 1682.

Prowse, Anne. *Of the Markes of the Children of God.* London, 1609.

R., W. *Advice to Lovers.* London, 1680.

[Ramesay, William.] *The Gentleman's Companion.* London, 1672.

[Redford, Elizabeth.] *The Love of God Is to Gather the Seasons.* London, 1690.

————. *The Widow's Mite.* London, 1690.

Reflexions on Marriage and the Poetic Discipline. London, 1673.

Remarks Upon Remarks, or A Vindication of the Conversations of the Town. London, 1673.

Remarques on the Humours and Conversations of the Town. London, 1673.

Restored Maidenhead. A New Satyr Against Women, The. London, 1691.

Rich, Barnaby. *The Excellency of Good Women.* London, 1613.

Rich, Mary, Countess of Warwick. *Autobiography.* London, 1848.

Rogers, Daniel. *Matrimonial Honour.* London, 1642.

Rolph, Alice. *To the Chosen and Betrusted Knights . . . the Humble Petition of.* London, 1648.

[Rowe, Elizabeth Singer.] *Friendship in Death, in Twenty Letters from the Dead to the Living.* London, 1728.

———. *Miscellaneous Works in Prose and Verse.* 2 vols. London, 1737.

———. *Poems on Several Occasions, Written by Philomena.* London, 1696.

Rowlands, Samuel. *The Bride.* London, 1617.

Rowlandson, Mary. *A True History of the Captivity and Restoration of.* London, 1682.

Russell, Rachel Wriothesley, Lady. *Letters.* Edited by Lord John Russell. N.p. 1853.

S., J. *A Brief Anatomy of Women.* London, 1653.

St. Hillaries Teares, Shed Upon All Professions. London, 1641.

Savile, George, Marquess of Halifax. *The Lady's New-Year's-Gift: or, Advice to a Daughter.* London, 1688, reprinted 1700.

Sawyer, Elizabeth. *The Wonderful Discoverie of Elizabeth Sawyer, a Witch.* London, 1621.

Scarborow, Ann. *A Looking-glass for Maids.* n.d.

Schurman, Anna Maria van. *The Learned Maid; or, Whether a Maid May Be a Scholar. A Logic Exercise Written in Latin by That Incomparable Virgin Anna Maria van Schurman of Utrecht.* London, 1659.

Shannon, Francis Boyle, Viscount. *Several Discourses and Characters Addressed to the Ladies of the Age.* London, 1688.

Sharp, Jane. *The Midwives Book.* London, 1671.

Simmonds, Martha. *A Lamentation for Lost Sheep.* London, 1655.

Sowerman, Ester. *Ester Hath Hanged Haman: or, An Answere to a Lewd Pamphlet, Entituled, The Arraignment of Women.* London, 1617.

Speght, Rachel. *A Mouzell for Melastomus, the Cynicall Baiter of, and Foule Mouthed Barker Against Evahs Sex.* London, 1616.

Sprint, John. *The Bride-Woman's Counseller: Being a Sermon Preached at a Wedding.* London, 1700.

Stiff, Mary. *The Good Womens Cries.* London, 1650.

Swetnam, Joseph. *The Arraignment of Lewd, Idle, Froward, and Unconstant Women; or the Vanity of Them, Choose You Whether. With a Commendation of Wise, Virtuous, and Honest Women.* London, 1615.

Swetnam, the Woman-hater, Arraigned by Women. London, 1620.

Sylvia's Complaint of Her Sexes Unhappiness . . . the Second Part of Sylvia's Revenge. London, 1688.

Sylvia's Revenge, or A Satyr Against Man; in Answer to a Satyr Against Women. London, 1688.

Tate, Nahurm. *A Present for the Ladies: Being an Historical Account of Several Illustrious Persons of the Female Sex.* London, 1692.

Taylor, John. *Divers Crab Tree Lectures.* N.p. 1639.

———. *A Juniper Lecture.* N.p. 1639.

Ten Pleasures of Marriage, The. London, 1682.

T[heophilus], D[orrington]. *The Excellent Woman Described by Her True Characters and Their Opposites.* London, 1692.

Thornton, Alice. *Autobiography.* London, 1873.

T[orshell], S[amuel.] *The Womans Glorie.* London, 1645.

Town-Misse's Declaration and Apology; or, An Answer to the Character of a Town-Miss, The. London, 1675.

Trapnel, Anna. *The Cry of a Stone.* N.p. 1654.

Triumphs of Female Wit in Some Pindaric Odes: or, the Emulation. Together with an Answer to an Objector Against Female Ingenuity, and Capacity of Learning. London, 1683.

Trye, Mary. *Medicatrix, or the Women-Physician.* London, 1675.

Tuvil, Daniel. *Asylum Veneris, or A Sanctuary for Ladies.* London, 1616.

Venn, Anne. *A Wise Virgins Lamp Burning.* N.p. 1658.

Verney, F. P., and Verney M. M., eds. *Memoirs of the Verney Family During the Seventeenth Century.* London, 1907.

Vertuous Wife is the Glory of her Husband, The. London, 1667.

Vincent, Margaret. *A Pittilesse Mother.* London, 1616.

Vincent, Samuel. *The Young Gallants' Academy.* London, 1674.

Virgins Advice to the Maids of London, The. London, 1695.

Virgins Complaint, The. London, 1642–43.

Vives, Juan Luis. *Vives and the Renascence Education of Women.* Edited by Foster Watson. London, 1912.

Walker, Mary. *The Case of.* London, 1650.

Walsh, William. *A Dialogue Concerning Women, Being a Defence of the Sex.* London, 1691.

Wandring Whore, A Dialogue, The. London, 1661.

[Ward, Edward.] *Female Policy Detected.* London, 1695.

Warren, Elizabeth. *The Old and Good Way Vindicated.* London, 1646.

———. *Spiritual Thrift,* London, 1647.

Waters, Margaret. *A Warning from the Lord.* London, 1670.

W[eamys], A[nna.] *A Continuation of Sir Philip Sydney's Arcadia.* London, 1651.

Webb, Mary. *I Being Moved of the Lord.* London, 1659.

Wentworth, Ann. *The Revelation of Jesus Christ.* London, 1679.

Wharton, Anne. *Examen Miscellaneum.* London, 1702.

———. *A Miscellany.* London, 1695.

Whately, William. *A Bride-Bush; or, A Direction for Married Persons.* London, 1617.

White, Dorothy. *An Alarum Sounded Forth.* N.p. 1661.

Whitehead, Ann, and Elson, Mary. *An Epistle for True Love.* 1680.

Whitrowe, Joan. *Faithful Warnings.* London, 1647.

Whole Duty of a Woman, The. London, 1696 (this edition, 1708).

Whole Petition to London Prentices, The. London, 1668.

Wife: Now the Widow of Sir Thomas Overbury, A. London, 1614.

Woman's Advocate, The. London, 1683.

Women's Sharpe Revenge, The. London, 1640.

Wonders of the Female World, The. London, 1683.

Woolley, Hannah. *The Gentlewoman's Companion; or A Guide to the Female Sex.* London, 1675.

——. *The Queen-like Closet.* 5th ed. London, 1684.

Wotton, William. *Reflections upon Ancient and Modern Learning.* London, 1694.

Wright, Thomas. *The Female Vertuosos.* London, 1693.

Wroath, Lady Mary. *The Countess of Montgomeries Urania.* London, 1621.